A.McNAIR
CELTIC F.C.
J. Bennett. A. M'Nair. D. M'Leod. J. Young. D. Adams. W. Orr. R. Templeton.
J. Bauchop. W. Loney. J. Quinn. A. Wilson.
D. Hamilton. J. M'Menemy. P. Somers. R. Craig.
CELTIC F.C., 1906-07.
Maclure, Macdonald & Co.
(Half Back)
A McNAIR
CHURCHMAN'S CIGARETTES.

David Potter

ALEC McNAIR

CELTIC'S ICICLE

ALEC McNAIR

CELTIC'S ICICLE

by David Potter

Foreword by John Fallon

THE CELTIC STAR

Alec McNair - Celtic's Icicle
by David Potter

Published by The Celtic Star in cooperation
with Matt Corr Media.

First Published in the UK in 2021 by The Celtic Star.

ISBN 978-1-8380207-2-9

A catalogue for this book is available from
the British Library and the Irish Library in Dublin.

Cover & page design and typesetting by Stephen Cameron.

Edited by Matt Corr.

Publisher - David Faulds. Email. editor@thecelticstar.co.uk

Contents

Appendices

Dedication

For my late father and grandfather
Angus Potter and David Potter
who have been dead for many years
but still talk to me every day about Celtic

Acknowledgements

A few words of thanks from your author…

John Fallon for kindly writing the foreword.

Matt Corr and David Faulds for editorial,
design and publishing input.

Stephen Cameron for his book design expertise.

Mark Lewis for provision of rare photographs
and his excellent collage

The Celtic Wiki, which is a great research tool
for anything regarding Celtic

British Newspaper Archive for its
voluminous collection of newspapers

An unknown lady, whom I met by chance one day in September 2020 in Larbert Cemetery, who showed me where Alec McNair's grave was located and told me a great deal about Stenhousemuir

Visit - https://thecelticstar.com

Shop - https://celticstarbooks.com

Introduction

I'm not really sure where you would begin to describe Alec McNair and his contribution to the success of Willie Maley's first great Celtic sides.

Perhaps you could think about a combination of Danny McGrain and Billy McNeill, those defensive and leadership qualities allied with a career-spanning devotion to Celtic.

The rocks upon which great Celtic teams were built and flourished.

Revered 'one-club' legends, who operated at the top-level of football over two decades, captaining club and country and winning medals for fun in those cherished Hoops.

Men who commanded respect from far beyond the Celtic community, on and off the field. Humble but classy. Fabulous role models and ambassadors for Celtic and everything we stand for.

Then throw in the coolness and composure of George Connelly and the authority and presence of Virgil Van Dijk.

Now we might have Alec McNair, the best defender in the world in his day.

The story of Celtic's Icicle is quite remarkable.

Great stories require great authors to tell them properly. Someone who can get under the skin of the main characters, feel and share their joy and their pain and take you as the reader into the story itself.

Fortunately, we have David Potter in this role. A man whose lifelong devotion to his beloved Celtic would sit comfortably beside any of the great names mentioned above.

The eminent Celtic Historian is in his element here.

In many ways this is a football love story written by him about one of the greatest Celts of all time, and the social and political context and insight which supports the narrative is fantastic. It really brings Alec's story to life, as we kick every ball with the early Celtic greats.

Jimmy Quinn and Patsy Gallacher.

'Sunny Jim' Young, 'Napoleon' McMenemy and Charlie Shaw.

James Edward McGrory and the first set of McStay brothers.

What a supporting cast that is.

I thoroughly enjoyed this wonderful trip back through a record-breaking period in Celtic's history.

You will too, I'm sure.

MATT CORR

Foreword

It gives me great pleasure to write a foreword for this book written by David on one of the true all-time Celtic greats, Alec 'Eck' McNair. Even though it is now almost 100 years since the man known as 'The Icicle' retired from a glorious playing career which spanned more than two decades at Celtic Park, a captain and vital member of some of Willie Maley's greatest-ever sides, Alec's name still remains famous among Celtic supporters everywhere.

If you know your grand old history, you will most likely know something about Alec McNair.

Like so many Celtic supporters of my vintage, as a youngster I was told about the 'Holy Trinity' of Shaw, McNair and Dodds by the older members of my family, and now at last these and so many of Alec's other contemporaries have been brought to life in print. I would wager that if you ask someone from a Celtic background to name all 12 Apostles, in many cases they would probably struggle to do so. However, without exception they would almost certainly be able to recite the names of the first Celtic team they ever saw play. For the era of Alec McNair, that might be the first Celtic team that our grandfathers or great grandfathers watched live! And for anyone who followed the Hoops either side of the First World War, this would always include McNair. For the best part of two decades, 'Eck the Icicle' was a virtual ever-present in Maley's teams, starring beyond his 40th birthday as he amassed more than 700 competitive first-team appearances for Celtic.

Alec was a truly wonderful player, playing in truly wonderful Celtic teams. Nothing has happened in the best part of a century which has elapsed since he last wore the Hoops with such distinction to even remotely diminish his value and contribution to the success of our club.

Alec McNair, Celtic's Icicle. Coolness personified. One of the best players and finest men ever to don that famous green-and-white jersey.

A man who loved the club, who had a medal collection to die for and who created records as a Celt which stand to this day.

A man who experienced and overcame personal tragedy, whilst continuing to give his all for Celtic.

This is his story, and what a story it is.

JOHN FALLON

CHAPTER ONE

BIRTH AND STENHOUSEMUIR

It is curious how often football books get things wrong about births and deaths. Many books will tell us that Alexander McNair was born in Bo'ness on Boxing Day 1883. In fact, as the Scotland's People website will make clear, he was born in Stenhousemuir, in the Parish of Larbert, on Christmas Eve 1882. He was registered on Boxing Day 1882, and that may explain where some of the error came from, but why was it a year out, and why the wrong town? Although Bo-ness is in the same general area as Stenhousemuir, Alec was certainly Stenhousemuir born and bred – and very proud of it!

He was the son of James and Agnes McNair. They had been married in Falkirk in April 1877, (the marriage certificate says 13 March 1877, although it is clear from other sources that it was 13 April) and Agnes had the most un-Celtic maiden name of Boyne! James is mentioned as being an iron moulder and was illiterate, in that he just made a cross on the certificate (education was only made compulsory in Scotland in 1872). In the 1881 Census, there are five McNairs listed as living at 164 Church Street, Stenhousemuir, and by 1891, there were eight of them, parents James and Agnes, and their children Agnes, James, William, Alexander, Lilias and John. They had moved to 209 Church Street, presumably to a larger house. James was still an iron moulder, and the eldest daughter Agnes was by now a domestic servant.

By 1901, the daughter Agnes had left the house and there were now eight children. The family had moved again but still lived in Church Street, at number 182, and Alexander, now aged 18, is described, like his brother William, as a grate fitter. James junior was listed as a tinsmith, Lilias was a dressmaker and John was a baker's apprentice. The others, Mary, Maggie and Janet, are still described as 'scholars' and they all attended Larbert Central School. Alec then started to serve his time at the Larbert Foundry with Messrs Dobbie, Forbes and Co. Ltd. By this time, he had developed an interest in football, and it was obvious from an early stage that he had an aptitude for the game.

In the three successive seasons of 1900/01, 1901/02 and 1902/03, Stenhousemuir FC won the Scottish Qualifying Cup. That statement actually needs to be adjusted because in December 1902, the club thought that they had won the trophy, by beating Motherwell at Celtic Park for the third year in a row, but, Motherwell objected on the grounds that Stenhousemuir had fielded an illegal player. The objection was upheld and Stenhousemuir, who had been presented with the trophy at the Alexandra Hotel in Glasgow, were required to hand it back. The final was replayed at Ibrox, and this time Motherwell won! In each of these three finals, Stenhousemuir had a McNair playing for them on the left wing, but the Scottish Referee, in its preview of the 1901 game, tells us that this was James McNair, and not Alec. This was almost certainly Alec's elder brother James. Alec was still playing for juvenile teams like Stenhouse Hearts and Stenhouse Thistle at that time.

Because they had done so well in the Scottish Qualifying Cup, Stenhousemuir were admitted to the Scottish Cup proper and in early 1903 they had a good run, beating Partick Thistle, for example, and getting as far as the semi-final, where a record crowd of 8,000 came to Ochilview on Saturday, 7 March 1903 to see Stenhousemuir take on Rangers. We are not too surprised to read that there was no giant-killing act and that Rangers won that match 4-1. There is a McNair listed as playing centre-forward for Stenhousemuir that day, but, once again that is probably James rather than Alec. Nevertheless, it must have been a great occasion for the small town and its small, but ambitious football team. Rangers had been, of course, the Scottish League champions for the past four years, and they would go on to win the Scottish Cup that year.

Stenhousemuir FC are one of the oldest clubs in Scotland, having been founded in 1876. They play at Ochilview, a ground whose name says it all, in that one has an excellent view of the Ochil Hills from there. On a nice day, it can be a beautiful ground. They are by no means the best-supported club in the country, nor are they the most successful, but they have kept going. Not far from the football ground is the ground of Stenhousemuir Cricket Club, who play at The Tryst, and the cricketers' record is noticeably better than that of their football counterparts! They too have fallen in bad times in recent years, but their record is a proud one, with many Scotland Internationals having cut their teeth at The Tryst, that fine ground which now adjoins an equally fine golf course.

It would be season 1903/04 before we hear of Alec McNair playing for Stenhousemuir FC, alongside his brother James, to whom he was very attached. We know this because Alec was the best man when James got married on Hogmanay 1903. The pair of them were very close all their lives, James surviving Alec by only a few months in 1952.

Meanwhile, in 1903, Celtic were in trouble. The club had not won a major trophy since 1899, if one ignores the Coronation Cup of summer 1902, often referred to as the British League Cup. Yet Secretary/Manager Willie Maley was searching, spreading his net far and wide to find replacements for men like Dan Doyle and Sandy McMahon. In June 1902, he had signed a young man from Rutherglen called James McMenemy. The boy had talent but was not quite good enough to force his way into the first team yet, so Maley farmed him out on loan for a spell at Stenhousemuir in March 1903. McMenemy played well for the Warriors, losing narrowly to East Stirlingshire in a replayed Stirlingshire Cup final, before he was recalled in April 1903, but the significance of this, as far as McNair was concerned, was that contact had been established between the two clubs, and it may be that Maley happened to ask someone at Ochilview if there were any talented youngsters going around.

Someone, possibly McMenemy or local boy Donnie McLeod, who was now right-back for Celtic, may have mentioned Alec McNair, the brother of James. According to McNair himself, who wrote a series of articles on his career in The Sunday Post in June 1920, it was Donald (sic) McLeod who approached him on Willie Maley's behalf in April 1903 and asked if he would like to play in a friendly for Celtic. Alec was flattered and even a little puzzled, for McLeod cannot have seen him play very often, but of course someone from Maley's network of spies probably had!

Celtic had agreed to play a friendly at Broomfield against Western League side Airdrieonians on Saturday, 9 May 1903. Young Alec McNair, under the pseudonym of Woods, played at left-half. Why he played under a pseudonym, we know not, but it may be that either he or Maley did not want Stenhousemuir to know that Alec was playing for Celtic. But he certainly played at left-half and Celtic won 6-0. McNair was then asked if he wanted to play in another friendly against Hibernian, but, he had a previous commitment, namely that Stenhouse Hearts were playing in a cup tie. He then signed for Stenhousemuir for season 1903/04, possibly feeling in any case that he was not yet quite ready to move on to Celtic.

Alec had a good first season for Stenhousemuir and one is struck by his versatility. He played mainly on the left side of the field at left-half, inside-left and outside-left. The team finished fourth in the Northern League, which was satisfactory, but not as good as some seasons lately with the high-profile Scottish Qualifying Cup triumphs. McNair consistently earned praise in the local press, The Falkirk Herald, and this was clearly enough for Willie Maley to have another look at this lad.

Maley had a huge network of contacts and spies but liked to do his scouting himself. This was clearly impractical if Celtic were playing on the same day, so he would sometimes send an injured player, a committee man or even a volunteer supporter to have a look. He had long since realised that relying on the word of the Press was not necessarily the best method of assessing a player, even though The Falkirk Herald was one of the better newspapers, with reasonably lengthy and detailed comments on how the local teams – Falkirk, East Stirlingshire and Stenhousemuir - were faring. It was mildly supportive of all three teams, but, when things were going badly, it said so, and did not miss and hit the wall instead.

1903/04 was a better season for Celtic themselves. A good side was coming together, and it was often said that this was a "launching pad" or a "springboard season" for what was to come. A new half-back line of Young, Loney and Hay had emerged, and on Saturday, 16 April 1904 at the brand-new super Hampden Park, Celtic had won the Scottish Cup with a Jimmy Quinn hat-trick. On that very day, both the McNair brothers, James and Alec, were in the Stenhousemuir team which lost the final of the Stirlingshire Consolation Cup to Camelon at Brockville. Alec was playing on the left wing that day and naturally was disappointed with the result, for it meant that Stenny had won nothing that season.

It was soon after this game that Willie Maley made another indirect approach to Alec McNair, asking if he would like to join Celtic. If McNair had ever said something like "it was a dream come true and naturally I jumped at the chance," or "I grabbed my cap and ran all the way", or, indeed, described Celtic as "the only team I ever wanted to play for…", it would not have been true. Maley himself tells us that McNair said he would like to think of it. But the Celtic manager liked his 'sincere look' and did not rush him.

It was a big step for Alec, although the thought of professional football was an attractive one – earning money for doing something that he loved! – and, in addition, he had now seen the cheerful and genial Willie Maley in the distance on several occasions and been very impressed by what he had heard of him. However, the first time that the two men really met was when McNair actually signed the documents. He still had a couple of questions that needed answered. One was the rather obvious one of where was he likely to fit in? Would he be good enough to replace the excellent Davie Hamilton on the left wing? And the other was the slightly more embarrassing and sensitive matter of whether he would be able to cope with the undeniable Irish and Catholic atmosphere that prevailed at the club, when he was Alec McNair from a Scottish United Free Church background.

He did, of course, know someone who was in that Celtic team. This was ex-Stenhousemuir man, Donnie McLeod, who was still high in the clouds having played in that 1904 Scottish Cup final of just a few days ago. They did not know each other all that well, (McLeod was several years older) but his brother James knew him better and both McNairs sought Donnie out to ask about Alec's concerns.

The second question, about religion and background, Donnie laughed at. He said that it was never an issue. In fact, he did not honestly know the religion of most of the players – still less did he care – but he did say that the two wing-halves who had done as much as anyone to lift the Scottish Cup, Jimmy Young and Jimmy Hay, were both Protestants from Ayrshire and despised any religious bigotry. Celtic players, however, were likely to be called "Papist" and "Fenian" by some not very bright young men at some grounds, St Mirren, Hearts and (incredibly) Queen's Park being the worst. As for his other question, Donnie said that no-one could guarantee anything about getting a place in this excellent team, which was really going somewhere. The place buzzed with anticipation and Willie Maley made no bones about the fact that he intended to have the best team in the world, with everyone desperate just to wear these green-and-white horizontal stripes, which they had now worn for a season. "Basically, Eck, just you join us. Celtic Park is the place to be!"

By late April 1904, Alec McNair had joined Celtic. Rather surprisingly, The Falkirk Herald does not have anything to say on the subject. Alec may have had a few qualms about whether he had made the right decision, but probably reckoned that if it didn't work out, he could just give up and return to play for Stenhousemuir or for some junior team. Financially, he also had his trade to fall back on if things didn't work out. But the thought of being a full-time professional football player was a very attractive one, especially for the team that had just won the Scottish Cup!

CHAPTER TWO

THE MULTI-PURPOSE MAN (1904-1908)

There is value in being versatile and Alec McNair was just that. Willie Maley would say that McNair played at one time or other in every position in the Celtic side, except goalkeeper. This was not exactly true, unless we count reserve games, testimonials, friendlies with English or Irish teams and tour games. He arrived at Celtic Park at the end of April 1904 as a forward, but gradually it appeared that he was a better defender with a distinct preference for the right, rather than the left, and it was a long time before he became the world's greatest right-back.

The Celtic Park that Alec arrived at was an exciting and excited place, and not just because of the stand on the Janefield Street side of the ground, which was burned down on 9 May 1904, a fortnight or so after he arrived! The Scottish Cup final triumph over Rangers on Saturday, 16 April had lit up Celtic and their support in the same sort of way that a similar occasion in April 1965 would do. The cup finals themselves, in both cases, had been glorious and the heroes Jimmy Quinn and Billy McNeill were duly feted and hailed as the demigods that they were, and each side had a manager at the height of his powers who stressed that this was only the beginning. Indeed, the future in both cases would be something to savour and the actuality scarcely believable in its consistent glory.

One of the great qualities of Maley, at this stage of his life at least, was his ability to welcome people. This extended to opposition teams, journalists, SFA officials, referees and supporters. A week after Celtic's great triumph at Hampden, the Celtic boss had been at the Crystal Palace with the Manchester City party (his brother Tom, another early Celt, was the City manager) to see them win the English FA Cup, beating Bolton Wanderers 1-0 thanks to a Billy Meredith goal. Willie had been charm personified there, and his brother's success as well as his own caused him to glow with pride. It was unparalleled in history (and would remain so) for one brother to manage a Scottish Cup-winning team one week and another brother to do likewise with an English FA Cup-winning side a week later!

In later years, Willie Maley developed a certain hardness and aloofness, which did not endear him to his players, but, in 1904, he was cheerful and pleasant, albeit not without the ability to be tough and even brutal if he had to be. Once again, the parallels between Maley and Jock Stein are striking. But Maley took an immediate liking to Alec McNair, both as a player and as a character.

So, what would have been McNair's feelings as he met this mighty man and was introduced to his teammates? It is often said that McNair was a Rangers supporter when he joined Celtic. Alec, in 1920, was honest enough to admit this. Whether he did that in 1904 is another matter! But he did say, in an article in The Sunday Post in June 1920, "I had a fancy for a particular team and followed them with great eagerness, being happy when they won and downcast when they lost." This was Rangers, and he goes on to say that it was ironic that he became so indelibly identified with Celtic. But by "followed them with great eagerness," he does not necessarily mean that he was a regular attender at Ibrox. He was too busy playing the game for his juvenile side in any case. It possibly means only that he read their reports in the newspaper. To be fair, Rangers were not a bad side, for they had won the Scottish League from 1899 to 1902, and then the Scottish Cup in 1903.

On the other hand, although not a Celtic supporter, McNair would have heard about all the great Celtic players of their 16-year existence – men like Sandy McMahon, Dan Doyle, Jimmy Blessington and Johnny Campbell. He was, therefore, in awe of the current players, or at least he would have been if they had not been so humble and unpretentious. He already knew Donnie McLeod - known as 'Slasher' for his scything tackles - and Willie Loney and Davie Adams were both from his part of the world. There was the sociable and knowledgeable wee man from Rutherglen, Jimmy McMenemy, a comedian and entertainer called Peter Somers, the loud but cheerfully welcoming man from Ayrshire whom everyone called 'Sunny' and the tough-looking captain Willie Orr.

An enigma was Alec Bennett, a refined-looking, gentlemanly character from Rutherglen and a friend of McMenemy. Bennett had a few problems, not least that Rangers were trying to sign him with some of his family very keen on the idea and not above using a little emotional blackmail, including the vile card of sectarian religion, to persuade him to go to Ibrox. Bennett wanted to do that, but he also loved being at Celtic. Nevertheless, he was so unsettled about all of this that Maley had decided to drop him from the 1904 Scottish Cup final, concocting a story about flu that no-one believed.

Bennett also had another problem, which Alec McNair would have identified with. He was not sure about his best position. Centre-forward was where he normally played, but now that Jimmy Quinn had scored a hat-trick in the cup final from that position, how could he get that job back? Willie Maley moved him to the right-wing, and that seemed to solve the problem, at least for a spell. He very soon earned the nickname 'The Artful Dodger,' as distinct from his opposite number on the left, Davie Hamilton, who was known as 'The Dancer.'

But, conversely, the hero of the hour was the almost paranoically shy and self-effacing Quinn. He did not say much but thought a great deal and was an acquired taste, with only Willie Loney getting anywhere close to him. Jimmy came from Croy, which was not all that far away from Stenhousemuir, and so he and McNair had a certain amount in common. In time they would become firm friends, but, for a while, Alec almost felt a frisson of fear when he met Quinn in the corridor or on the park, not because he was afraid of Quinn in a physical sense (although no-one would take any liberties with the tough miner) but simply because he would have had very little to say to the great enigmatic character. Quinn was the man who dominated every topic of conversation in sporting Scotland but would say very little himself. Indeed, Jimmy Quinn was sometimes called 'Jamie The Silent.'

And what did McNair himself bring to the table? He had been watched by Willie Maley in a few games for Stenhousemuir, but also by one or other of Maley's wide network of spies and had clearly impressed on the left-wing. The funny thing is that The Falkirk Herald, one of the many good newspapers in Scotland at the time for giving detailed football reports, never singles Alec out. Occasionally, one gets an oblique reference to a "strong left flank" or "good forward play," but he never seems to shine. Nor is he singled out for condemnation either, however.

But Willie Maley remembered that he had played well in the friendly for Celtic the previous summer, and felt he was worth a chance. Maley did like young McNair's attitude. He was shy without being timid, assertive but not aggressive and displayed an apparently phlegmatic attitude to life which did not hinder or hide his desire to do his best and to win football games. He fitted well into the team.

An immediate delight for Alec came when he was invited to join the club tour of the Highlands. This was good enough for the lad from Stenhousemuir, staying in Highland hotels and enjoying good food and company as well as doing what he really loved, playing football, but there was in addition at the end of May and into June a trip to Europe

– trains, steamboats, more hotels, foreign countries! It was more than a lad from Stenhousemuir could even contemplate, and it was possibly his own insecurity at this point that caused him to say that he preferred trips to the Highlands far more than trips to the Continent. But this was life for the Edwardian Celtic – the team that already considered itself the best club on earth and would soon prove it.

Alec's first game for the club was on Monday, 2 May 1904 at Pittodrie. It was a tour match with McNair given a game at left-half, possibly just to give Jimmy Hay a rest. It was a rare trip for Celtic to the Granite City. Aberdeen FC had only been in existence for a year, an amalgamation of another team called Aberdeen with two others, Orion and Victoria. They clearly had aspirations to play Scottish League Division One football (they would be elected to Division Two for season 1904/05) and it was a great occasion for them to host the Scottish Cup-holders on their Monday Spring Holiday.

Sadly, the game which was due to kick-off at noon had to be postponed until 4.00pm because of torrential rain, and although conditions had improved by then, there was a meagre crowd of barely 2,000 inside Pittodrie to see the following Celtic team, which was a mixture of rugged experience and callow youth;

Adams, McLeod & Strang; Young, Loney & McNair; McConnachie, McMenemy, Gilligan, Somers & Quinn.

Celtic won 3-1, and nothing is said about McNair, although The Dundee Courier says that "play was very uninteresting and almost devoid of incident." However, £45 was raised, and Alec McNair had apparently fitted in well.

McNair then missed the next game at Dundee but played at Kingsmills Park, Inverness on Wednesday, 4 May 1904 against an Inverness XI, a combination of men drawn from Clachnacuddin, Caledonian and Citadel. It was a 5-1 victory and comments include "play as brilliant as any ever witnessed in the North" and "the clever tactics which characterised the movements of the Glasgow team delighted the two thousand spectators," with Hamilton and Bennett singled out for praise. That night, Alec was introduced to another aspect of playing for Celtic, attending a 'smoker' at the Palace Hotel in Inverness, at which the various cups were presented by Willie Maley to the Highland clubs who had done well this season. "Nothing was left to be desired," in terms of the hospitality on offer.

Alec may well have been disappointed not to be chosen for the two Glasgow Charity Cup games, held later that month of May 1904, but watching from the stand at Hampden he would have seen another, less pleasant side of playing for Celtic, when Jimmy Quinn was badly injured in a tackle by the brutal Nick Smith, which split his thigh open. To the Celtic party, it looked like a piece of revenge for the Scottish Cup final. There was generally a good relationship between Celtic and Rangers players, but, things took a dip after that for a spell. Sadly, poor Smith died of the enteric flu which ravaged Ayrshire in early 1905, while Quinn became the most famous football player in the world.

And so to the tour of the Austro-Hungarian Empire! It was a world totally alien to most Scottish young men, including 'Sunny Jim' Young, who managed to get lost! Such tours were interesting to see a bit of the world, but in footballing terms, they were a little overrated perhaps. Football was primitive in Vienna and Prague. The pitches were usually hard and dry, and the standard of refereeing was poor. Celtic won all four games played, with Alec featuring in at least two of them (sometimes the teams are not given in newspapers) and he returned in early June as an established Celtic player.

Such was the quality of the team, however, that he could not be guaranteed a place, albeit his enthusiasm for training and hard work and his willingness to play anywhere in the team meant that he was already looked upon as a valuable member of the Celtic Park set-up. It was what is now called 'having the right attitude.' Alec kept up his fitness over the summer and returned to Celtic Park at the beginning of August, determined to fight for his place.

He was given a run in the team in the practice matches. One was against Royal Albert, but the other was a return to his old stomping ground at Ochilview, to play Stenhousemuir in a Benefit match for James McBride. Unfortunately, it was a very rainy Wednesday night and only 2,000 spectators appeared at the game. McNair was playing at inside-left (he had been at inside-right on Saturday) and scored twice in the first half to the delight, presumably, of any of his relatives and family watching in the meagre crowd, but it meant very little. He was tried at wing-half as well, but by the time that the League games started, he failed to win a place. Alec was not downhearted about his, and Willie Maley was there to encourage him, telling him that his time would come.

McNair was given a game on Saturday, 10 September 1904 on the left-wing, to take the place of the injured Davie Hamilton, for a Glasgow Cup first-round tie against Queen's Park at Celtic Park. Celtic won comfortably 3-0, and The Scottish Referee states uncompromisingly that "McNair is a better forward than Hamilton, for he is less fancy, and a telling shot." This was quite a compliment to the nervous McNair, who tells us that he needed to be buoyed up by the encouragement of Donnie McLeod and the cheerful banter of Peter Somers, who kept cracking jokes in the dressing-room.

It was quite a remarkable game. It was the first time that Alec had played in front of a crowd anything like as big as 23,000, and there were actually four men from Stenhousemuir playing in that game – McNair and McLeod for Celtic and Leslie Skene, the Queen's Park goalkeeper, and Johnny McLean the right-winger of the Spiders. The game was rather hard, but it was generally felt that English referee Mr Lewis of Blackburn was a trifle too histrionic when he halted play, called all the players to the centre circle and told them to cut out the rough stuff! He was particularly sharp with a few offside decisions as well, including once when Alec actually scored but was pulled up for offside. It was an unusual baptism.

McNair played a couple of League games, against St Mirren and Hearts, then dropped out when Davie Hamilton returned from injury. In the meantime, Celtic continued to play well, winning the Glasgow Cup and looking comfortable at the top of the League. Alec's first game against Rangers took place on Monday, 2 January 1905, and it was an odd one. It all came about because Willie Orr was out, Jimmy Hay, therefore dropping back from left-half to left-back, leaving a space for McNair to come in at left-half. The opposition was Rangers, and the venue was Ibrox. Would it be a Happy New Year for Alec?

It transpired to be anything but happy. The game had to be abandoned because of crowd encroachment. It turned out that 40,000 spectators paid to get into Ibrox. However, a crowd attacked the exit gates, broke some of them down and another 20,000 people surged inside. This made the actual attendance 60,000, far more than Ibrox was likely to be able to accommodate, and at several points, even before the players came out, the supporters had crossed the somewhat primitive fences. After a delayed start, the first half commenced, but, the crowd kept on appearing on the field, and when the ball went out of play, there was a problem getting it back. The game was quite farcical, and some of the crowd began to fight with each other (not necessarily anything sectarian here but, it being New Year, an awful lot of alcohol had been consumed) and they kept spilling onto the park in spite of the heroic efforts of the police to push them back. At half-time, the players could not even reach the sanctity of the pavilion, and simply turned round.

Not surprisingly, with all of this going on, football became impossible. Amazingly, referee Mr Lewis kept the game going until the 70th minute when, after consulting the respective managers, Willie

Maley and William Wilton, he decided that enough was enough and invited the players to run the gauntlet through the crowd into the pavilion. They all managed it, albeit not without a few alarms, but it was an absolutely awful way for Alec McNair to start his competitive career against Rangers.

McNair was not yet called 'The Icicle,' as he would be referred to in his later career, but, his temperament was able to deal with all this, and he was back in the team for the following day's game, a trip to Airdrie. This was another disappointment, albeit for different reasons. There were no crowd disturbances this time, but Celtic suffered a rare defeat, going down 2-3 to the home side, Airdrieonians. Alec felt that he had played well enough, but crucially Jimmy Hay missed a penalty when the score was 2-2, and ultimately it was a sore defeat for Celtic.

So, it was back to the reserves for McNair. He was taken to Seamill Hydro for special training for a few days in January with the regulars, and this seems to mean that he was considered to be a first-team man. He also would have been upset by the death of Barney Battles, who succumbed to the flu in early February. It was a massive Celtic funeral. Alec did not know Barney well, but he still trained with Celtic, even though he was now playing for Kilmarnock, and McNair had been, like everyone else, in awe of the great Barney Battles.

It was in February 1905 that the next opportunity presented itself for Alec in the first team. Sunny Jim Young had been given a lengthy suspension after an incident with Doug Sommen of Partick Thistle, and after Willie Black had been given a couple of games and had failed to impress anyone with his fitness, Willie Maley turned to Alec McNair, now well enough known by everyone to be called 'Eck.' As it happened, the game on Saturday, 18 February was the replay of the New Year encounter with Rangers. This time, there was no problem with the crowd; the problem was the wind and the rain. But Eck had seen some rain in his time at Stenhousemuir and was magnificent at right-half as Celtic lashed Rangers 4-1, Jimmy Quinn and Davie Hamilton with two goals apiece.

There followed progress in the Scottish Cup, as Celtic, with McNair outstanding as they beat Partick Thistle 3-0 - "Young was hardly missed." And then he scored his first goal for the club on Saturday, 4 March 1905, as Celtic won 6-2 at Motherwell on a muddy pitch. This was, in fact, the club's final Scottish League fixture of the season (There were only 14 teams in the League and so 26 matches were played). At that stage, Celtic had reached 41 points, but Rangers still had three games to play.

Alec would have been disappointed to miss out on the Scottish Cup semi-final at Celtic Park against Rangers on Saturday, 25 March 1905, when Jimmy Quinn was unjustly sent off, and the angry crowd invaded the park, but, he was probably better out of that game. He continued playing the occasional friendly and Glasgow League games (an insignificant tournament used by clubs to blood their reserves) and then at the end of the season, he was given a great opportunity.

The Ibrox side had lost the 1905 Scottish Cup final to Third Lanark but had won their three remaining League matches. This meant that Celtic and Rangers were tied at the top of the table on equal points, and as no-one had yet thought of goal difference or goal average in those days, the precedent based on the first-ever year of the League in 1891 seemed to be to declare the teams as joint champions. But it so happened that Celtic were due to play Rangers on Saturday, 6 May 1905 in a Glasgow League game. The Scottish League decided to make this match the League decider as well, both teams agreed, and it was duly moved to Hampden.

To some supporters, this had all the hallmarks of a device to earn more money, and in spite of a fine day, only 30,000 spectators appeared. Sunny Jim Young seems to have picked up an injury in the Holiday Monday game, the week before against Queen's Park, and thus Alec McNair was given an opportunity to play in his first game where a trophy was at stake. He may have been nervous, but The Scottish Referee states that "McNair was in great form for Celtic at right-half," the ever-modest Alec himself later singling out right-back Hugh Watson as the best player on the field. In the event, Celtic won 2-1 with goals from Jimmy McMenemy and Davie Hamilton.

Although the game itself was, in some ways, an anti-climax, Alec had the satisfaction of knowing that he had played his part in Celtic winning their fifth League title. He had, technically, not played enough games to earn himself a Scottish League medal, nevertheless, he had played in a Celtic team that had beaten Rangers twice, and because he had played in the League decider, he was most probably given a medal. That was a source of some happiness to Alec, as he boarded the LMS train to Larbert that night at Buchanan Street Station. The team also won the Glasgow Charity Cup that season, beating Partick Thistle 2-0 in the final at Hampden, on Saturday, 27 May 1905, albeit Alec was not chosen for that game. There was a McNair listed on the right-wing, but, that appears to have been Alec's namesake, the unrelated Willie.

Celtic had, thus, won three competitions out of four in this season, and it was clear that this was indeed a splendid team. Alec was, of course, happy to be part of all this, but the very success of the team was what caused him a problem. How was he to break into this great side? He hated the thought of being a permanent reserve, waiting (and in spite of himself, perhaps hoping) for someone to get injured so that he could get a game. He felt that he was worth regular first-team football, and Willie Maley agreed. He kept telling Alec to bide his time and that his great days at Celtic Park were yet to come. It was a mark of McNair's character that he did not throw a tantrum, demand a transfer or storm out. Sometimes in football as in life, one simply has to show patience.

The next campaign, 1905/06, saw him make a total of 26 appearances for the club, almost always as a cover for injuries and never in the position in which he became famous, namely right-back! Sunny Jim tended to be out quite a lot this season, and Alec played 13 times at right-half, five times on the right-wing, twice at centre-half, twice at inside-left, twice at inside-right and twice at left-back. Mr Versatile indeed! In another age, he would have been an ideal substitute. Of all these positions, he preferred centre-half, presumably because he liked to be in the centre of the action.

Other players might well have complained about this sort of thing, but not Alec McNair. He considered it to be so much of an honour even to get a game for Celtic, and he never felt that he was being harshly treated. To be called 'McNair of Celtic' was itself a great privilege! This team, which retained the Scottish League title with a couple of games to spare when they beat Queen's Park 6-0 at Hampden on Saturday, 10 March 1906, was a difficult one to break into, and it was hard to point the finger at anyone and say that he was not up to standard. It was notable, however, that when someone was injured and Alec took his position, there was no diminution of the team's performances.

Alec was honest enough to blame himself for losing the League game at Dens Park, Dundee on Saturday, 3 February 1906. He was playing on the right-wing that day, and the team were 0-1 down when he allowed a cross ball from Davie Hamilton to go past him, thinking that the ball was going in for a goal anyway and that he might spoil everything by being offside. That might have made it 1-1, but as it was, it became one of Celtic's very few defeats that season.

McNair's performances on the field reflected his personality off it. He was phlegmatic, calm, principled, sincere, intelligent, sociable, and he thoroughly enjoyed being part of the social set-up of this team. On the weekends away at Seamill and Highland retreats –

one of the perks of the job, even though it was hard work training – Willie Maley always insisted that everyone did their party piece to entertain the other guests. This was not necessarily Alec's strongest suit – it was more to the taste of show-offs like Young and Somers - but he was usually coaxed and cajoled into doing a recitation or a song.

On the field, we find a reluctance on the part of the newspaper reporters to say anything about him. He was never spectacular nor flamboyant. One wonders how he managed to fill the shoes of Sunny Jim Young, when he was out injured or suspended. Sunny was loud, aggressive, 'in your face,' and his fair hair was never far away from the action on the field, always riling an opponent and usually managing to upset the supporters of the other team by a hefty challenge or two. Such was Sunny's passion and commitment to the club. Eck, on the other hand, was quiet, efficient, never in trouble with a referee and hardly noticed by anyone. He tackled well and fairly and always was a great reader of the game, knowing where he should be at any given time and in any given set of circumstances. His 'peripatetic' role of playing in every position when required, gave him a wide knowledge of the dynamics of a football field and how a team should play. Of course, he had so many good players around him to help, and he was in a perfect position to spot and analyse their many strengths and their few weaknesses.

Alec had a bad time at the end of February and early March 1906, losing two vital games. One was at Celtic Park, on Saturday, 24 February, when Willie Maley's side went out of the Scottish Cup to Hearts after being 1-0 up at half-time. Eck was at right-half that day in place of the injured Sunny Jim. The other match took place a week later, when he was (prematurely) given his first Scottish cap against Wales at Tynecastle. Scotland did have a tendency to underestimate Wales and Ireland, often awarding caps to men who would not be given such an honour against England. This is what happened here, Scotland deciding not to field any players who were based in England, apart from Tommy Fitchie of Woolwich Arsenal, who was an amateur and could more or less play when and where he liked.

Three Celtic players - Donnie McLeod, Alec McNair and Jimmy Quinn - had taken part in this International which saw Wales win 2-0 to secure a first-ever victory on Scottish soil. The Welsh were a good side, but Scotland simply had too many inexperienced players, McNair included. The Scotsman says that "McNair was throughout cool and clever, if a trifle over-anxious," a curious and even contradictory statement, but in any case, McNair was not chosen again for Scotland that season. He would enjoy some great games for Scotland among his 15 International appearances, but, this was not necessarily one of them. It was probably a step too soon. Nevertheless, it was a first step.

Another disappointment for Alec came in the 5-3 defeat by Rangers in the Glasgow Charity Cup semi–final, played at Celtic Park on Saturday, 5 May 1906, but, the main thing was that the League title had been won, and that this time he certainly qualified for a medal. The season finished with two tours, once more to the Highlands and then again to Germany and Austro-Hungary, in which McNair quite often found himself playing at centre-half, as Willie Loney was injured. It was a role that he would find himself in regularly during the next campaign, 1906/07, one of the best seasons in the history of the club up to this point.

The summer of 1906 was one which Eck would have enjoyed once he returned from Europe at the end of May. The previous season had brought a few frustrations and disappointments, but, the Scottish League-winner's medal made up for it all, and he was now an established Celt, albeit he had not yet found a regular berth in the team.

But great changes were also beginning to happen in Scotland and in the United Kingdom. The Liberals had been returned to power with a huge majority in the General Election, held in the early part of 1906, with a benign although ageing Prime Minister in the Scotsman Sir Henry Campbell Bannerman. There were also two very dynamic characters in the Welshman David Lloyd George and the engaging but unpredictable Winston Churchill (who had suddenly decided to be a Liberal after cutting his teeth with the Conservatives), and they were beginning to change the old regime and to bring in some much-needed social reforms. Already there was talk of free school meals for poor children and other such almost revolutionary matters. The Prime Minister was the MP for Stirling Burghs, and that was close to Stenhousemuir.

Life continued to be hard for Alec's family. In a sense they were fortunate, in that Great Britain had an insatiable appetite for iron and steel, particularly for supplying the shipyards of the Clyde, now that competitors to Britain's hegemony were arising in Germany and the United States of America. But the workers were ill-organised and insisted on hamstringing themselves with silly internecine arguments like demarcation disputes, and so wages remained low while the social conditions were appalling. In a small industrial town, things were not so bad as in Glasgow, but, Alec was appalled at some of the dreadful poverty that he saw on his daily journey from Larbert to Glasgow, not to mention within Glasgow itself.

King Edward VII, that overweight, self-indulgent, hedonistic but in some ways loveable rogue, had been on the throne for five years now. Unlike his self-obsessed mother, he did occasionally seem to show some concern for his people and did try to encourage friendly relationships between Great Britain and the rest of Europe. It was no great secret, however, that he and his nephew, the Kaiser of Germany, did not like one another. Nor was it any great secret that Edward was still very fond of quite a few ladies other than Queen Alexandra!

Season 1906/07 was the first year that Alec played in more or less every game for Celtic. He was fortunate in the sense that Willie Loney broke his arm, and that, therefore, Alec was drafted in as centre-half for most of that season. Eck fitted in seamlessly and played a large part in the successful season which was the best in the club's history hitherto. No club had ever won the Scottish League and the Scottish Cup in the same season. Preston North End and Aston Villa had both done so in the last century in England, but, it seemed beyond anyone in Scotland. Rangers had come close in 1899, winning the title, but being defeated by Celtic in the Scottish Cup final. Willie Maley was determined that his fine young, rapidly developing side should be the first to do this 'Scottish Double,' or, as the punters asked for in the pubs, a 'double Scotch.'

The forward line of Bennett, McMenemy, Quinn, Somers & Hamilton did not get a chance to play together as often as Maley would have liked, for there were always injuries, whilst Jimmy Quinn was out for a long time after the New Year, serving a suspension that Celtic supporters considered unjust. The Celtic paranoia complex about everyone being against them was very strong in the 1900s and perhaps had a little more justification at that point in history, but, the point was that although Celtic missed the incredible talent which was Quinn (how could they not?), the available cover was adequate, and the team won through anyway.

We will soon see how Alec McNair stepped in to cover with a great deal of success for Willie Loney, but, at the start of the season, the main Celtic problem seemed to be with the goalkeeping role. Davie Adams had been playing in a game at Ibrox for Finlay Speedie's benefit, when he caught his hand on a nail on the post. Davie was then out injured for several weeks, albeit Rangers were decent enough (as the accident had happened at their ground) to offer Celtic the services of their reserve team goalkeeper, Tom Sinclair. The offer was gratefully accepted, and Tom Sinclair of Rangers went on to become Celtic's best-ever goalkeeper, statistically speaking!

Tom played nine games and kept eight clean sheets! Indeed, it would be his ninth and final game before he lost a goal. He then conceded two in one game and, according to McNair, he was very upset about that, but there was a distinct sweetener in that it was the Glasgow Cup final against Third Lanark, played, ironically, at Ibrox on Saturday, 6 October 1906, and Celtic won 3-2, thus giving Sinclair a medal which, frankly, would have escaped him had he stayed at Rangers. According to Alec, he actually lost three goals in that Glasgow Cup final when Sunny Jim beat him with a pass-back for an own goal! Fortunately, the whistle had already gone for an earlier infringement! It was actually a good game, with referee Mr Lewis of Blackburn living up to his reputation for being strict by continually penalising Sunny for taking foul throws. But Willie Orr took a good penalty and Young (at the right end!) and Peter Somers scored the other two goals for Celtic to win well.

There was then a further development in this strange season for Tom Sinclair, for he was transferred to Newcastle United and played a few games in their goal as they won the English First Division title in the spring of 1907!

It would be fair to say that Tom Sinclair's success at the start of the 1906/07 season owed a great deal to the fact that he was seldom troubled. If you have defenders of the likes of Donnie McLeod, Willie Orr, Sunny Jim Young, Jimmy Hay and Eck McNair in front of you, you are less likely to be under pressure. Alec was playing in various defensive positions, as the situation demanded, and was now thoroughly enjoying his football. He was also humble enough to appreciate that he was still learning his trade at this level. In addition, no-one in this Celtic squad could take anything for granted, as far as a position in the next week's team was concerned, and the supporters were now responding to the football played by this terrific side.

The Glasgow Cup was now safely in the bag, and Celtic did not lose another game until the New Year. This was the controversial game which took place on Tuesday, 1 January 1907, in which Jimmy Quinn was sent off at Ibrox after he tried to jump over a Rangers player, Joe Hendry, and slid into him on the wet ground. In spite of efforts to support Quinn by the more honest members of the Rangers establishment, Jimmy was suspended for two months, and Celtic felt ill-done by.

It is at times like this that level-headed characters like Eck McNair come into their own. Things might well have become really silly in that game, and in the immediate aftermath, but, thankfully, he was on hand to calm things down. The events at Ibrox were unfortunate, Alec reckoned, but as long as Celtic won their other games, all would be well. And this is what they proceeded to do, although they made a real meal of some of their Scottish Cup-ties, Maley's men requiring three games to beat Morton then another three to beat Hibernian.

Celtic lost only one game en route to winning their 'double Scotch,' and, significantly, that happened on a day that Alec McNair wasn't playing. On Saturday, 16 March 1907, Celts went down to Third Lanark at Cathkin whilst Eck, Alec Bennett and Peter Somers were a mile or so away playing for Scotland in a 3-0 win over Ireland at Celtic Park. The week before that had seen a situation which demanded the tact and diplomacy of McNair at his best.

It was the Scottish Cup quarter-final tie against Rangers at Ibrox, and as luck would have it, it was the first game back for Jimmy Quinn following his lengthy suspension. Glasgow was all agog to see how Quinn would react. Eck, who had now managed to get through to Jimmy (never an easy job, and one where he had to persevere!) talked things over with him, correctly pointing out that Rangers would try to provoke him and would have him heavily covered, so that he would not have the satisfaction of scoring against them. But that, as Eck said, meant that there would be fewer Rangers to mark the other Celts. All that Jimmy Quinn had to do was to stay out of trouble.

And so it turned out. Quinn did all that was required of him, sometimes taking three men with him, and that left gaps all over the place for Jimmy Hay, Davie Hamilton and Peter Somers to score the goals in what was a rather easy 3-0 victory, the only real threat to Celtic being the snow which fell late in the game as the Rangers crowd were heading homewards, leaving the Celtic supporters to sing "The Wearing O' The Green" in praise of their great team.

Celtic then needed three games to get the better of Hibernian – and this did little to silence the vicious tongues who suspected it had something to do with making money – but, eventually they turned it on to beat the Easter Road men 3-0 and set up a Scottish Cup final against the other Edinburgh team, Hearts, seven days later, on Saturday, 20 April 1907. As it happened, Celtic beat the Tynecastle side 3-0 as well, in a game that was significant in the subsequent history of both clubs.

For Celtic, it was the first step of their Double, as the League was more or less won by this time. For Hearts, it was the game which condemned them to almost 50 years of trophy famine and a pronounced inferiority complex about Celtic, which they have never lost. For Eck, it was his first big game at Hampden. Glasgow Cups were all very well, but, it was the Scottish Cup which was rightly called 'The Blue Riband' and looked upon as the number one trophy in the country. Although Hearts had their captain, Charlie Thomson, out through injury, they still had a fine forward-line, in Bauchope, Walker, Axford, Yates and Wombwell, and Eck and the rest of the defence knew that they would have to keep Bobby Walker quiet. Walker was commonly known as 'Houdini' (the great escapologist of the day) for his tricky play and was generally reckoned to be the cleverest player in the land at the time.

The following teams lined up before 50,000 spectators at Hampden Park;

Celtic: Adams, McLeod & Orr; Young, McNair & Hay; Bennett, McMenemy, Quinn, Somers & Templeton

Hearts: Allan, Reid & Collins; Philip, McLaren & Henderson; Bauchope, Walker, Axford, Yates & Wombwell

Referee; Mr D Philip, Dunfermline

The weather was "of the most disagreeable description," according to The Scotsman. It was a typical Scottish spring day, with heavy, violent showers punctuated with some sunshine. The weather was probably responsible for reducing the crowd to 50,000, although there had been no lack of travellers from Edinburgh, sometimes called the 'capitalists.' This sounded like the oppressors of the working classes, but, all it meant was that they came from Edinburgh, with their crawmills, rattles, flags and a few huge hearts with "Don't Lose This" written on them. There was no lack of confidence from Edinburgh, for they were the cup-holders, had eliminated Celtic from the Scottish Cup, the previous year, and recalled the final of 1901 when they had beaten Maley's Bhoys 4-3. Celtic's support, on the other hand, were quieter, not at all impressed by their problems in eventually defeating Morton and Hibernian.

The kick-off had to be delayed for some time to allow the Hearts goalkeeper, Tom Allan, to get through the crowd, his horse-driven taxi having been held up by the mass of spectators outside Hampden, and the first half which followed was "of an unsatisfactory description," both teams sizing each other up, afraid to give anything away. Early in the second half, Celtic were awarded a penalty, after Jimmy Quinn had been pushed off the ball in the box. Hearts disputed this award, and for years afterwards would add it to their collection of "we wuz robbed" stories, but Mr Philip from Dunfermline had no hesitation, and neither did Celtic's captain Willie Orr, and now Celtic were 1-0 up.

A fightback was expected from Hearts, who were now playing with the wind behind them towards the King's Park end, but, the defensive rock of Alec McNair, Donnie McLeod and Willie Orr proved impenetrable, and Celtic slowly took command with Jimmy McMenemy and Alec Bennet proving a strong right-wing. Hearts made the same mistake as Rangers had done a month previously, by concentrating too much on Jimmy Quinn, leaving space for Peter Somers, a grossly undervalued player, to score two fairly easy tap-ins for a final score of 3-0, as Celtic finished the game well on top.

It was a great moment for Eck and his family. This was his first Scottish Cup-winners medal, given to him that night at the Alexandra Hotel in Bath Street, in Glasgow's city centre, and as he caught the late-night train back home, he realised just what a great team Celtic were in every respect. He was cheered all the way from Bath Street to Buchanan Street Station by people who did not necessarily have all that much going for them. The Scottish League title was then won at Meadowside with a 2-0 victory over Partick Thistle, in circumstances of anti-climax on the following Wednesday afternoon, and so Willie Maley's Celtic had won the first-ever Scottish Double or 'Double Scotch.' In fact, it was a Treble because they already had the Glasgow Cup from the autumn, and it might even have been a Quadruple but for a complacent performance against Rangers in the Glasgow Charity Cup final in May.

A mystery surrounds the tour of Denmark in the early days of June 1907, for Alec McNair was not there. We were told he was "getting married," but, something must have happened because Eck did not wed Mary Niven until the summer of 1910. Did the couple fall out in 1907? Was he to marry someone else and it didn't come off in

1907? Perhaps the matrimonial motif was simply a rumour, and McNair was injured, or he was just needing a rest. Maybe there was some family problem, that we are unaware of, involving illness of relatives, for example? There is a mystery here!

Whatever it was all about, McNair was back in action for the start of the 1907/08 season, a season that turned out to be even better than the one just ended, and which can possibly be described as the best in the entire history of the club. Certainly, it stands comparison with 1966/67, in that Celtic won every competition for which they entered – the Scottish League, the Scottish Cup, the Glasgow Cup and the Glasgow Charity Cup. Eck also played twice for Scotland and once for the Scottish League.

And yet Alec McNair still had to fight for his place at Celtic! Willie Loney was back, and he was a mighty centre-half, and the other position that he would eventually make his own was right-back, where he found it difficult to dislodge (although he eventually did so) 'The Slasher,' Donnie McLeod, his friend from Stenhousemuir.

This was also the season that saw the appearance of the old Jungle on the north side of the ground. There had been a grandstand there until it was burned down in 1904 (shortly after Eck arrived at Celtic Park), but now there was a huge, ugly-looking barn structure, which would last, in one form or another, until 1966. Presumably in 1907, there were not the holes which appeared in the roof in the 1940s and 1950s, and the structure did provide shelter from the elements for at least some fans.

It was during this season that Eck discovered his best position was right-back. He was playing in that position when Celtic won the first trophy of the season – the Glasgow Cup – beating Rangers at the third attempt, after two draws. The third game was played at Hampden, on Saturday, 26 October 1907. Celtic were two up at half-time with goals from Peter Somers and young Davie McLean, before Rangers staged a terrific fightback in the second half and although "one goal was conceded, a second was not," and Celtic held out to win the Glasgow Cup for the second year in a row. Eck, at right-back, had Rangers star left-winger Alec Smith to deal with, but he did so admirably.

It is not often that Eck is singled out in newspaper reports for excellent play. A right-back or centre-half of McNair's style seldom hit the headlines, but, this season saw him mentioned several times with honour in The Glasgow Observer. On Saturday, 7 December 1907, Celtic beat St Mirren 4-0 at Parkhead. McNair scored the first goal, which was not entirely surprising as in those days centre-halves doubled up and exchanged places with centre-forwards, and mention was made of the "short, dribbling runs... sharp, low, skilful passes" which characterised his play.

Alec is also well-mentioned in the New Year's Day game against Rangers, played at Celtic Park on Wednesday, 1 January 1908, which Celtic won 2-1, McNair reported as "gobbling up everything that came down the middle." This day was dominated by the news that captain James 'Dun' Hay was seriously ill with appendicitis. Hay had had his operation, however, and was on his way to recovery by Saturday, 18 January 1908, when McNair played his part in rescuing Celtic from defeat at Fir Park, Motherwell. It was quite simply a rare poor game for Celtic, as without Loney, Quinn and Hay, they lost two early goals to a nippy home side, who were holding on comfortably until, with 12 minutes to go. At that point, Eck, everything else having failed, tried a "long drooping ball" which the goalkeeper ignored, thinking that it was going over the bar, only to watch it creep in. Then Peter Somers equalised. Celtic might even have snatched a winner, but, 2-2 was the final score.

It was McNair's performance in the Scottish Cup second-round tie against Rangers at Ibrox on Saturday, 8 February 1908 which suggested to the Scottish sporting public that Eck had arrived as a right-back. This was a game played before a much lower crowd than normal of 23,000, hosts Rangers having decided, unilaterally, to double the admission fees. A surly, angry crowd turned up, unable to afford the price, and threatening to break down exit gates as they had done in the past. It needed 240 policemen to disperse them. Inside the ground, a very close game was won 2-1 by Celtic (still without Jimmy Hay and Jimmy Quinn - who was out with a poisoned toe - albeit both were actually at the game and looked quite healthy) after a mistake by Rangers' John May allowed ex-Ibrox star Willie Kivlichan to score the winner from a very tight angle. McNair was praised for his "resource, coolness and judgement" and totally dominated Celtic's right flank, repeatedly sending passes to Alec Bennett and Jimmy McMenemy.

The excellence of the Celtic flank that day no doubt played a part in all three of McNair, Bennett and McMenemy being chosen to play for the Scottish League against the English League on Leap Year's Day 1908 at Villa Park, Birmingham. Eck, who had excelled at either right-back or centre-half all season for Celtic, now found himself playing once again at right-half, such was his versatility! And he played well, even if the Scottish League lost 0-2. In his absence, Celtic could only draw 1-1 with Third Lanark at Parkhead, the same afternoon.

The Scottish League v English League game was an annual event and was often looked upon as a trial match for the 'big' International in April. Only domestic players were eligible, of course, but, the games were looked upon as important, and Alec had played well enough to win a place for the full Scotland team for the next game, against Wales at Dens Park, Dundee, seven days later, once again at right-half!

The Courier was of the opinion that McNair was one of the best players in Scotland's 2-1 win, "both in tackling and feeding his wings, he was a star," and he was rewarded for all this by being chosen to play for Scotland in the most important match of the year, the international against England at Hampden on Saturday, 4 April 1908. This time he was at right-back! The game attracted an astonishing crowd of 121,452 and it was generally agreed to be the largest ever assembled for any sporting fixture in the history of the world! It kicked off at 4.00pm and the gates had to be closed at 3.15pm with thousands (estimated at 15,000) turned away and denied admission. The Scottish Referee goes into raptures about the crowd and the spectacle on this fine spring day, saying that "Rome and Athens and all their gladiatorial and Olympic grandeur approached" Hampden on that day, especially when the pipers started to play patriotic and stirring Scottish tunes.

Alec McNair, although he picked up an early injury, held his own in this game which ended in a 1-1 draw, many Scottish supporters convinced that the English goal was unjustified in that the ball did not cross the line. Certainly, goalkeeper Peter McBride was of that persuasion. Quinn had a good game as well, and it must have been a barely believable experience for the two young men from Croy and Stenhousemuir to play in such an arena on such an occasion. About a mile away, at Celtic Park, their club teammates were playing before just 3,000 spectators as they beat Morton 2-0.

Two weeks later, Eck was back at Hampden, this time before a crowd of about half that of the international match to see Celtic take on St Mirren in the Scottish Cup final. Celtic had reached that stage by beating Aberdeen at Pittodrie in the semi-final, in a tight game decided in the last minute. This match could not have been more different. It was a nice, bright, breezy day and Celtic controlled the game from start to finish, as they beat the Buddies 5-1. St Mirren's only possible grounds for complaint would be that they thought there had been an infringement before Alec Bennett's second goal. However, they then committing the cardinal error of stopping and waiting for referee Mr Ferguson to do something! Yet it was their own player who had fouled Quinn, and the Falkirk official wisely played advantage. Eck was once again outstanding in defence. "McNair was, as usual, judicious, clever and cool," said The Scottish Referee. Celtic had now won the Scottish Cup six times, and it was Alec's second Scottish Cup medal to go with the one he won the previous year.

The teams at Hampden on that afternoon of Saturday, 18 April 1908 were as follows:

Celtic: Adams, McNair & Weir; Young, Loney & Hay; Bennett, McMemeny, Quinn, Somers & Hamilton

St Mirren: Grant, Gordon & White; Key, Robertson & McAvoy; Clements, Cunningham, Wyllie, Paton & Anderson

Referee: Mr J Ferguson, Falkirk

And this very eventful and successful month of April 1908 had not yet finished. Celtic, without McNair, beat Hearts 6-0 on the Monday, and this meant that the League could be clinched at Ibrox on Saturday, 25 April, the date that just happened to be manager Willie Maley's 40th birthday. The game was, quite frankly, a disgrace, with some awful tackling by Rangers, and a few of the Celtic men not above a little retaliation. The main target was, naturally, Jimmy Quinn, but, Davie Hamilton and Eck McNair were also injured. Quinn had to go off, but McNair limped on bravely, in so doing putting himself out for the rest of the season. He had the satisfaction of seeing Alec Bennett score the only goal of the game, and thus Alec McNair had won his fourth Scottish League winner's medal.

Maley's Celtic had won their back-to-back Doubles, and this season they also won the Glasgow Charity Cup to complete their Quadruple. Eck's injured leg meant that he was out of that competition, albeit he enjoyed sitting in the stand and watching his men do the necessary. Could life get any better for the quiet, dignified man from Stenhousemuir? He was often seen on the train, looking dapper and even elegant, polite but not effusive, and with the appearance of a business gent travelling to and from his office. He was however aware of other passengers nudging each other and saying sotto voce, "That's McNair." "Who?" "McNair of the Celtic, and Scotland!"

CHAPTER THREE

REPLACING SLASHER (1908-1910)

Donnie McLeod was a tremendous right-back. He came from the same part of the world as Alec McNair, and the two became great friends, with the man known as Slasher reputed to have played an influential part in persuading Eck to join him at Celtic Park. McLeod was the regular right-back at Parkhead until 1908, although McNair was an able deputy when required. The value of McNair, however, was his sheer versatility.

In the Scottish Cup final of 1908, Donnie McLeod was injured, and Alec McNair was the right-back, but, the start of the 1908/09 season would see Slasher's departure. The circumstances are strange. McLeod played in the first five games, two of which were defeats to Dundee and St Mirren whilst another was a 4-4 draw in the Glasgow Cup against Queen's Park. It seems that McLeod was blamed for some of the goals lost in the Glasgow Cup game, and possibly a few intemperate words were exchanged between the player and Willie Maley. In any case, in October 1908, Donnie McLeod was on his way to Middlesbrough, one of many to have played with distinction for both Celtic and Boro, Jamie Weir, Neil Mochan, Willie Fernie and Tony Mowbray being others. McLeod became a regular and a great hero at Ayresome Park, took over The Lord Byron pub in Middlesbrough, but then met his death at Passchendaele in October 1917, having been conscripted very much against his will.

Eck McNair was naturally sorry to see Donnie go to Middlesbrough, although he immediately spotted an opening for himself at right-back. He was, privately at least, getting a little fed up with being a 'utility man,' and hated himself for hoping that one of his friends would get injured, so that he could get a game! But he immediately seized this opportunity and remained Celtic's right-back from 1908, more or less, until 1925, an astonishingly long time, especially when one considers the horrific things that happened both to the world, and to Eck personally in these awful but momentous 17 years.

The 'Donnie McLeod business' also highlighted another aspect of Willie Maley's character, in that he did not like failure. In spite of Maley's specious statements about "the game's the thing" and pompous verbiage like "as well as enjoying the fruits of victory, we must also sometimes taste the bitterness of defeat," and even "we are delighted for our friends at Ibrox" for the benefit of the Press, his players all knew that he was a very bad loser, who would shout at them if and when things went wrong. Even in the middle of the very successful 1907/08 season, he had taken a dig at Donnie, using words like "adipose" (a euphemism for "fat"), and he clearly made McLeod the scapegoat for the comparatively poor start to the season.

David McLean tells the story of how Maley charged into the dressing room after this 4-4 game in a "black rage and pitched into them." There were, of course, other people to blame as well (Alec Bennett had now gone to Rangers, for reasons that defy explanation, and Bobby Templeton to Kilmarnock). However, Donnie McLeod was there and, apparently, he bore the brunt of it. He may well have felt, in any case, that it might be time to move on, and this was what decided him. In any case, Middlesbrough came in for him just at the right time, and McLeod was soon on his way.

Donnie McLeod and Alec McNair were different kinds of fullbacks. McLeod was not called The Slasher for nothing. He went in hard and found himself, now and again, on the wrong side of the referee for the occasional reckless tackle. He could occasionally be caught out of position (as clearly happened against Queen's Park), but, he was generally a competent right-back, as his four Scottish caps would tend to indicate.

In contrast, McNair was far more refined. A very intelligent man off the field, Eck revealed a great deal of brain power on the field as well. In those days, the positions were slightly more rigid than they are now, and each defender knew who he had to mark. Eck believed in doing his homework on his direct opponent and would spend the first quarter of an hour of a game sizing him up, noticing his strengths and weaknesses, and determining how best to play him. McNair tackled well, scorning the nasty tackle and reckoning that most referees would possibly allow one or two before cracking down on him, as they did with Sunny Jim Young, for example, when his enthusiasm got the better of him.

McNair had good positional sense and had a healthy respect for the basics of the game, such as keeping fit, preparing in advance and not talking too much, certainly not to the Press. Willie Maley tended not to give lengthy or detailed team talks, but, Eck believed in carrying out such instructions as had been given. Football, he reckoned, was a simple game. Keep yourself between the ball and the goal, tackle at the right time, try to pass accurately and if in any doubt, there was never anything wrong with a punt up the park, on the grounds that, even if the ball did come straight back, the defence had a few extra seconds to re-organise.

But Celtic were having a bad autumn in 1908. Such things often happen after a phenomenally successful season. The Glasgow Cup was a nightmare for more reasons than one. They needed two games to beat Queen's Park, another two to defeat Rangers and then in the final they actually lost to Third Lanark in the third game! The common perception in Glasgow at the time was that they were 'at it,' deliberately drawing games in order to get another big gate in the replay, with bookmakers, all-pervasive although illegal, involved as well. Seven games had been required to finish where only three were strictly necessary!

More than a hundred years later, it is difficult to deny or accept such allegations. The sheer amount of drawn Cup ties is certainly suspicious, but, it is very difficult to 'fix' a football match, as with so many people having to be involved, the odds are that someone would 'snitch' and leak it all to the Press. The Glasgow Herald and The Scottish Referee, two very respectable newspapers of the time, tend to think that most games are straight, although the amount of space that they devote to the issue shows that the idea was very current at the time, and needed to be addressed.

There is also the question of players' integrity. It is hard to imagine men like McNair with his quiet probity, Young with his unbounded professional aggression and Quinn with his moody but determined introversion going along with anything so deliberately dishonest. On the other hand, one can never deny the inordinate and sometimes obvious greed of the clubs themselves and their desire to make money. On balance, one would have to conclude that corruption was not the issue, but, the important thing was that people at the time thought that it existed. There would be appalling consequences of this popular perception in the following spring.

One game that certainly was not fixed was the third game of the Glasgow Cup final. Deprived of a third Saturday and compelled to play on the afternoon of Wednesday, 28 October 1908, Celtic appalled the 17,000 crowd with a 0-4 collapse, something that tended to hint at some trouble at Celtic Park itself. It could, of course, be quite simply that Celtic were exhausted after their heavy schedule and played badly, whilst Third Lanark, no mean side in 1908, played well, scored their goals at the right time and thus won the day. In addition, Celtic suffered a severe blow in the serious injury to influential left-winger Davie Hamilton, who was carried off after only 30 minutes. Nevertheless, the comprehensive nature of the defeat of that great team of 1908 caused no little concern and puzzlement among the Celtic support.

The wonder is, however, how quickly Celtic recovered. It was almost as if something bad had to be got out of one's system, so to speak, and that the team, still a great one, had to move on. Sensible players like James Hay - the captain, Eck McNair, Jimmy McMenemy and Peter Somers realised that Celtic's reputation had been badly damaged by the events and rumours of the autumn, and that a major blow had been landed, but, it was now time to turn round and fight back, while others like Sunny Jim Young and Jimmy Quinn were determined that it must never happen again. The next seven games were won, all of them competently but unspectacularly, with McNair playing his part and occasionally we find a reference to his "clean tackling" and "crisp passing". It was also around this time (the weather was cold!) that we find, for the first time, references to 'The Icicle' as a nickname for him.

The run was brought to an end on Boxing Day 1908, in a narrow 0-1 defeat to neighbours Clyde on a snow-covered pitch, in conditions that were clearly unsuitable. That this was only a temporary reverse, however, was shown in a good 3-1 win over Rangers at Ibrox on New Year's Day 1909, (the weather having improved beyond all recognition) in which the home wingers were played out of the game by McNair and Weir, the Celtic full backs. The duel that attracted the most attention was on the Rangers right wing, where ex-Celtic player Alec Bennett, booed and catcalled mercilessly by the Celtic fans, was marked out of the game by Jamie Weir. However, no less significant was what happened on the other flank, where Alec Smith was barely given a kick of the ball by the excellent Alec McNair, and when the ball did come to him, Smith was compelled to get rid of it and to pass or cross prematurely.

One wonders, however, what the professional McNair made of the events the following day at Kilmarnock. The win over Rangers had come at the cost of an injury to goalkeeper Davie Adams. Celtic, as it happened, and surprisingly given the normal methodical approach of Willie Maley, did not have a reserve, specialist goalkeeper. It would have been in order for Maley to ask for a loan from another club (we recall the heroics of Rangers' Tommy Sinclair in 1906) or to approach one of the myriad of Glasgow Junior clubs whose goalkeeper would have given his eye teeth to play a game for Celtic. Instead, he did something odd, and which he later regretted.

Sunny Jim Young had missed the New Year's Day game at Ibrox with an injury, from which he was gradually recovering, although not yet feeling fully fit enough to play in his normal right-half position. He approached the Celtic boss and suggested that, although he could not play in his conventional position, why couldn't he take over from Davie Adams in goal? In the goal, you did not need to run about quite so much and "they boys in front o' me wad keep the ba' awa'." Astonishingly, Willie Maley agreed to this.

To be fair, in 1909 it was probably not quite as extreme a proposal as it seems to us well over 100 years later. The goalkeeper had to be nominated as the man who was allowed to handle the ball in his own area, but otherwise played as a defender, indeed, it was not until about 1911 or 1912 that goalkeepers began to wear a different coloured jersey from the rest of the team. The Scottish Referee does not make a big issue of this in its report of the game, saying quite blandly that "Jim Young was in goal for Celtic…His work at the start was sufficient to dispel any uneasiness that the Celts might have felt for the safeness of their citadel." Yet, nevertheless, it must have amazed McNair and a few others that Maley allowed this. Not surprisingly, Celtic lost 3-1 at Kilmarnock that day, although the newspapers go out of their way to exonerate Young from any blame. The real reason for the defeat was possibly euphoria from the previous day's result and a certain feeling of complacency. Plus of course, the simple fact that Kilmarnock played well!

Celtic had simply to bite the bullet, learn a few lessons and move on. Increasingly, captain James Hay was finding that he was turning to Alec McNair for advice. He did not feel that McNair was in any sense a rival to himself as captain (although McNair had in extremis done the job now and again, when Hay was off injured) because Eck, although his knowledge of the game was second to none, lacked the ability to shout, cajole and even swear at players. All captains needed to have this capacity! Willie Maley, too, always felt that any suggestion from Eck McNair was worth listening to.

The Scottish League this year was strange. The title challengers were not so much Rangers, who were far too capable of off days, as Dundee, who led the table for most of the season. Celtic were behind but had many games in hand because of their extensive and prolonged Glasgow Cup campaign. Not unnaturally, this caused a little apprehension and resentment in Dundee. Their team was often likened to a traveller heading towards his destination hotel called 'the Scottish League Championship' well ahead of everyone else, but with a shadow called 'Celtic' coming up behind him.

The Dundee Courier, an odd publication which, of course, had to keep Dundee supporters happy without in any way antagonising the huge Irish population in the city which followed Celtic, is quite outspoken about how unfair it was on both teams. Celtic would know how many points they needed at any given time in the run-in; on the other hand, they would have to play all of their games close together.

Eck, not normally an injury-prone player, sustained a bad knock in a Scottish Cup-tie against Airdrieonians in mid-February and had to go off early in the second half. Although the team still managed to win, Eck was then out for a month, returning for the Scottish Cup semi-final against Clyde, which was drawn (tactlessly) the first time but won in a replay. On the Monday following that 2-0 victory, Celtic beat Partick Thistle 1-0 in a dull game at Celtic Park, which owed a great deal, once again, to the hard tackling of their full-backs, Alec McNair and Jamie Weir.

This brought us to the end of March, with Celtic in the Scottish Cup final against Rangers and the League table showing Dundee top, having played 32 and amassing 46 points, Rangers second with 27 and 39, and Celtic third with 24 and 36. In total, 34 games were to be played, and with two points on offer for a win in 1909, Celtic could, therefore, overtake the leading pair of Dundee and Rangers, albeit an awful lot of football remained to be played in the April. Celtic would reasonably be expected to overtake Rangers, Dundee, but, did seem to be just a shade too far ahead.

It is always true that April is a very busy, important and exciting month, but, no-one could ever hope to guess just exactly what was going to happen that month in 1909. McNair played a total of 12 games, every single one of them important and vital. One sometimes has to laugh at the way modern players are protected and cossetted, with everyone worrying about them playing too much football!

For Alec McNair, the eventful month started at the Crystal Palace in London on Saturday, 3 April 1909, and it was a disappointing day as Scotland went down 0-2 to England. It was not one of McNair's better performances, but then again, that may be something to do with the fact that he was playing once again for Scotland at right-half, rather than his now normal place of right-back. The two chosen full-backs were little known Anglo-Scots called John Cameron and James Watson, from Chelsea and Middlesbrough respectively, and they were out of their depth. England got the goals, and Jimmy Quinn up front never really got going.

It was a heartbreak for Scotland, and Eck McNair as much as anyone, except that he had the consolation of a trip to London to appear at the 'Palace of Doom', where Scotland seldom played well. The Palace of Doom phrase was first used by Newcastle United supporters, who had lost three English FA Cup finals there, but, it could have been applied to Scotland as well. Unaccountably, only 27,000 spectators were there on a fine day to see it (there had been almost 100,000 more at Hampden the previous year) but amongst the meagre crowd was HRH The Prince of Wales (the future King George V), paying a rare visit to a football match.

McNair himself tells the story of how Scotland were awarded a penalty kick late in the game, and several Scottish players were reluctant to take it, Alec Bennett, Jimmy Quinn and Peter McWilliam all apparently so dispirited that they lacked confidence. So, captain Jimmy Stark of Rangers had to take it himself and he shot straight at Sam Hardy in the England goal. It was no-one's finest hour.

It was now time for Alec McNair to get back to Scotland and win the League Championship and the Scottish Cup for Celtic. On the day of the England International, Celtic minus McNair and Quinn had beaten St Mirren 1-0 at Love Street, but Dundee had also won, so effectively there was no change.The Scottish Cup final now appeared on the horizon, Celtic v Rangers, the fourth final between these two, Celtic having won in 1899 and 1904, and Rangers having been successful in 1894.

One would have thought that Celtic might have played off one of their outstanding League matches in the week between the International and the Scottish Cup final, but, for some reason the club did not do so, preferring to train quietly at Parkhead for the coming date at Hampden. Alec McNair and Jimmy Quinn, who had played in the game against England at Crystal Palace were possibly glad of the rest from competitive football.

The Scottish Cup final, played at Hampden on Saturday, 10 April 1909, itself attracted a large crowd of 70,000 spectators and they saw a fairly even competition. Celtic were definitely on top in the first half and led 1-0 at half-time, with a good goal well-taken by Jimmy Quinn. Indeed, they might have scored more. Then, about halfway through the second half, Rangers made a key positional switch by moving Alec Bennett to centre-forward. Bennett had not been a success on the right wing against Jamie Weir, but, he made more progress in the middle against Joe Dodds, who had been preferred to Willie Loney for fitness reasons. Dodds still lacked experience, and subsequent history would indicate that a better position for him would be at left-back. Bennett got the better of him, feeding Tom Gilchrist to equalise in the 75th minute and then a few minutes later scoring himself to put Rangers ahead.

Things now looked bleak for Celtic. However, they kept pushing forward, leaving Eck McNair to cover the defence whilst left-back Jamie Weir and centre-half Joe Dodds went forward in an attempt to grab the equaliser. To the enormous relief of their supporters in the crowd, they did so with only seven minutes to go, and it was a funny one. Rangers' goalkeeper Harry Rennie caught a high ball, then out of the corner of his eye, saw Jimmy Quinn rushing at him. A shoulder charge was legal in 1909 and often goals were scored by the keeper being bundled into the net, so Rennie moved back out of the way, as he thought, but in so doing managed to lose balance slightly and crossed his own line with the ball in his hands. Referee JB Stark, never the best-loved of referees in Celtic eyes, on this occasion correctly gave a goal.

Rennie's own goal was much argued about that night, and it was unfortunate, in the context of later events, that a contentious and disputed goal led to a draw. It escaped no-one's notice that a draw meant another large crowd the next Saturday, and eyebrows were raised as newspapers made innuendoes in the Press on Monday with pointed and barbed references to the power of the 'Old Firm' (as they were now called) to attract large attendances.

Perhaps aware of these undercurrents, (they were in fact a lot stronger than undercurrents), Willie Maley asked publicly if there was to be extra-time in the event of the scores being level at the end of 90 minutes in the replay. He thought that might be an idea, and there is a certain amount of evidence that Rangers might have backed him up, but, the competition organisers, the SFA, being sticklers for the rules as always, would not bend. Crucially, however, they did not make their decision sufficiently public. The result was that a significant amount of the 60,000 spectators went along to Hampden that fateful Saturday afternoon of 17 April 1909, thinking that there might be extra-time in the event of another draw, whereas the SFA's decision would have been a third game, and referee Mr Stark was so instructed.

There was an added issue as far as Celtic were concerned, in that they still had eight League fixtures to play. It seems that everything had to be finished by the end of April, otherwise there would be huge problems with players' contracts. How were Celtic going to play eight games in a fortnight? And that was reckoning without the possibility of a third Scottish Cup final! It was a problem of the club's own making, of course, thanks to those Glasgow Cup replays, but it was a severe problem, nevertheless.

In the meantime, Celtic had dropped a point on Monday, 12 April 1909, as they edged towards the League flag in a disappointing performance against Third Lanark at Cathkin. Rangers also drew, which meant that the top three positions now showed Dundee 33 - 48, Rangers 30 - 44 and Celtic 26 - 39. Any progress on that front would have to wait until next week when the Scottish Cup was decided.

Once again, a huge crowd, slightly down on last week but still over 60,000, saw an even game. Jimmy Gordon scored for Rangers in the first half, and Jimmy Quinn equalised from a Davie Hamilton cross after the break. Neither team could then score a winner, with Celtic's full backs McNair and Weir effectively blotting out Rangers dangerous wingers Bennett and Smith, and the Rangers defence similarly able to concentrate enough strength to snuff out Jimmy Quinn.

A feeling of disappointment was prevalent as Mr Stark blew for time up. Clearly the players themselves were not sure whether there would be extra-time or not and stayed on the field looking up to the stand for guidance. Guidance came there none, and Mr Stark, who had been told there was to be no extra-time, hung about on the field with the ball under his arm, quite correctly waiting for the players to make their way to the pavilion, it being the referee's job to be the last man off the pitch, not unlike the captain having to be the last man to leave a sinking ship.

Alec McNair himself, years later, sums it up in his memoirs by saying; "What a pity someone didn't take the trouble to make a definite statement regarding the position." A clear statement in the Press on the morning of the game might have clarified matters. There was a "howl of rage and chagrin," as the confusion stayed for a few minutes. Some of the crowd decided to go home, muttering about "another bloody fix", but, a few others saw a chance to at least talk to men like McNair and Quinn and jumped over the low surround. Then more arrived, and with still no-one taking a grip of the situation, they began to throw cinders (which were on the earth terracing steps to prevent the spectators from slipping) at each other for fun. And then more fans come onto the field for a laugh.

Things then took a more serious turn, and the players, to coin a phrase, 'scarpered.' Eck was adamant that no violence was ever at any stage offered or threatened to the players or the referee, nor was there even any violence offered to each other by either support. The wearing of colours, usually rosettes, was not unknown, but, it was not widespread either, and there was certainly no sectarian or partisan element in what followed.

What happened then, in some ways, defies description. Whisky was poured on goal posts, the better to make then burn! Ambulance men were stoned. Fire men were attacked, and their hoses cut. Turnstiles were set on fire, and serious damage was done to the pitch and to the steps of the terracing. Hampden would not recover for a long time.

Men like Alec McNair (and indeed Scottish public opinion in general) would struggle to make out what this was all about. In so far as one can make any sense of it, it revealed two things – one was the definite perception that they were being 'had' by the clubs wanting more money out of them, and the other was the sheer love of football and the consequent anger when they were being deprived of half an hour's extra-time. But of course, ochlocracy or mob rule is, by its nature, irrational and volatile. Sociologists could analyse it all and talk about the "revolutionary tendencies" of the underprivileged and how Edwardian society was not as stable as it wanted to portray itself to be, but, in fact, all it revealed was the ability of the urban mob to turn violent and enjoy itself doing so, when an opportunity presented itself.

The important thing was that, although there were quite a few injuries and an awful lot of damage to property, there were no deaths. The Scottish Cup itself was rescued and taken away to safety by Alec Maley (Willie's brother), the players were safely escorted to charabancs and taxis, and at a meeting on the Monday night, the SFA decided to withhold the Scottish Cup that year. Apart from anything else, Hampden was now unusable and no other ground (other than Celtic Park or Ibrox) was able to hold the crowd. There are times when the modern expedient of penalty shoot-outs does not seem to be such a bad idea after all!

Another thing that must be stressed is that there was never any political element to this. It is tempting for some historians to see things like Irish Home Rule or No Popery involved here. Some historians, confusing 1909 with 1980 (which was indeed a sectarian riot between two sets of mentally-challenged youths) make out that it was Celtic youths who started it, or Rangers youths who were worse than their counterparts. This was absolutely not the case! If there was any cause, for which anyone was fighting, it was against the authorities who would not allow them to watch more football!

So, sadly Celtic could not win the Scottish Cup for the third year in a row. But what about the League? On the same night that the SFA decided to withhold the Scottish Cup, important events took place in Edinburgh. It was the local Holiday Monday, and Celtic beat Hearts 2-1 at Tynecastle with two goals from Jimmy McMenemy, whilst across the city, Rangers blew up and lost what little chance they had of winning the title by going down 0-1 to Hibernian. This only left Dundee, who now could do little other than stand and watch, hoping that the other teams could do them several favours.

Basically, after the riot Scottish Cup final, Celtic had to play eight games in the last 12 days of April – on Monday 19, Wednesday 21, Thursday 22, Saturday 24, Monday 26, Wednesday 28, Thursday 29 and Friday 30. A total of 16 points were available, of which 12 would be sufficient for Celtic to retain their title, assuming Dundee won their game in hand, as they duly did. It was still a tall order, but, Celtic buckled down to the job in hand. They lost one game (to Hibernian at Easter Road), drew another two (Hamilton Academical and Airdrieonians at home, funnily enough) but won the remaining five, over Morton and Motherwell at Celtic Park and against Hearts at Tynecastle, Queen's Park at Cathkin rather than the ruined Hampden, and finally, on a lovely spring night, in the presence of off-duty soldiers from the nearby barracks accompanied by well-dressed young women, Celtic beat Hamilton Academical 2-1 at Douglas Park. This gave Celtic a total of 12 points from their eight games, enough to win the Scottish League for the fifth year in a row, and, indeed, for Eck McNair to secure his fifth League medal.

The Press are united in their admiration for this achievement. In circumstances like these, people look to men like Eck McNair to provide leadership. This he did, his quiet, serene, yet determined nature bringing a sense of reality to a situation that could have gone wrong, and badly so. He was of course puzzled and saddened by what happened at Hampden back on 17 April, but, he realised that it had happened and was now behind them. The Scottish League was now the important thing, and the fact that Celtic had now won it for five consecutive seasons meant that they had now beaten Rangers record of four-in-a-row, achieved between 1899 and 1902. Eck, by his own admission having supported Rangers in these four years, was now proud to have been part of the side which broke that particular record!

Davie Adams, Alec McNair, Jamie Weir and Jimmy Quinn played in all eight of those epic 12 games. It was a feat that more or less defied description and we would have thought they would have been tired. Not a bit of it! Three of them were playing the following day in Aberdeen in a Charity game! The season did take its toll on Eck, though. He missed the Glasgow Charity Cup semi-final against Clyde, played at Celtic Park on Saturday, 8 May 1909, and looked slightly out of sorts in the final, seven days later, in which Rangers got some sort of revenge by beating Celtic 4-2 in a game with more policemen than anyone could ever remember seeing before. It was just as well that there was no foreign tour that year. Eck McNair was badly in need of a rest.

The year of 1909 was an important one in British politics. There was what might be termed a constitutional crisis, as the House of Lords refused to pass the Budget of David Lloyd George. The Liberals, who had been in office since early 1906 (the Prime Minister, the amiable and respected Henry Campbell-Bannerman had died in 1908 and been replaced by Herbert Asquith), and had passed some welcome and much needed social reforms including, for example, free lunches for poor children at school. This needed to be paid for, and Lloyd George produced a Budget which unashamedly hit the rich hard. The Conservatives and the House of Lords resisted, two General Elections were held in 1910, and the Liberals lost their huge majority... but they won their point.

For Celtic and its supporters, this had implications about Ireland, for it had been the House of Lords which had stymied previous Liberal attempts at Home Rule. As a Scotsman from Stenhousemuir, this hardly impacted Alec McNair, but, he was very aware that it did affect the support and other members of the team. Another thing that affected McNair and Celtic as the 1909/10 season started was the death of one of Celtic's most renowned of administrators, chairman John H McLaughlin. He was only 46, but, his effect on the development of the club had been profound. John McLaughlin and Eck McNair had a deep respect for each other.

The season started well, if unspectacularly, with Celtic winning the first four games, but then Eck suffered a bad blow, on Friday, 10 September 1909, when his father James died at the age of 55. He had been ill for some time with carcinoma of the liver. James McNair was living in Church Street, Stenhousemuir at the time. He is a shadowy figure about whom very little is really known, but, it would be a fair bet that he was very proud of his son. Eck's mother, Agnes, survived her husband by many years and would play a vital and supportive role in helping her son deal with the tragedy that would befall him in later years.

Obviously, Eck could not play against Morton at Cappielow the following day and it is perhaps significant that Celtic sustained a rare loss that day. Otherwise, the form of the team was very good, with October bringing a Scottish League cap for McNair against the Irish League, and another Glasgow Cup medal. The latter was secured on Saturday, 9 October 1909 at Hampden, and Celtic's opponents once again were Rangers. In the context of what had happened five months earlier, much discussion took place about whether the game could go ahead or not. But all was well. More police were deployed, it was made more difficult for anyone to get onto the park at the now-renovated Hampden, and tactfully, it was not another draw! Celtic won 1-0 with a strange goal, following a skied clearance from a Rangers defender, Jimmy Quinn getting there as it landed before four Rangers defenders converged upon him! In the second half, the Celtic defence of Adams, McNair & Weir; Young, Loney & Hay then defied everything that Rangers could throw at them, enabling the Glasgow Cup to be regained.

Otherwise, the New Year of 1910 was reached without any significant alarms for either Alec McNair or Celtic, other than that he missed the game at Kilmarnock on Christmas Day with a twisted ankle. From his seat in the Rugby Park stand, Eck saw the only goal scored by Jimmy Quinn, the 'Croy Express' running almost the length of the field, beating man after man, to score a goal that was still being talked about 50 years later! Celtic finished the calendar year of 1909 well ahead of Rangers in the Scottish League, their closest rivals at that time being Falkirk, the near neighbours of the McNairs of Stenhousemuir.

Celtic were having a good 1909/10 season. They still missed Alec Bennett on the right wing, albeit Dan Munro and Willie Kivlichan were good enough. The only other change of note was that Peter Johnstone from Glencraig, in Fife, had replaced Peter Somers at inside-left. McNair played in the New Year's Day game against Rangers, a bruising battle which ended up 1-1 (The Scottish Referee, tongue firmly in cheek talks euphemistically about "over-eagerness!") before 60,000 spectators at Celtic Park, but, he aggravated his ankle and was out injured for most of the rest of January. His place was taken by Jimmy McIntosh, an adequate player who performed much the same role as McNair himself had done a few years earlier as a utility defender.

It then so happened that Eck's return on Saturday, 29 January 1910 saw a dreadful game and Celtic's first defeat since 11 September 1909. Games between St Mirren and Celtic at Paisley were seldom pleasant ones, and Willie Maley's side finished this one with only nine men, Davie Hamilton having been injured and Sunny Jim Young sent off for making a few comments which referee Tom Dougray did not appreciate. The pitch was barely playable, and at several points the crowd seemed to be threatening an invasion, but, one man stood out above everyone else. "McNair was in a class by himself as a back, his superb coolness under pressure and general deportment marking him out from the others. When the occasion demanded, he came through the Saints forwards single-handed, and always disposed of the ball to advantage." This comment, from The Scottish Referee, is typical of so many written about McNair at this time, even though in this case, it was in a losing cause.

February was a better month, with progress made in both League and Scottish Cup, and for McNair the satisfaction of playing in a Scottish League side that beat the English League at Blackburn. It was the first full International of the year, however, which had long term implications for Celtic. The International was played at Rugby Park, Kilmarnock against Wales, and Scotland, with five Celts on board (McNair playing once again for Scotland at right-half!) won 1-0. The Welsh did not take very kindly to this, and Jimmy McMenemy (far and away the best player on the park) was badly crocked, ruling him out of the next week's Scottish Cup semi-final against Clyde at Shawfield.

The problem was that McMenemy joined a number of other key players who were not playing. Sunny Jim Young was suspended, and goalkeeper Davie Adams was ill with pneumonia. Celtic still did not have a reserve goalkeeper and hired Leigh Roose of Sunderland (who had played for Wales against Scotland in the previous week's International) to take Adams' place. Sadly, Roose proved to be an eccentric extrovert (not what one needs in a grim Scottish Cup-tie between two Glasgow rivals) and Celtic lost their first match in the competition in over four years. Roose insisted on running out to shake the hand of Jackie Chalmers, the Clyde forward who had scored against him, something that did not go down at all well in the eyes of the ultra-professional Alec McNair.

Some people thought this was the moment that Willie Maley's first great Celtic side began to break up. Maybe so, but, it was no disgrace to lose to Clyde, who had also defeated Rangers and would go down only narrowly to Dundee at the third attempt in the Scottish Cup final at Ibrox in April. It meant, however, that as far as Celtic and McNair were concerned, the season would now fizzle out. The Scottish League was won, anti-climactically, before a crowd of 2,000 at Celtic Park in a 0-0 draw against Hibernian one Monday afternoon at the end of April, after Maley's men could have done so more spectacularly against Falkirk (their main title rivals) at Brockville on the Saturday. Anti-climax or not, Celtic had now won six Scottish League Championships in a row, and Alec McNair had played magnificently in all six of those.

No-one, however, seemed able to understand why McNair was not chosen for the remaining Scottish Internationals that season. The right-back place was held by George Law of Rangers, a good player in all truth but not as good as the super cool Icicle. In fact, Celtic would play a very large part in Scotland's 2-0 win over England – Jimmy Quinn and Jimmy McMenemy scored the goals – but Eck was watching from the Hampden stand that day. He also missed (through injury) Celtic's only Glasgow Charity Cup game that year, as they went down 0-1 to Third Lanark. It was a very flat end to the season for the man now reckoned to be one of the best players in the British Isles.

But midsummer brought personal happiness. On Thursday, 16 June 1910, at Greenfield Place, Stenhousemuir, Alec McNair of Church Street, Stenhousemuir married Mary Niven of Greenfield Place, Stenhousemuir, the service conducted by Reverend

Spence, the Minister of the Larbert East United Free Church. Interestingly, the marriage certificate describes Alec as a grate fitter, rather than a professional football player – which makes one think that he had returned to his trade in the summer months – whereas Mary was described as a shop assistant, the daughter of an iron moulder, the same profession as Alec's late father. It would prove to be a very strong and very happy marriage, albeit short and full of tragedy as well.

CHAPTER FOUR

MARGINAL DECLINE (1910-1913)

All good things must come to an end, it is said, and Celtic's run of six League Championships in a row duly finished in 1910. Rangers won the League in 1911, 1912 and 1913. Some Celtic historians often talk about these three years as if they were some sort of disaster. This is putting it too strongly. It is true that the great days of 1907 and 1908 had gone. Some players had left, for example Alec Bennett and Peter Somers, whilst others such as Willie Loney, Jimmy Quinn and Davie Adams had declined and, in some cases, retired or left Celtic at this time, but, gradually during this three-year period, a new team was developing, possibly an even better side than in 1907 and 1908. A few key players – Sunny Jim Young, Jimmy 'Napoleon' McMenemy and Eck McNair - straddled both eras, and there were new ones like Andy McAtee and Patsy Gallacher fast developing.

Yet were these three years a total disappointment? The Scottish Cup, still considered the most prestigious trophy of them all, was won in both 1911 and 1912, and the Glasgow Charity Cup was won in 1912 and then again in 1913, in a game which hinted at better things to come. Against that, League form was disappointing - Celtic were actually 5th in 1911! - whilst the Glasgow Cup failed to reappear at Celtic Park, twice being lost to Rangers following painful final defeats at Hampden.

In other respects, as well, things were changing. The Liberals were still in power following the General Election of January 1910 but with a thin majority and now dependent on the Irish Nationalists to keep them in power. When the result was repeated in December 1910, it was clear that the Liberals had won their prolonged battle against the House of Lords, but, it was also clear that Ireland was now going to be a major item on the political agenda. Those who claim that this did not raise the tension in Glasgow, as far as Celtic and their supporters are concerned, are guilty of naivety, though it must also have amused men like Eck McNair and Sunny Jim Young, neither Irish nor Catholic but now both Celts to the core. Trouble was clearly brewing in Ireland.

On 6 May 1910, King Edward VII died. A rumour swept the streets of Glasgow that it was Jimmy Quinn who had passed on, apparently after someone had seen a newspaper billboard heading "Death of Great Man." Fortunately, it was "just" the King. There was a certain grudging respect for this unashamedly gluttonous hedonist who had reacted just too much and gone too far in the opposite direction from his awful mother, Queen Victoria. He did have some concern for the poor, and he had tried, misguidedly but with the best of intentions, to create alliances in Europe for Great Britain. His replacements, his son King George V and his Queen Mary (who had married him in undue haste after his elder brother had died), were more austere and in some ways a throwback to the grim old 'Granny Vic,' as those with less respect for the monarchy would have put it.

But back in the reality of Scottish football, Celtic's players and manager Willie Maley came in for a fair amount of criticism in season 1910/11. This was disappointing but is as one would have expected. Celtic supporters have not really changed in their intolerance of their team if results turn bad. Those of us who stood on the Celtic Park terracing of the 1960s and 1990s will know what I mean here, when vitriol and filth are mingled in a dreadful cocktail of irrational inanity. It can become too much for some players, whereas others simply cope with it. Eck McNair himself was seldom blamed for his own or someone else's shortcomings, but, when the crowd did turn on someone like Andy McAtee, John Hastie, Paddy Travers or Ebenezer Owers, it was noticeable that McNair would be seen to pat the players concerned on the shoulder, and to do something to cheer them up.

Eck's own form remained predictably solid and even, on occasion, impeccable and he still remained in contention for Scotland caps before often, to the amazement of Celtic supporters, being passed over. He was often de facto captain of Celtic. He had done it before, when Jimmy Hay or Jimmy Young were injured, but after Hay left for Newcastle United in 1911, the captaincy passed to Sunny Jim Young on the grounds, presumably, that although Eck was perhaps temperamentally better suited for the job, Sunny was more of a leader on the field with his famous war cry "Face the ball, Celts" or his more even more basic "Tak a man apiece" a well-known feature of Celtic Park and other grounds. For these reasons, Young was a good choice as captain, but, he had been known to 'lose it' now and again, and in these circumstances, wise old heads like Alec McNair and Jimmy McMenemy were required to be around to help him out.

But back in season 1910/11, Jimmy 'Dun' Hay was still Celtic captain. He was a man, though, who some thought was beginning to be feeling a little impatient and intolerant of the bullying tactics of Willie Maley. Hay was, of course, a great player, but, in 1910/11 he found himself at left-back partnering Alec McNair whilst his left-half place was taken by Joe Dodds. Historical hindsight would, of course, suggest that this would have been better the other way round, but, sometimes one simply has to try things and find out.

The first indication that things were not going to go so well for Celtic this year came in the loss of three successive games to Falkirk, Morton and Kilmarnock in late August and early September 1910. Frankly, Celtic never really recovered from that blow and although they stabilised for a spell after that, early October saw their first-ever defeat by Raith Rovers on Kirkcaldy's Holiday Monday, then a 1-3 defeat by Rangers in the Glasgow Cup final. From now on, all causes seemed lost, and New Year 1911 was reached with Celtic nowhere, and although there was the occasional good goal from Jimmy Quinn or Jimmy McMenemy, even those great players were pulled down by the general mediocrity. The team had quite simply lost its sparkle, as can happen after a long period of sustained success, and the appetite was not there. Those readers who can recall the 1974/75 season will appreciate this. A certain "lack of new worlds to conquer" ennui sets in.

It was, of course, Alexander the Great, the King of Macedon in the 320s BC who sat down to weep because there were no new worlds for him to conquer. The other Alexander the Great however, McNair, was still at his best at right-back, albeit excellence in his position was not quite what Celtic needed. They did not concede many goals, the problem was that they did not score many either. Celtic found themselves at the end of January with only the Scottish Cup to play for, a situation that they had not found themselves in for a while.

That Scottish Cup campaign encapsulated Celtic's season. Not a single goal was conceded, but, there were never any commanding victories. All the games were played at Parkhead, apart from the final and the replay, which were both staged at Ibrox. The best game was possibly the first one against St Mirren, when they won 2-0. There followed three successive 1-0 wins against Galston (!), Clyde and Aberdeen, then in the final Celtic drew 0-0 with Hamilton Academical in an awful game, before winning the replay 2-0 seven days later. It was all pretty undistinguished stuff. Meanwhile, Eck McNair had a major tragedy to deal with at home.

Shortly after Eck played in the Scottish League v English League game in early March 1911, his wife Mary gave birth to a baby girl, to be called Helen. Naturally, they were both delighted, but, soon after the birth, the baby showed signs of what was commonly known then as 'failure to thrive,' and then at the age of one month, baby Helen developed what looked like a severe cold, from which tragically she never recovered. The death certificate says that she died of rhinitis and laryngitis. She did, however, live long enough to be enrolled on the 1911 Census which took place on 2 April. The family was living at 12 Victoria Place, Stenhousemuir, and Alec, Helen's father, is described as a professional football player.

Such tragedy was far from uncommon in 1911, but, it was a severe blow nevertheless, and Eck, one can imagine, was devastated. But one of the benefits of living in an extended family in a small Scottish town was that everyone rallied round, and maximum comfort was given to Eck and Mary from his mother, sisters and brothers, and from Mary's family as well.

The baby had died early on the morning of Tuesday, 11 April 1911. The Scottish Cup final against Hamilton Academical had been played on the Saturday before, and the replay was scheduled for the following Saturday, 15 April. Eck had the difficult decision to make about whether he wished to play or not. On the one hand, he was very upset and unhappy. There was even a feeling in Scotland at that time that it was in some way 'disrespectful' to do anything other than mourn. Queen Victoria had, of course, led the way in this self-indulgent introspection by sulking solidly for 10 years after her husband died in 1861, until her Scottish gillie John Brown found ways of cheering her up. On the other hand, life sometimes has to go on, no matter how tragic the circumstances are.

One of the features of Eck's family was that they always rallied round and supported each other. We can imagine him talking to his wife, his mother, her parents, his brothers and sisters and agonising over this issue. Celtic manager Willie Maley, of course, was also very supportive. He himself had lost a young daughter in similar circumstances about ten years previously, and one can imagine Maley coming to Stenhousemuir for the funeral and telling the man who in some ways had become his favourite player that the decision was Eck's and Eck's alone, and that he would support him in whatever he chose. But he hoped he would play.

One of the salient characteristics of Alec McNair was his stoicism. His play on the field reflects his character. Not for nothing was he called The Icicle. Not for him was the desire to display emotion. This did not mean that he did not feel things strongly. It meant, however, that prolonged grief had to give way to a sober realisation that although he had sustained a blow, in this case a severe one, he had to take it on the chin, fight back and make the best of things. There was simply far too much grief and sorrow going around, and he always reckoned that there were others a lot worse off than he was.

In the end, McNair decided to play. It is interesting - and perhaps a comment on Scotland in 1911 - that this whole business is not mentioned in newspapers. Today's tabloids would not only have mentioned it but would have gone to the other extreme. Perhaps the Press had a code of conduct in those days that they would not mention such private matters; perhaps child mortality was simply so common that it did not merit any great attention in the Press; perhaps the McNair family quietly and without any great fuss decided that they wanted the whole business to be kept quiet.

In any event, Alec's brave decision was rewarded with a victory and his third Scottish Cup-winner's medal. The first game against Hamilton Academical had been a shocker, played on a hard, bumpy Ibrox pitch with very little good football on view and generally reckoned to be one of the worst cup finals of them all. The replay was only marginally better, but, the victory was still celebrated to an enormous extent by the Celtic masses who had endured a poor season and really needed something to cheer them up. It was particularly feted in the village of

Croy, where three local men played in that team – the great Jimmy Quinn (of course) and two men of virtually the same surname – Andy McAtee on the right wing and Tommy McAteer at centre-half. The village of Croy in 1911 had about 70 houses, and three of them had produced Scottish Cup-winners! The other notable point about this success was that Celtic had actually won the trophy without conceding a goal. For this, men like Davie Adams, Eck McNair and Jimmy Hay deserve a great deal of credit.

The conditions were atrociously typical of Scotland in spring, with several heavy downpours, which did at least help the pitch which had been far too bumpy last week, a strong westerly wind and periods of bright, warm sunshine. Celtic played into the gale first half, and possibly were happy that Hamilton had not scored when they had the benefit of the wind. Goalkeeper Davie Adams was singled out for praise, but, Jimmy McMenemy, writing in The Scottish Referee a few days later, is in no doubt that "McNair again was our best defender and is playing just now at the very top of his form." The second half saw Celtic on top but unable to convert until two late long-range efforts from the two Crojans, Jimmy Quinn and Tommy McAteer, brought home the bacon. The disappointing crowd of 25,000 had something to be happy about, at last, although Alec McNair's celebrations were necessarily muted.

The cup final line-ups were as follows:

Celtic: Adams, McNair & Hay; Young, McAteer & Dodds; McAtee, McMenemy, Quinn, Kivlichan & Hamilton

Hamilton Academical: J. Watson, Davie & Miller; P. Watson, W. McLaughlin & Eglinton; J. McLaughlin, Waugh, Hunter, Hastie & McNeil

Referee: Mr T Dougray, Bellshill

The 1910/11 campaign now fizzled out. The Glasgow Charity Cup saw a win over Third Lanark, then a 1-3 defeat by Rangers in the final, something that emphasised that, in spite of the Scottish Cup triumph, Celtic were only second best this season. Some would complain that Rangers won through their time-honoured tactic of targeting Jimmy Quinn, but in fact, most Celtic historians agree that in 1911, Rangers were the better team. The big talking point among Celtic supporters that May, however, was the departure of skipper James Hay. There is an air of mystery about this one, for he had been a great player and captain. Possibly he fell out with Willie Maley and the Directors about money, possibly he simply felt that he wanted a change and to try English football before he got too old. In any case, by the start of the next season, Jimmy Hay was at Newcastle United, (in 1911, by some distance the best team in England) and Sunny Jim Young became Celtic's new captain. Some felt that Alec McNair might have been a better choice, but, Alec, phlegmatic as ever, supported the decision and continued to give his utmost for the club.

In the circumstances of his family life, and also to allow him time for a few physical injuries to be healed at the same time as emotional wounds, Alec was allowed to miss part of Celtic's forthcoming European tour. The main party left for Germany and Austro-Hungary in mid-May, whilst McNair and Davie Hamilton joined them at Lucerne and played a couple of games in Switzerland and France on the way home.

The Coronation of King George V in midsummer passed without incident, and Alec and the other Celtic players returned for the 1911/12 season. If it hadn't been true before, it was now certainly the case that Scottish football tended to be about Celtic and Rangers. As far as Rangers were concerned, the sectarianism which would become the cornerstone of their existence in the 1920s had not really become a serious issue, although it was growing, and was not helped by the 1912 arrival on the Clyde of the Belfast firm

Harland and Wolff, which, notoriously, refused to employ Roman Catholics. Rangers and their supporters began to find themselves pushed towards taking a 'Protestant' position, using words like "loyal" and "sovereign," mainly because Celtic fans, and their Board of Directors, unashamedly supported the campaign for Home Rule for Ireland.

But the problem for Celtic at the start of the 1911/12 season was that Rangers were good, deserved champions of 1911, as Alec Bennett now looked as if he was starting, at last, to find form with them. There remained little doubt that he had been a far better player for Celtic than he ever was for Rangers, and he may often have asked himself whether he would not have been better, after all, staying at Parkhead. Rangers were indeed the champions, although they were now beginning to develop a complex about the Scottish Cup, which they had not won since 1903.

Celtic were in the throes of transition. Paddy Travers, Andy Donaldson, Willie Nicholl and John Brown were all given extended runs in the first team but had not, as yet, shown any signs of making an impact. Peter Somers had gone, as had Jimmy Hay, Willie Loney, Davie Hamilton and Jimmy Quinn were ageing and increasingly injury-prone, and the form of the team was depressingly inconsistent. Home form was acceptable, even good on occasion, but, before the turn of the year, Celtic had gone out of the Glasgow Cup to Partick Thistle and there had been away defeats to Dundee, Hearts, Hamilton Academical, Rangers, Motherwell and Third Lanark in the League. It was clear that, unless something extraordinary were to happen, Maley's team would not regain the League Championship.

But on Saturday, 2 December 1911, the Celtic manager introduced a new forward to the side, a small, thin-legged, consumptive-looking youngster, "more like an admission to a sanatorium than a football team," called Patsy Gallacher. Amidst all the comments from Jimmy

Quinn and Willie Loney (who should have known better), such as "Maley should be done for manslaughter for playing this wee guy," and "the last time I saw legs like that there was a message attached to one of them" (a reference to the pigeon post), captain Sunny Jim Young (whose bulk was about twice that of Patsy) and the wise Alec McNair went out of their way to make him welcome. In a few months, no-one made fun of Gallacher. He was variously described by The Glasgow Observer as "tricky," "elusive," "possessed of no great physique but a favourite from his first match," "control and passing comparable with McMenemy," "cool artfulness and judgement of a veteran" and "no superior in the passing of a ball."

With eulogies like that, McNair was aware that one of his jobs would have to be to keep Patsy Gallacher's feet on the floor, and Eck also had another new colleague to introduce gradually. This was goalkeeper John Mulrooney, brought in because Davie Adams was prone to arthritis and had, in any case, reached his peak. Mulrooney was a strange-looking character, with protruding ears and a funny jerky way of running, but, he soon settled in with McNair and Joe Dodds, and a feature of this Celtic season, once again, was that very few goals were scored against them.

There were a few great days. One of them was New Year's Day 1912, when Willie Maley wisely decided to omit the young Gallacher, of whom everyone was already talking about, and Celtic beat Rangers 3-0, all the goals coming from Jimmy Quinn, who clearly felt that he still had a point to make to all those who had written him off as being 'past it.' It was a result as surprising as it was decisive, but, the tragedy was that Celtic could not capitalise, drawing 1-1 with Clyde then Hearts in the next two games, something that was all the more galling because Rangers too had a form slump, losing 5-0 to Hibernian and then 2-1 to Clyde in successive weeks.

Indeed, Clyde, whose trainer was a tough character called Willie Struth, were a good side that year, as we shall see. For Celtic, now that the League had gone, the Scottish Cup, as last season, assumed a great deal more significance. The first opponents were Dunfermline Athletic, on Saturday, 27 January 1912. The Fifers were making their first-ever competitive trip to Celtic Park. Dunfermline, recently admitted to the Scottish League Second Division, had won the Scottish Qualifying Cup, and on a rather unpleasant day, played one of their best games and lost only by 0-1. They claimed that the ball was over the line and out of play before Sunny Jim Young crossed for John Brown to score, and it certainly was not a great Celtic performance at a desolate Parkhead, before a very disappointing crowd of 6,000.

Two weeks later, Celtic received another home tie against apparently easy opposition in East Stirlingshire. This time though, they made a better job of it, by winning 3-0 with a couple of goals from Jimmy Quinn and another from Paddy Travers, but, that was hardly the main news of the day. That came about a mile away from Celtic Park, at Shawfield in the Clyde v Rangers game. The crowd was huge, and the ground was on the small side but seemed to have settled down, until with 20 minutes to go, and Clyde winning 3-1, a section of the Rangers support invaded the field with no other intention than to get the game stopped and played again.

It is, of course, fanciful and a gross over-simplification to link all this with what was going on in Ulster at this time. Nor was there the slightest similarity to the Hampden Riot of 1909, where there was some sort of rationale or excuse for it in that the supporters had been misled or manipulated. The events on this day, Saturday, 10 February 1912 were simple thuggery, and a form of blackmail with threats of violence. Rangers manager William Wilton was mortified by all this, and the Ibrox club conceded the tie. Thus, Rangers exited the Scottish Cup again, and Clyde emerged as one of the leading contenders for the trophy. It was poignant for Celtic boss Willie Maley, as the manager of Clyde was his brother, Alec Maley.

The following week, Eck McNair was away with the Scottish League at Middlesbrough. It was not one of his happier moments, as the Scots went down 0-2, albeit it was generally agreed that he had a good enough game. The Scottish Cup continued on the Saturday after that, with Celtic given a difficult quarter-final tie at Pittodrie against Aberdeen. It was a fascinating game of football watched by 23,000 at a crowded Pittodrie in excellent conditions, and at one point, soon after half-time when Celtic went 0-2 down, it looked very much as if Maley's side were on the way out. But inspired by a huge Celtic support, who had been arriving in Aberdeen all morning on special trains, they fought back. Andy McAtee had already missed a penalty, when Celtic got another spot kick, this time taken by Jimmy Quinn. The goalkeeper saved his first attempt, but Jimmy netted the rebound, and then fairly soon after that, a fine move involving Quinn, Brown and finally McAtee earned Celtic a replay. Indeed, they might have won the tie, for there were chances at both ends in the final few minutes, but the match ended with the teams still level at 2-2, and so it would go to a replay at Celtic Park.

Eck McNair now had a remarkable month of March. He played five games, two of them difficult cup-ties and three Internationals, winning four of them and drawing the other (the International against England). His first game was on Saturday, 2 March 1912 at Tynecastle, when Scotland beat Wales 1-0. It was a tight game, with Jimmy Quinn grabbing the late winning goal. The next International was two weeks later at Windsor Park, Belfast and Eck was given the unusual honour of being made captain of Scotland, when he was not even the skipper of his club! McNair must have made a good job of it, leading Scotland to a 4-1 win, for he was then re-appointed captain for the main International of the year against England at Hampden. This was even more unusual because in the team was his old club captain James Hay, now with Newcastle United! Not only that, but Eck was given the honour over Charlie Thomson of Sunderland who had been the captain in the game against Wales!

The ways of the SFA Selectors were indeed odd.

In some ways, it was the greatest moment of Alec McNair's career to lead his country out on the Hampden turf before a crowd of 127,307, a remarkable turnout given the fact that the country was at this time bedevilled by rail strikes. It was generally agreed to have been one of the closest Internationals of them all, eventually finishing as a 1-1 draw. Both teams scored in the early stages of the game, with neither able to force a winner even though Scotland had men like Jimmy Quinn, Davie McLean and Bobby Templeton up front. But it was at least satisfactory as far as Scotland were concerned, and McNair was much commended in the Press for his usual calm and elegant play as well as his general deportment and demeanour.

A humble man, Eck was honoured and proud to have been made the captain of his country, but there was also a Scottish Cup to be won as well. On the Saturday between the Wales and the Ireland games, 35,000 spectators were at Celtic Park to see the Scottish Cup quarter-final replay between Celtic and Aberdeen. Once again it was a close game, with the Dons, a team who had been in existence less than 10 years, by no means overawed by being at Parkhead, and putting up a great fight. Jimmy Quinn was targeted, as he often was, but, this allowed Paddy Travers to score two opportunist goals at the end of each half, and cup-holders Celtic were now through to the last four.

The semi-final against Hearts, played on Saturday, 30 March 1912 attracted a crowd of 43,000, the attendance still affected by the rail strike, which meant that Hearts' supporters from Edinburgh had to leave early in the morning to catch what few trains there were, or to club together and hire what few autobuses, charabancs or even horse-drawn brakes there were to take them to Ibrox (This was the first year that neutral venues were used for semi-finals).

For Celtic, Paddy Travers had been injured, and this created an opportunity for young Patsy Gallacher. It was an opportunity that he seized, but Celtic's star on the day was one of the 'Bhoys from Croy,' Andy McAtee, who set up all three goals, two for Jimmy McMenemy and one for John Brown in what was a comprehensive 3-0 win. Alec McNair was "dashier than usual," according to The Scottish Referee, and the fact that Hearts 'Houdini,' Bobby Walker, was tamed into insignificance really says it all. Willie Loney, a man who had suffered more than his fair share of injuries and illnesses over the years, was now back, and the defence of Mulrooney, McNair & Dodds; Young, Loney & Johnstone was a mighty one.

But now it was the Scottish Cup final at Ibrox against near neighbours Clyde on Saturday, 6 April 1912. Clyde, a club with whom Celtic traditionally had a good relationship, were enjoying a good spell under the firm leadership of Alec Maley and Willie Struth. They had suffered bad luck in 1910 when they were within a minute of beating Dundee in the first game of the Scottish Cup final, and of course, this year they had defeated Rangers in that notorious game destroyed by hooliganism.

The days leading up to the game were dominated by talk about the great new ship that was about to cross the Atlantic Ocean. It was called Titanic and was rumoured to be a floating palace and totally unsinkable. There was nothing unsinkable about Celtic, even though their general play had improved beyond all recognition of late. Clyde, on the other hand, had solid defenders, creative half-backs and tricky forwards, and Celtic were constantly reminded about how it was Clyde who had defeated them in the last Scottish Cup-tie that they had lost, back in March 1910.

The cup final teams at Ibrox that afternoon lined up as follows;

Celtic: Mulrooney, McNair & Dodds; Young, Loney & Johnstone; McAtee, Gallacher, Quinn, McMenemy & Brown

Clyde: Grant, Gilligan & Blair; Walker, McAndrew & Collins; Hamilton, Jackson, Morrison, Carmichael & Stevens

Referee: Mr T Dougray, Bellshill

The match itself was dominated by the wind, which had been a problem at previous Scottish Cup finals at Ibrox – last year certainly and notoriously in 1900, when the game had been known as the 'Hurricane Final.' People who had watched that game were convinced that the 1912 Scottish Cup final was just as bad for wind, and it may even have had an effect in reducing the crowd to 48,000 when a few more might have been expected. It was Alec McNair's fifth Cup final, and he was aiming for his fourth winners' medal, the famous old trophy having been withheld after the riot in 1909.

Sunny Jim Young won the toss and chose to play with the wind in the first half. The wind, as usual at Ibrox, was blowing from the west towards what is now the Copland Road end of the ground. Celtic were clearly on top all of the first half, albeit finding themselves frustrated at not being able to score because of a combination of wind, some stubborn Clyde defending and their own inability to cope with the ball. It was often said that Jimmy Quinn was not at his best while playing with the wind. Today was maybe an example of that.

But eventually, in the 37th minute, Celtic were awarded a free-kick outside the box. Eck McNair took it, judged the situation perfectly by hitting it not too hard and not too high, and the ball eluded two Clyde defenders before it dropped in front of the feet of Jimmy McMenemy. Napoleon had a fairly easy tap in from about five yards.

Thus, it was 1-0 to Celtic at half time, and Alec McNair trooped off wondering if that would be enough. It would be a different story in the second half, though, as the wind, if anything, was intensifying. It would be a severe test of the ability of Eck and the rest of the

Celtic defence to keep out this good Clyde team. Eck was also aware of another point. The fallout from the 1909 riot Cup final was still there. The last two Scottish Cup finals – Dundee v Clyde in 1910 and Celtic v Hamilton Academical in 1911 had both been draws first time round. Eck, himself scrupulously honest and convinced that there had been no 'fix' in any game that he had been involved in, was determined not to let Clyde score to make it yet another replay. It was not nice to hear supporters turning on their players and shouting things like "cheat" and "crook" at them.

Thankfully, it did not happen this year. Eck and the rest of the Celtic defence realised that the tackling and the blocking would have to be good, but that something else was required. It would be folly to boot the ball downfield. Far better to keep the ball on the ground, and in McNair's case, to try to find the eager Andy McAtee with short passing. This indeed was what happened to bring about Celtic's second goal. McAtee made a run up the right wing, crossed to John Brown, whose header goalwards lacked sufficient power. A Clyde defender got in the way of it, the ball breaking to Patsy Gallacher. Patsy had scored before for the club, but this was the first time in an important game.

A quarter of an hour remained, enough time for Clyde to mount a last desperate attempt to get back in the game. However, the Celtic defence was well organised with that "they will not pass" look about them. On one occasion, goalkeeper John Mulrooney was beaten before McNair managed to get his body in the way of it. On several other occasions, Clyde looked to have opportunities but shot high or wide. Full-time came to a tremendous cheer from the Celtic supporters, who had now seen their team win the Scottish Cup eight times. They were fast catching up on Queen's Park's record of 10 successes.

It was generally agreed that Celtic were the better team and might have won a great deal more comfortably if the conditions had been better. The Scottish Referee was an admirable newspaper, reporting all games in Scotland and coming out on a Monday morning. It was certainly not a pro-Celtic newspaper in the way that The Glasgow Observer was, or in the way that The Glasgow Herald clearly favoured Queen's Park (curiously, and perhaps differing from other ages, in the 1910s no newspaper had any obvious liking for Rangers!). On Monday, 8 April 1912, however, whilst also making the somewhat caustic or waspish point that "the feature that the public like most about this final is that it was finished in one match and on one day, thus there is no re-draw on the public purse…", The Scottish Referee goes into ecstasy about Celtic.

Patsy Gallacher, Andy McAtee, Jimmy McMenemy and Jimmy Young are all singled out, as indeed they deserve to have been, but, their encomia diminish when compared with what is said about Alec McNair, "who has discovered a dash and a devil superior to his past that warrants one declaring that, as a back, the present is his best season in his cool and consistent and modest career. Celtic owe him a lot for this joyful cupful, for his steadiness and headiness (sic) allowed young Mulrooney to win his spurs as a keeper…"

It was as well that Eck was always a steady, modest, 'feet on the ground' sort of man, for the same newspaper chooses him for their Portrait Gallery this Monday morning, saying things like "there is none worthier than this able, manly and modest artist… when you have, as is happily the case with McNair, ability of the first degree as a player, allied to a most likeable personality, you have a duality of power that makes for popularity. As a player he is a gentleman and an artist, scorning low methods, and earning as much respect from his foes as he does from his friends. To the old and the young in this sport, we can point to no finer exemplar or model on and off the field than Alexander McNair."

The year 1912 thus saw Eck at the pinnacle of his career. Captain of Scotland, and the winner of six Scottish League medals and now four Scottish Cup medals, there was little wrong with the world as he saw it. His 'pinnacle,' as we have put it, we are glad to say, was more like a plateau than a sharp point. He still had a considerable time to run at the top. He was not yet 30 years of age, and he would still be donning his now-beloved green-and-white jersey when he was over 40!

Indeed, spring of 1912 had not finished with him yet. We have seen how the previous year, Alec and Mary were delivered a most dreadful blow in the death of a child. This year, there was better news, when in the early morning of Tuesday, 7 May, Mary McNair gave birth to a baby boy to be called James. This baby was healthy and, indeed, would himself grow up to play professional football with Falkirk and Stenhousemuir, although, as he would cheerily admit himself, he was not as good as his illustrious sire. Everything was, for the moment, happy in Victoria Gardens, Stenhousemuir.

There was still some more football to be played, with the Glasgow Charity Cup to be competed for. Three days before the birth of James McNair, his father had played in the Celtic team which beat Queen's Park in the semi-final, a tight 2-1 victory with goals from Jimmy Quinn and Patsy Gallacher. This put Celtic into the Charity Cup final on Saturday, 11 May 1912, to face Clyde again, a Shawfield team now exclusively under the command of this bright young fellow called Willie Struth.

A crowd of 25,000 appeared at Hampden Park for this game. Once again, there was a strong wind, albeit it was a bright and sunny day. It was an odd final, for Celtic won it without scoring a goal! It had been decided that, in the event of a draw, the number of corner kicks awarded would be decisive, and at the end of the goalless match, Celtic duly won by seven corners to nil, figures which give some indication of how far on top they were. Alec McNair and the rest of the Celtic defence played well, not even conceding a corner to the Clyde attackers! It was Celtic's 10th victory in the Glasgow

Charity Cup, but oddly enough the first for McNair, who had missed the previous triumphs of 1905 and 1908. It was nice now for Eck to have a complete set, as he already had winner's medals from the League Championship, Scottish Cup and Glasgow Cup.

And season 1911/12 had still not finished with him! After a short break, there was a Celtic tour of Denmark and Norway in early June. Eck could have claimed compassionate leave if he wanted to, his wife having recently had a baby, but, presumably after consulting Mary, he decided to go, knowing that his large and supportive extended family would rally round to help, particularly his mother and his sisters.

The year 1912 was the year of the Stockholm Olympic Games, and Celtic would have the privilege of playing against the Olympic XIs of both Denmark and Norway. Surprisingly, they lost to the Danes before defeating their Norwegian counterparts and winning another other three games on the tour. The Celtic party returned to Hull on 12 June, and now, at last the close season had arrived. Time for Alec McNair to recharge his batteries and to return for the new campaign fully refreshed.

Sadly, the next campaign, 1912-13 would not turn out to be so good. Eck missed all of August with a 'strain.' It seemed to come upon him suddenly, for the morning papers of Saturday, 17 August 1912, the opening day of the season, contained no hint that he would not be playing, and it was only when the teams ran out at Falkirk that supporters noticed that there was no McNair, and that in his place was the earnest young Tommy McGregor.

What the word 'strain' meant exactly in 1912 we cannot be sure, as it was used to cover a multitude of possibilities. It may have been a hamstring injury, in any case, it was certainly an injury. Eck would not have been dropped because he was such a consistently good player, and he is even less likely to have been suspended or be out of favour for picking a fight with Willie Maley. He simply was not that kind of player!

Celtic's two draws in their opening League fixtures in August, 0-0 at Brockville then 1-1 at home to Hibernian, meant that they were off to a bad start. Although they gradually picked up, their form could still be infuriatingly inconsistent. It was no disgrace to lose 3-1 to the good Dundee side at Dens Park in September, but, a 2-1 defeat to Raith Rovers at Stark's Park the following month was less easily shrugged off, as was their other loss before the New Year, by the same score at home to Motherwell in November, a game which showed how much they missed the injured Jimmy Young.

But the big defeat was to Rangers at Hampden on Saturday, 12 October 1912 in the Glasgow Cup final, a competition which Celtic had recently shown every sign of falling out of love with, having last won it in 1909. The crowd was a huge one, approaching 90,000 on a crisp autumn day, and it is reported in all newspapers as being one of the best games between the "two Glasgow protagonists" of them all. Celtic were without Jimmy McMenemy whilst Rangers had four first-team players missing. Moreover, the Ibrox side had Jacky Robertson carried off after an accidental collision with Andy McAtee (for which Andy was unfairly barracked by the Rangers crowd) and Celtic scored first through Jimmy Quinn.

Unfortunately, things then collapsed in the second half, with The Scottish Referee making the telling comment that "Celtic were missing McMenemy more than Rangers missed their four players!" Willie Loney was also taken off injured, and the Celtic defence, good though it was, was simply overwhelmed. Inexperienced goalkeeper Bob Boyle (John Mulrooney was out injured) had a bad attack of nerves and was responsible for the loss of two of the three goals that Rangers scored in the second half.

It was perhaps with all this in mind that on the Monday afterwards,

Alec McNair travelled down to London to play in an unusual game for the Scottish League against the Southern League at New Cross, the home of Millwall. The Southern League was a collection of London teams with aspirations to join the Football League. On that day, they were outclassed by the Scots, but still won 1-0, thanks to their excellent goalkeeper. This was an embarrassing result for the Scottish League, and particularly for McNair, who conceded an extremely rare own goal! But hiding his disappointment after the game, Alec got talking to the Southern League goalkeeper, who was, in fact, Scottish and McNair vaguely remembered him. He was called Charlie Shaw, he had played for Port Glasgow Athletic before moving to Queen's Park Rangers, and he was a Celtic supporter from Twechar, who knew men like Jimmy Quinn and Andy McAtee. He gave Eck to understand that he would not be averse to a move back to Scotland.

Alec McNair naturally reported this back to Willie Maley, and he was quoted in newspapers as saying that "Southern League possess in Charlie Shaw one of the cleverest custodians of the day..." Maley, shrewd as always, got in touch with a few of his contacts in London to ask their opinion of Shaw. They all agreed with McNair's assessment, and very soon wheels were set in motion to put in place the first three names of the great Celtic litany of Shaw, McNair and Dodds.

Not quite yet. McNair had had an awful week after the loss of the Glasgow Cup and now this game against the Southern League, but, like most great men, he fought back as indeed did Celtic. They beat Rangers 3-2 in the League game on Saturday, 26 October 1912 at Parkhead, with goals from John Brown, Patsy Gallacher and Jimmy Quinn, and by the time that they defeated them again at Ibrox on New Year's Day 1913 with another Quinn strike, then beat other three other Glasgow teams Clyde, Partick Thistle and Queen's Park in quick succession, they were four points ahead of Rangers and looking like winning back their title, Alec frequently singled out for his "usual calm, methodical play."

But then things began to go wrong. Sometimes in football, such things happen. Those of us following the team in a more modern time will recall with anguish the years of 1980, 1983 and 1987, when Celtic, from a position of strength managed to 'throw away' the title following a series of bad performances. Sometimes one defeat leads to another, a player loses fitness or form (or more often a series of players lose their touch at the same time), luck or refereeing decisions go against them, while crucially, their opponents win.

This was what happened here. Rangers kept winning while Celtic lost at Hibernian, drew fecklessly with Airdrie at Parkhead and were comprehensively dumped 3-0 at Pittodrie. The Aberdeen Press and Journal, which had previously, on many occasions, been in awe and admiration of Celtic, is perplexed. "True, the one and only James Quinn was absent...but the tired and seasoned veterans, heroes of many a hard-won and glorious victory, like McNair and Young, were no better than the rest." Maley's men found it difficult to cope with an Aberdeen team that had lost last week at Dumbarton. It was, quite simply, a poor team performance. It still need not have been fatal, had the team rallied and fought back.

The League title was then comprehensively lost in March, during which the team went down to Motherwell (who thus completed a rare double over Celtic) and Falkirk (their first-ever win at Celtic Park), in the aftermath of the worst result of all, the home defeat by Hearts in the quarter-final of the Scottish Cup on Saturday, 8 March 1913. That month, thus, saw three successive Saturdays in which any hope of success for the team disappeared up in smoke. Had Celtic still been in the Scottish Cup when they faced Motherwell and Falkirk, it might well have been a different story, but, the 1-0 loss to the Tynecastle side signalled the arrival of the Parkhead 'death wish,' which so often in the past and in the future, a defeat by Rangers would bring. Back in March 1913, it was Hearts who were the catalyst.

Yet, the Scottish Cup game against Hearts featured some hard luck as well. Edinburgh-based The Scotsman is little given to sensationalism and hyperbole in its football reporting. Its sober account of the proceedings (in brilliant weather before a 65,000 crowd at Parkhead, which resulted in the gates having to be closed) admits that Celtic had bad luck. Willie Loney had a fine shot saved by the Hearts goalkeeper and there was one goalmouth scramble where the ball might just have crossed the line to produce a goal for Celtic. The visitors had scored in the first half through Bobby Walker, while Celtic's talisman Jimmy McMenemy was still recovering from injury and really ought not to have played. The second half was a great battle, see-sawing from goal to goal, but, in the end, Hearts just managed to keep Celtic out and thus gained revenge for last season's 3-0 defeat at the semi-final stage.

There was, thus, to be no third successive Scottish Cup for Celtic, something that they had wanted to achieve because Queen's Park and Vale of Leven had both previously managed it, the Hampden club on two occasions. There would be no Scottish Cup for Hearts either, as they went out in the next round - the semi-final stage - to Falkirk, who had earlier beaten Rangers at Ibrox. The Bairns then went on to win the trophy, beating Raith Rovers 2-0 at Celtic Park in an unusual final. The victory of near-neighbours Falkirk in the Scottish Cup may not have gone down very well in Stenhousemuir.

Eck McNair did enjoy one big moment that season though, when he was invited to play for Scotland against England at Stamford Bridge on Saturday, 5 April 1913. It was, by all accounts, a great spectacle, with Scottish supporters entertaining the English crowd with their dress, music, singing and dancing. A close game was won 1-0 by England, and it was a pity that the match had to be decided by a controversial goal when Joe Hampton of England bundled Scotland goalkeeper Jimmy Brownlie over the line in what was then a perfectly legal shoulder charge. McNair was obviously disappointed, albeit he had the personal satisfaction of knowing that he had played a great game. The Scottish Referee says that "Alec McNair kicked well and tackled acutely...McNair's tactics were safety to the core." Eck had apparently realised that his direct opponent, Joe Hodkinson, was faster than he was, therefore mitigating that by concentrating his ideas on simply keeping himself between Hodkinson and the goal.

McNair had, thus, consolidated his International position, even though there would be no Scottish Cup or League Championship medal for him this year. Things at Celtic Park were not so good. There had been plans to make this a celebratory season, for it was, of course, the club's Silver Jubilee of 25 years. Such celebrations, as existed, were distinctly muted, as the club experienced its worst season since Alec had joined the club. This was a shame because Celtic had a great deal to celebrate – 10 Scottish League Championships and 8 Scottish Cups was not bad going for 25 years!

As always happens with Celtic, there was no lack of finger-pointing and blaming. Jimmy Quinn was slowing down. Patsy Gallacher, though clearly prodigiously talented, had not yet learned the discipline of playing for a team and what is now termed 'game management.' There was still a major goalkeeping problem, in that neither Bob Boyle nor John Mulrooney was completely reliable. John Brown had been inconsistent and had been more or less replaced by his near-namesake John Browning, a wild boy who was still learning the game. John Mitchell and Peter Johnstone were quite simply not Celtic class. Willie Maley was far too dictatorial. All these things (some of them grossly unfair and just pure wrong) were said, albeit it was noticeable that some players evaded criticism. These included Sunny Jim Young, who was excused a few mistakes because of his wholehearted approach, Jimmy McMenemy because he was normally so good, and Alec McNair, as he was simply Mr Reliable and The Icicle.

And yet there was a sting in the tail, or light at the end of the tunnel, and the morning star of a really great side. This was in the Glasgow

Charity Cup in the month of May. The same competition some 10 years earlier, in 1903, had provided an excellent launching pad for the career of Sunny Jim, and now, in 1913, goalkeeper Charlie Shaw was given an opportunity to show what he could do. Johnny McMaster also made his debut in the Charity Cup final, and the competition was the highlight of the very brief Celtic career of a man called Barney Connolly.

Celtic beat Clyde 1-0 in the first round with a goal from Willie Loney. Charlie Shaw - "a gem of a custodian" according to The Glasgow Observer - made his debut in the semi-final at Cathkin, as Celtic narrowly beat Third Lanark to set up a final at Celtic Park on Saturday, 10 May 1913 against Rangers. A crowd of 39,000 was present to watch a fine game on a good day. Celtic were 0-2 down before 10 minutes had elapsed, and a hammering was then expected, but, Celtic rallied. Patsy Gallacher pulled one back before half-time, then Barney Connolly equalised just after the restart. Late in the game, the same player notched the winner when he was on hand to deal with a rebound off the crossbar following a fierce Willie Loney drive. Thus, Alec McNair now had two Glasgow Charity Cup-winners medals! He had waited so long for one, and now there were two.

Thus, there was some balm in Gilead after all that season, and the handsome Charity Cup returned to Celtic Park, where Willie Maley was given a sum of 300 guineas for his services over 25 years. The Celtic manager had plans now for another great team to emerge, and he was beginning to see how he could do so. Charlie Shaw and Johnny McMaster were good recruits, Sunny Jim was still there, Jimmy McMenemy would soon get over his knee operation, and what potential there was in young Patsy Gallacher! At the back, there was no problem. Joe Dodds was solid, and Alec McNair, well, he was just Alec McNair! Seldom had Celtic been better-served by the ever-faithful, ever-reliable Eck McNair, now well over 30 years old but showing no signs whatsoever of slowing down! What a man!

Also, in May of that year, two cousins met in Berlin and were driven in their carriage around the streets to the cheers of the Germans. One was King George V of Great Britain, and the other was the Kaiser. They were great friends as well as cousins!

CHAPTER FIVE

SHAW, McNAIR & DODDS (1913-1915)

Season 1913-14 was, without very much doubt, one of the best in the history of the club. Celtic did not win everything this season, for they missed out on the Glasgow Cup, but, they did win the Double of the League and the Scottish Cup, thus emulating the teams of 1907 and 1908. Amazingly, it would be another 40 years before a similar thing could happen again. Not until season 1953-54, when Jock Stein was the captain of the club, did Celtic once again lift the Double.

It was, of course, the last season before the Great War, and it is at this juncture that we must point out an illusion that so many people, football historians not excepted, are under about this season. The impression is often given in history books that everyone knew that war was coming. One reads phrases like "Europe was a tinderbox," "Everyone knew that a small spark would ignite a conflagration," and "The world was living on borrowed time." Not so! No-one knew that a war was inevitable. They probably did, in totally different circumstances, in 1938 and 1939, but, in 1913 and even 1914, there was not an inkling of the approach of war until it all happened so suddenly. There was possibly a feeling that it might happen someday, but no feeling that it would.

There were, of course, undeniably two armed camps in Europe bound together by various alliances, ententes and understandings, but, everyone knew that, if restraint was exercised, war need not happen. All these countries had their own internal problems – in the case of Great Britain, poverty, Ireland and Suffragettes – but no-one predicted the events of August 1914 until about a week before! Indeed, the war could have been stopped if just one country, just one diplomat, just one member of an effete and decadent ruling imperial dynasty had had the courage and the perspicacity to say "No!" As it was, everyone was simply swept along in a heedless tide of folly. Those who did query the headlong dash to slaughter, like Ramsay MacDonald, were either ignored or pilloried.

A couple of months before the conflict, Celtic had been on a tour of Germany and Austro-Hungary. They had happily played football, enjoyed German food, drank German beer and flirted - no doubt with varying degrees of success - with German frauleins, with absolutely no sign of anything untoward about to happen. Years later, Willie Maley would say that he thought there were more Germans in uniform than on the club's previous visits. With respect to the grand old Celt, that was written with the benefit of historical hindsight.

The 1913/14 season started in August, with a Benefit for Alec McNair. Benefits were awarded as and when the club thought fit. It was usually a match in which a few fringe players or men returning from injury were given a game and it was usually very light-hearted. In Eck's case, the opponents were Rangers, who won 2-0 with a crowd of 3,000 who contributed £117 (a lot of money in 1913) for the McNair family. The crowd rose to Alec as he appeared out of the pavilion. It was a great and fitting tribute for what he had achieved. Benefits are usually given at the end of a career. McNair was now over 30 years old. No-one could have predicted that he had another 10 years to give Celtic!

The campaign did not start especially well for Celtic. In particular, there was a bad weekend in mid-September when the team unaccountably went down 0-2 to St Mirren at home – two freak goals, one a deflection off McNair, plus Sunny Jim Young voluble in his opinions that Celtic should have had about nine (yes, nine, said Sunny!) penalties, and then suffered another defeat by the same score to Hearts at Tynecastle on the Edinburgh Holiday Monday. Perhaps the worst of all results around that time occurred early in October, a 0-1 defeat by Third Lanark at Cathkin in the replayed Glasgow Cup semi-final, following a goalless draw at Celtic Park.

That Third Lanark goal came late in the game and ensured Celtic's dismissal from the Glasgow Cup to continue their recent poor form in this competition. It was scored by Third Lanark's McTavish and would begin to assume legendary status, for with the exception of one goal lost against Raith Rovers in December, it would be the last day of February 1914 before Willie Maley's men lost another. Such was the strength of Celtic's defence of Shaw, McNair & Dodds; Young, Johnstone & McMaster, although credit must also be given to Tom McGregor, who played cheerfully at either right or left-back when either McNair or Dodds was injured.

It was a tremendous defensive feat. We can, of course, parallel this achievement with the winter of 2013/2014, which was just as good as that of a century earlier. Fraser Forster and Virgil Van Dijk kept everyone at bay for a while that winter as well, at least in League games. European games, however, were a different matter altogether!

One hundred years previously, Alec McNair was at the apex of this Celtic defensive feat, but then again, he had always been there. Where he deserved particular credit was in his ability to knit together with the others. Joe Dodds had now developed into a fine attacking full-back, with a perfect understanding with McNair, and Eck knew how to cover for Joe's attacking forays. Peter Johnstone, who had started his Celtic life at inside-left was now a first-rate centre-half, and Johnny McMaster had fitted in perfectly, but, the huge difference was goalkeeper Charlie Shaw. Time and time again, we are told about "deafening roars of delight at Shaw's saves," or "the ground resounded with applause at Charlie's bravery," and he very soon became a Glasgow personality.

This was only half of it, of course, because up front a great forward line was developing. Barney Connolly sadly proved to be a flash in the pan after his Glasgow Charity Cup heroics and was replaced first by the red-headed Ebenezer Owers and then, more successfully, by Jimmy McColl from juniors St Anthony's, who in a few years' time during the war would earn the nickname 'Sniper.' Andy McAtee of the 'billiard table legs' and the ferocious shot was a great right-winger, and on the left wing, Johnny Browning, once a wild boy, had now been tamed and was toeing the line to produce the goods. McNair had played his part in developing these boys, as indeed had Jimmy Quinn, still registered as a player but realistic enough to realise that his most useful contribution now was to bring on the youngsters.

But the real entertainment from this brilliantly balanced side came from the two inside-forwards, Jimmy McMenemy and Patsy Gallacher. McMenemy had broken his collar bone early in the season, but, once he was back, he showed the world why he was called Napoleon. His goals, his passes, his humility were all sources of wonder and perpetual discussion among the Celtic faithful. Like Alec McNair, he seemed to be able to go on for ever. And then there was Patsy Gallacher. When he became the best player in the world was a matter of some debate, but there was very little discussion as to whether or not he was the best player in the world. Like most geniuses, however, Patsy, beneath all the bravado and bombast, was sometimes insecure and required a little encouragement. He needed to be constantly told that he was the best player in the world, and who better to do that than the man who was undeniably the best defender in the world?

A feature of this team was that they all got on well together. For this, of course, Willie Maley deserves most of the credit, albeit he was supported by so many of his great team, particularly the three who straddled the 1908 team and the 1914 team, namely Jimmy Young, Jimmy McMenemy and Alec McNair or 'Sunny, Nap and Icicle,' as they were known. They knew how success on a football field came about. Not only were they great football players, they were also successful human beings, and that, as any football man will tell you, is mightily important. The 'awaydays' that season at Seamill Hydro and elsewhere were great successes. Even training was fun!

Rangers presented few problems for Celtic that season. The League game at Ibrox, played at the end of October, was a 2-0 win for Maley's men, with a "crasher" of an opening goal from Andy McAtee, another from young loanee George Whitehead, and a fine defensive performance from the now impenetrable wall that was Charlie Shaw, Alec McNair and Joe Dodds. That was good enough, but then came New Year's Day at Parkhead, which saw Celtic at their best. The score was 4-0 and it really should have been more. The highlight was, without any sort of doubt, the goal that Jimmy McMenemy scored just before half-time, when he waltzed past about four defenders and crashed an unsavable shot past John Hempsey in the Rangers goal. It was simply sublime football, well remembered by anyone who saw it and talked about for decades afterwards. "It was possibly the best goal that McMenemy has ever scored," according to The Daily Record. And that is saying something!

The goal that Celtic lost in that long winter came at Kirkcaldy on December 13. It had been 13 games since their last defeat, and the year was 1913, so the jokes abounded about triskaidekaphobia. Willie Maley's side did not lose the match, in fact they won 2-1, but they conceded a goal scored for Raith Rovers by James Scott, a man who was fated to lose his life in the Great War. It was certainly not one of Celtic's better performances of the season, but, the team still rallied round to win.

Sometime during the game on Saturday, 3 January 1914 against Partick Thistle at Firhill, Eck McNair seems to have picked up an injury which troubled him off and on until March. He missed several weeks of football, albeit when he did return, he was more or less immediately put back into the Scotland team who drew 1-1 against Ireland at Windsor Park, in a game played in a pressurised atmosphere given the political tension, and then he was in the Scottish League team which beat the English League 3-2 at Burnley, whilst all the time Celtic were making progress towards their double.

McNair did seem to have a lucky escape from Belfast. In March 1914, there were two armed camps in the city as the Orangemen tried to resist the Irish Home Rule Bill. There was, thus, a supply of pistols readily available in the city, and Eck and Jimmy Brownlie, the Third Lanark goalkeeper, were convinced that they heard pistols being fired. Hopefully, it was not with live ammunition, but possibly it was. Just as well, then, that Ireland got a late equaliser, even though Sam Young looked well offside!

On Tuesday, 24 March, with Alec outstanding, Celtic drew 0-0 with Hearts at home in what was a good result for Willie Maley's team because Hearts had been challenging all season for the flag, but Celts were now ahead of them. Then on Saturday, 30 March, Celtic beat Third Lanark 2-0 in the Scottish Cup semi-final at Ibrox in front of a 50,000 crowd. Once again, McNair was magnificent, and April was destined to be another great month for both he and Celtic. To beat England at Hampden, win the Scottish Cup, then clinch the Scottish League, all in one calendar month, was no mean feat!

Scotland paid Celtic the ultimate compliment, when they chose the full-back duo of Alec McNair and Joe Dodds to face England at Hampden on Saturday, 4 April 1914. Eck was not the captain of his country that day, the honour going to Jimmy Gordon of Rangers. It was a not undeserved appointment it would have to be said. Gordon was a good player, almost the Rangers equivalent of Sunny Jim Young, perpetually 'in your face' and an encourager and cajoler of men, whereas Eck's approach to captaincy was more studied, and almost academic. Nevertheless, there were those, even in the Press, who felt that Gordon being appointed captain was a sop to the Rangers crowd, and that McNair might have been a better choice. To his credit, however, Eck rallied round Jimmy and supported him to the hilt in what was one of Scotland's best-ever triumphs over England. And Jimmy Gordon himself was very appreciative.

It was the other Jimmy – McMenemy – who was the Scotland hero with two goals in the 3-1 victory, albeit The Scottish Referee is full of praise about everyone. One gets the impression that the Editor would have wanted to print extra pages that Monday morning to include all he wanted to say about the game. The gates were closed quarter of an hour before the start with 105,000 spectators present. Hampden might have managed to squeeze some more folk in. However, sensibly, no chances were taken.

Alec's direct opponent that afternoon was the famous Eddie Mosscrop of Burnley. Mosscrop barely got a kick of the ball as a result of McNair's intelligent interceptions and tackles. There had been a few questions about Eck's lack of pace in some quarters but that was not obvious today. Similarly, on the other flank, Joe Dodds was equally successful in dealing with Freddie Walden of Tottenham Hotspur, who rejoiced in the unlikely nickname of 'Fanny.' At half-back, Jimmy Gordon and Jimmy Dun Hay, now of Newcastle United, excelled, whilst up front there was Napoleon, Jimmy McMenemy! He linked up well with the rest of the forwards, particularly Willie Reid of Rangers, scored twice and made the other, and that was no small achievement considering that the English defence contained men like Bob Crompton and Jesse Pennington, called, not without cause, 'peerless Pennington' for his great play and gentlemanly comportment on the field. Almost the English equivalent of the gentle man from Stenhousemuir, in fact!

Thus, was the whole country on a high for a long time afterwards, far longer, of course, than anyone could have envisaged at the time, but, more glory was on its way for Celtic in three games against Hibernian. Hibs were often a difficult team for Celtic. They both, of course, shared their Irish heritage, and it was often felt the Edinburgh club had been the midwife, as it were, or even the mother at the birth of Celtic, but there was always a residual feeling of jealousy at Easter Road that their Glasgow equivalents had left them so far behind. Hibernian were, of course, the only opponents where Celtic players could be guaranteed not to be abused with absurd inanities like "Papist" or "Fenian!"

Indeed, at the first of those three meetings with Hibernian in April 1914, the Scottish Cup final at Ibrox, the feelings of the whole crowd were made manifest with the fanatical and passionate singing of "God Save Ireland," a song about the Manchester Martyrs of 1867, and which now seemed relevant to the current situation where the much-cherished Irish Home Rule seemed about to be granted, before it was then was taken away. Britain might have saved themselves a great deal of bother in 1916 if Home Rule had been quietly conceded with appropriate guarantees to protect the interests of the Protestants in the north. As it was, the Asquith Government gave in to the demands of the northern minority and the country suffered for that piece of surrender for more than a century!

The singing was perhaps the highlight of the first match in the Scottish Cup final. The football was a massive disappointment to the packed 56,000 crowd, which had actually prevented the Hibernian charabanc from getting there on time! The game was dull and for the most part neither team looked vaguely like scoring, although Alec McNair once cleared off this line with Charlie Shaw beaten. Then, at the very end, Willie Smith of Hibs was through, but miskicked and Sunny Jim Young was able to clear without any real trouble. Full time came with a 0-0 draw the outcome.

Oh dear! Another cup final and another draw, this time with the added dimensions of comments such as "some Catholic charities have done well out of this," in popular conception or even "let's hope it's not going to buy guns for these Irish Volunteers" and other such vacuous rubbish. The replay played again at Ibrox the following Thursday night (incredibly Hibernian had a League game on the Wednesday and Celtic beat Queen's Park on the Monday) was a totally different story, however.

Celtic's game played on the Monday evening had been a 5-0 home thrashing of Queen's Park. It was significant in two respects. One was that it was a huge step in the direction of the Scottish League Championship, and the other was that Jimmy McColl was brought in to replace Ebenezer Owers and scored twice. Naturally, McColl was kept in the team for the Scottish Cup final replay.

That replay against Hibernian was simply a night on which Celtic showed why they were such a good team. Before 10 minutes were up, Jimmy McColl had scored twice from excellent service from Andy McAtee, Patsy Gallacher and Jimmy McMenemy. Johnny Browning them scored before and after half time, and although Hibs pulled one back, the game was over as a contest with Celtic playing out the game calmly, having no desire to humiliate their Edinburgh friends. Shaw, McNair and Dodds strolled through it all. "In this McNair was seen to great advantage, as he dodged past three opponents ere placing nicely down the field," says the adulatory The Scottish Referee. Full-time brought Celtic's ninth Scottish Cup success and Alec McNair's fifth Scottish Cup-winners medal.

The teams were:

Celtic: Shaw, McNair & Dodds; Young, Johnstone & McMaster; McAtee, Gallacher, McColl, McMenemy & Browning

Hibs: Allan, Girdwood & Templeton; Kerr, Paterson & Grosert; Wilson, Fleming, Hendren, Wood & Smith

Referee: Mr T Dougray, Bellshill

The aftermath of the game was the famous 'march back,' as Celtic supporters (those who could not afford the fare for the underground!) walked from Ibrox in the south-west of Glasgow to the east end of the city regaling everyone with the songs and good humour. Surprisingly, there does not seem to have been any reaction or violent behaviour, even though the demonstration was not without its political content. The centre of Glasgow that fine spring night in the gradually descending darkness was busy and animated, but we can imagine, can we not, a figure, an almost insignificant figure with a hat and raincoat carrying a small suitcase containing his boots, making his way through the crowds to Buchanan Street Station to catch his train back to Larbert? "Hey, Pat, that's Eck, is it no'? Eck McNair?" "Naw, dinnae be daft, John, that's no' Eck! He wadnae be here! That's just an ordinary man!" But Eck, as it was also said famously of Jimmy Quinn on many occasions, was a surprisingly ordinary sort of man!

McNair was back at Parkhead on the Saturday, two days later, to confirm the winning of the 1913/14 Scottish League championship. The Scottish Cup also appeared, and a photograph was taken, then Celtic went on to defeat Hibernian again, this time by 3-0 with two goals from Jimmy McMenemy and one from Jimmy McColl against a Hibs team who had given up the ghost. Even the English Press were impressed by this Celtic side, with favourable references to McMenemy and McNair - "a doyen of defenders" - and the Scottish newspapers like The Glasgow Herald, an unashamed lover of Queen's Park, simply having to throw up their hands in admiration of all that Maley had done at Celtic Park.

There remained the Glasgow Charity Cup, albeit it was won almost before a ball was kicked, such was the aura of the 'mighty Celts' and the knowledge that no-one was going to get through Shaw, McNair and Dodds. Queen's Park certainly didn't, as Celtic beat them 3-0, and then in the final on the night of Tuesday, 12 May 1914, Celtic hammered Third Lanark 6-0 at Hampden, a particular point of pleasure to Celtic for it had been Thirds who had eliminated them from the Glasgow Cup in October and had thus prevented Celtic from completing another clean sweep as secured in 1908.

Thus, ended a great season. However, Celtic were immediately off on a tour of Central Europe. Alec McNair did not go on this tour, and a mystery surrounds the reason why. Perhaps he had picked up an injury. Perhaps Willie Maley felt that Eck, who was never a great tourist and always loved his own bed in Stenhousemuir, deserved a rest and when he asked for an exemption, the Celtic manager, in whose eyes McNair was a great favourite, could not say no. Perhaps there was a more ominous reason in that Eck's wife Mary had not been keeping too well of late. Maley knew that she was a delicate woman. For whatever reason, McNair stayed at home. In any case, this would give a great opportunity for the earnest Tom McGregor who was good enough. After all, Eck, now 31 years old, could not go on forever. Could he?

Alec thus missed a great experience with many adventures, including perhaps a few that he did well to miss! He said his farewells to his friends and said he would see them again in late July or early August, when the football season started again. No-one, I repeat no-one, could have come close to guessing what life would be like in August 1914!

Up until Saturday, 1 August 1914, no-one really thought that there was going to be a World War. True, the Austro-Hungarians were shelling Belgrade as a result of that assassination a month ago of Archduke Franz Ferdinand in Sarajevo. That had started a week ago, but, there did not seem to be any reason why that should involve everyone. There had been frequent wars in the Balkans before, but newspaper leaders started saying things like "we may be drifting towards a war," and very soon "Balkan war" began to be replaced by "international crisis" and "grave situation for everyone."

The problem was the Czar of Russia. The Serbs had appealed to him for help against the Austrians. Only too keen to divert attention away from his own internal problems, the Czar obliged and mobilised his army and pulled in France to help under the terms of the Entente. Austria now played her part in the "Ah'll get ma faither tae ye" game and appealed to Germany to help. The Kaiser was similarly spoiling for a fight, and now the continent of Europe was at each other's throats. It need not have involved Britain, but the Kaiser decided, foolishly and pig-headedly, to attack France through Belgium, giving the mighty British Empire the excuse to join in under the specious pretext of defending a small nation under the terms of the Treaty of London 1839. Britain was never too keen to protect the interests of another small nation called Ireland!

Thus, with bewildering speed, Europe was suddenly at war, and by the time Celtic played their first League fixture of 1914/15 at Tynecastle against Hearts on Saturday, 15 August, the war was a week and a half old, and the British Army was already in the field defending Belgium at places like Mons. The world had suddenly gone mad, and when the Celtic party arrived at Haymarket, Edinburgh was full of posters urging young men to join up "before it was too late" and pressure was on the authorities to suspend professional football on the grounds that 22 young fit men should be in the army fighting for their country, rather than kicking a ball around on a Saturday afternoon. Celtic lost that game 0-2, albeit it was hardly the main topic of conversation.

Fortunately, Scottish football managed to survive being put to sleep for the next four years, but at severe cost. Full time professional football was not allowed, although players could still feature on a part-time basis as long as they also worked in a war-related industry. In Alec McNair's case, this meant a job in the Ministry of Munitions, where ammunition and armaments were made. We find the occasional reference to him working at a firm called Electrics in Stenhousemuir, but what precisely he did, we cannot say. His talents as a grate fitter were presumably put to good use and developed for some wartime purpose, and he was still able to get a train every Saturday lunchtime, having worked a shift in the Saturday morning in order to play the game that he loved for the team that he also loved.

McNair resisted the temptation to 'join up.' Superficially, there were attractions of adventure, glory and getting the opportunity to wear a kilt, but, there was also a serious danger of death and, in any case, army life with its drilling, saluting and being trained how to kill people was something that Eck did not fancy in the slightest. His job would protect him to an extent, and Willie Maley, the son of a soldier and for that reason perhaps more aware of the dangers than most (in spite of his bogus claims about patriotism), was able to ensure that most of his excellent side were in reserved occupations and working close to Glasgow. Maley probably did support the war, at least at this stage. However, he also wanted Celtic to continue to rule the roost in Scotland. He was also very aware that on the political front, things were more complex than perhaps seemed to the casual observer. There was general support for the war, yes, at the moment but it wasn't necessarily going to last. Labour problems might arise, and Ireland was certainly not going to go away.

There would be no full International games, although there would be League Internationals for a season, and the Scottish Cup was also put into cold storage. These were particular blows to men like McNair, who would have been heavily involved in both spheres, but, the Scottish League continued, as did the Glasgow Cup and the Glasgow Charity Cup on the grounds that these local competitions did not involve much travelling. Football was to be restricted to Saturdays and Monday holidays only. There would be no midweek football without special permission. Midweeks were required for munitions working, and Sundays were still naturally earmarked for religious worship.

All these restrictions were courtesy of DORA – the Defence of the Realm Act – and it all meant that football did survive in some way. Indeed, the historian must not shrug his shoulders and say "war-time football" as if it were a piece of excrement that one has just stood on. It was very important indeed for everyone's morale, for the civilian population, servicemen home on leave and even for servicemen abroad. Willie Maley, for example, was very careful to send a telegram with a result of a game to the War Office soon after it finished, so that soldiers could find out how the team had done within a very short time of the full-time whistle. Hence all the rhymes like "Along the line the signal flew, Rangers one and Celtic two!" As it happened, Celtic won almost everything during the war.

The major opponents in the first year of the war were not Rangers but Hearts. Hearts had a fine side and had indeed got themselves off to a great start by beating Celtic 2-0 on the opening day of the season at Tynecastle. However, it is important to debunk a myth that still exists today in Gorgie circles. This was the belief that Hearts would have won the League Championship in 1915 if their first team had not decided en masse to enlist in late 1914. This is simply not so.

In the first place, it is right to pay tribute to the brave Hearts footballers who joined up. Rightly are they honoured in their special memorial stone at Haymarket Station for their brave, if possibly misguided, decision. So many of them did not return, and the country and the world were so much the poorer for all that. But for the remainder of the 1914/15 season, in a two-horse race for the title, they were still doing their basic training in Scotland and were, to a very large extent, available for most games. The reason they did not win the League Championship was simply that Celtic were better and wore them down by constant attrition, as we will see.

Alec McNair and the rest of the Celtic team would have been very upset to hear of the passing of John Mulrooney on 26 July 1914. He had been Celtic's goalkeeper in 1912 and 1913 – a good custodian between the posts and a great character in the team. Mulrooney had lost his place to Charlie Shaw after being diagnosed with a rheumatic condition (by no means unusual in goalkeepers of this era) and was now playing for St Johnstone. He was a much-loved character on the social side of the club and was rumoured to be able to wiggle his large sticking out ears at will. He died suddenly of heart failure at his home in Hamilton. He was not quite 28 years of age when he passed away.

It was a particular loss to Eck, who had built up a great understanding with him. Shaw was clearly the better goalkeeper, but John Mulrooney was a personal loss to all the team. It was a timely reminder of the fragility of human life at a time when it was going to become a great deal more fragile, both for McNair himself and for the human race in general.

McNair missed three games early in the 1914/15 season through injury. Unfortunately, one of these games was the Glasgow Cup-tie at Shawfield against Clyde, which was lost 0-2. Said to have caused "consternation in the trenches" (a rhetorical anachronism, one feels, for the trenches had hardly been dug yet!), this result was a bad one for Celtic, and Eck was sadly missed. Tom McGregor, his replacement, was "not so strong in the tackle" as McNair, and it seems no accident that Charlie Shaw chose this game on 12

September to have a bad day and conceded two goals. Clearly, he needed Alec McNair to be beside him.

Eck, however, came back into the side the next week and stability returned until early October, when Celtic dropped a point away to Raith Rovers on the Holiday Monday and then went down 0-1 to Ayr United the following Saturday, on the day that Antwerp fell to the Germans. Reports also reached the newspapers that Paris was being shelled from the ground and, amazingly, bombed from the air. Any remaining vestige of belief that the war would be "over by Christmas" had now been well and truly dispelled. Hearts were now five points ahead of both Celtic and Ayr United. Ayr's goal that day at Somerset Park had been scored by a young man by the name of Joe Cassidy. The hosts were fortunate in that many soldiers were based in that area doing their basic training, and therefore Ayr United were able to pick up quite a few useful players.

From now on, however, until the New Year, Celtic rallied, winning 11 games in a row and, as with the previous year, conceding very few goals with the 'Holy Trinity' of Shaw, McNair & Dodds once again well to the fore in supporters' conversations, including suggestions that the Germans would never get through them in France! A large crowd of 35,000 - including soldiers in military uniforms home on leave - was inside Parkhead on Hallowe'en to see a good 2-1 victory over Rangers, with Jimmy Quinn, widely written off as "finished," "too old," and "overweight," nevertheless playing a large part in the win. The military uniform may not have won the heart of young ladies (as was widely claimed) but it did protect young men from any taunts of being a "shirker," "dodger," "lead swinger" or, in the common neologism of the time, a "scrimshanker."

The last game of the eventful and scarcely believable year of 1914 saw a 3-1 win over Hamilton Academical, a particularly poignant occasion. Just one month previously, the two clubs had been well represented at the funeral of Peter Somers, who had played for both

Celtic and Hamilton. Peter was still in his mid 30s and his death followed the amputation of part of his leg. Somers is sometimes under-rated in the catalogues of Willie Maley's great teams, but not in the assessment of Maley himself nor in the opinion of Eck McNair, who considered him to be a superb player and an integral part of Celtic's great side of 1907 and 1908.

The win over Hamilton Academical meant that Celtic had continued to recover from their poor start, albeit, unfortunately, Hearts were winning as well and were still four points ahead. The odds would have to be on the Tynecastle side winning the Scottish League, and those odds shortened considerably when Celtic went down 1-2 to Rangers at Ibrox on New Year's Day 1915. 'Brigadier' of The Daily Record has no hesitation in nominating Alec McNair as the best full back of the four on view and praises his judgement, particularly against the strong wind, although he then blames him to a certain extent for losing the ball to Cairns in the build-up to the Rangers winning goal. Eck, like most of the 50,000 crowd, had thought that the ball was going out of play.

Celtic, however, quickly recovered from this defeat, and Hearts also dropped two points in January, so the gap was still four points when the teams met at Celtic Park on Saturday, 30 January 1915 for what was billed as "the game of the season." A crowd of 45,000 turned up, 10,000 of them wearing khaki according to one estimate, and they saw a very close game, "something between an International and a Cup-tie," according to one opinion in The Scottish Referee. It would turn out to be a 1-1 draw – Hearts scoring through Graham early in the first half and Celtic equalising through Andy McAtee early in the second. This was generally regarded as a fair result, although Hearts were "fortunate in effecting a draw," according to The Glasgow Herald. But it was de facto a victory for Hearts, who were still four points ahead, with both teams having 11 games to play but none of those against each other.

Although no-one realised it at the time, this game turned out to be Jimmy Quinn's last game for Celtic. The great man, by now in his late 30s, was just too old and too slow, but he accepted things graciously and did all he could to encourage his successor, Jimmy McColl.

The team needed encouragement. What does one do in such circumstances? Those of us who were alive and recall the similar circumstances of 1968 will relate to this. All one can do is win all one's own games as convincingly as one can, and trust that the other team will crack under the psychological pressure of all this. Rangers cracked under the pressure of 1968, and some 53 years earlier, Hearts similarly broke under the Celtic onslaught. The newspapers said that it was other teams who took the points from Hearts, but, everyone knew that it was the almost psychic and supernatural power of Willie Maley and Celtic that broke them from a distance by a sort of magical telekinesis!

Celtic were fortunate in several respects. One was that Maley was able to keep more or less the same team every week. This involved 'having a quiet word' with an employer or a foreman to secure a player's release, the organisation of transport (not always easy in 1915) and other logistic details. He was also lucky in that Jimmy McColl hit top form, scoring another 12 goals between the beginning and the end of the season. The third factor had less to do with luck and more to do with good judgement. It was Shaw, McNair & Dodds.

Celtic now proceeded to win their next 10 games, drawing the 11th when the League was well and truly won. They scored 27 goals and lost just five. It was better, for psychological reasons, for Celtic to win all their games comfortably. This they proceeded to do, 5-1 over Hibernian, 4-0 over Third Lanark and a couple of 3-0 victories brought much needed comfort for the Celtic fans and piled the pressure on Hearts.

As it turned out, it was Rangers, of all people, who produced the first crack in the Tynecastle edifice. The Ibrox men had not enjoyed the best of seasons. They had their good days, like New Year's Day for example, and now Saturday, 20 February 1915, when they defeated Hearts. It was a strange game, though. Rangers were well on top, and with their team losing 4-0 with 10 minutes to go, the Hearts fans were streaming out of Tynecastle. But then suddenly Hearts came back into the game and scored three goals. Sadly, for the conspiracy theorists, they couldn't score a fourth and the game finished 4-3 for Rangers. At the very death, Hearts forced a corner kick and "the whole stand rose" to cheer them on, before the Rangers defence cleared. Meanwhile, across in Glasgow, Celtic beat a determined Dumbarton side 1-0 thanks to a good goal from Jimmy McColl. "McNair was never at fault with his judgement," as the Sons staged a late rally.

The Sunday Post, a fledgling newspaper which had first appeared in the autumn of 1914, now asked the question, "Who Wins The League Flag Now?" Indeed, the pressure was now on Hearts, and the constant adulation of the Edinburgh press (because they had so many men now in the army) did not really help. Celtic knew how to win, as they proved when they beat Hibernian 5-1 on Saturday, 6 March 1915, one week after the Easter Road men had taken another point away from Hearts in an exciting Edinburgh derby. On that same day, Celtic had beaten Partick Thistle 2-0 to cut into the gap.

There was a brief pause in the title race in March. Although there were no full Internationals that year, there was a clash between the Scottish League and the English Leagues at Celtic Park. In the circumstances, it was considered to be just as important as a full International. It would be the last such occasion for some time, and in view of the score, that was perhaps just as well, for the English won 4-1. It was not a great day for McNair, and his mood would not have been helped by the news that Hearts, who had dropped another point the week before, beat Partick Thistle 3-1. Indeed, it was quite a sombre day all round, for reports were appearing in newspapers of heavy British losses at a place called the Dardanelles, with many people asking the obvious question of what on earth they were doing in the Aegean Sea when they were meant to be fighting the Germans in Europe?

On Saturday, 27 March 1915, both teams won as expected against poor opposition, Celtic beating Raith Rovers 3-1 at Parkhead and Hearts overcoming Clyde by 2-0 at Tynecastle. Thus, we entered April with Celtic having five games to play, Hearts three, and the Gorgie men now four points ahead. It was certainly an exciting race. If Celtic managed to win their two games in hand, it would be level-pegging, and if the teams finished equal on points, it would be a shared Championship.

But April and the spring weather won it for Celtic, who won four of their five games (the last one at Motherwell was drawn in a game that no longer mattered), scoring 11 goals without reply, whereas Hearts simply blew up. A feckless 0-0 draw at Pittodrie on Saturday, 3 April, whilst Celtic were beating Airdrieonians 3-0, gave Maley's side the edge. Then Celtic played off one of their games in hand on the Holiday Monday, defeating Queen's Park 3-0. Celtic were now just one point behind but with a game in hand, and most people at Tynecastle realised that the title game was up.

It was the following Saturday, 10 April 1915, which more or less won the League Championship for Celtic. A narrow 1-0 win over Aberdeen at Parkhead (the goal scored by the apparently omnipotent Jimmy McMenemy) owed much to the "calm demeanour and grim sense of purpose of McNair and Dodds," and then when a telegram arrived at Parkhead with news of Hearts' woeful and now almost predictable 0-2 defeat at Cappielow to Morton, the players celebrated, for Celtic were now clearly in the lead. To clinch the Scottish League flag for the 12th time, Willie Maley's Bhoys then went to Cathkin on Saturday, 17 April and treated a large crowd of 20,000 to a display of Celtic attacking football at its best, with two goals from Johnny Browning and one each from McMenemy and Jimmy McColl. It was Celtic's 19th clean sheet of the League season (50% of the games played) and it showed why they deserved to be champions, taking everyone's mind off what was going on in the Dardanelles. That day would, however, prove to be a poignant one in the 27-year history of Celtic Football Club, as word came through of the death in Dumfries of founder Brother Walfrid. The man born Andrew Kerins in Ballymote, County Sligo had passed away in Dumfries, just one month short of his 75th birthday.

This would prove to be Eck McNair's eighth Scottish League winner's medal, and life was not at all bad for the gentle genius of Stenhousemuir. His job in Munitions was hard, but it was better than being in the army, and there was always the sheer relief of his football on a Saturday afternoon. He would not have been human if he had not been upset with what was going on in Europe and, more particularly, in recent weeks in the Dardanelles, and he had already heard of some local casualties from Stenhousemuir and Larbert, young lads whom he knew and had played football with, in some cases. He could only hope and pray that it would all end soon.

But there was good news too. His wife Mary was pregnant. It had not gone entirely smoothly, but she was due soon, and his son James was now a sturdy three-year-old, whilst he had a large and supportive family around him. In any case, there was still the Glasgow Charity Cup to be played. In war time, this competition assumed more importance than normal, particularly as there had been no Scottish Cup.

The games were surprisingly close. Queen's Park put up a brave fight to lose 1-2 in the first round, and then Celtic could only be described as lucky to scrape through the semi-final against Partick Thistle by winning by 5 corners to 4. This, however, set up a final against Rangers, who won the toss for venue, 40,000 turning up to see what turned out to be a remarkable game on Saturday, 8 May 1915.

The final was played with a dreadful war event going on in the background, for the previous day, just off the coast of Ireland, German submarines had sunk the Cunard liner, RMS Lusitania. It was not yet known exactly how many had perished. However, the toll was high and most of the casualties were civilians. It was a shocking act of barbarism and cannot really be excused by the Germans saying that by taking out advertisements in American newspapers, they had warned people not to travel. Nor was the undeniable presence of military hardware bound for the British war effort a valid excuse either. Nothing could really legitimise what had happened, and Glasgow, a city made famous for its shipbuilding, was as shocked as anywhere. It would now be more difficult position for the anti-war people, and it remains a colossal blunder by the Germans, who now found that neutral opinion (and certainly opinion in the USA) was appalled by what had happened.

But this was of lesser importance for Eck McNair. He boarded his train that morning to Glasgow with a spring in his step, for a few hours earlier, Mary had given birth to a baby girl to be called Agnes Bennett Boyne McNair. It had been a difficult birth, but mother and baby were both well, and Eck who had left his wife and daughter in the caring hands of his family was congratulated by his teammates (and even a few of the Rangers players who were friends of his), although there might have been a joke or two about the baby's second and third names. Was the Bennett named after Alec, who had deserted Celtic for Rangers, and surely the third name couldn't have anything to do with any disreputable historical event?

The game was a fine one, played on a nice day, albeit with a little too much of the wind that was always associated with Ibrox. But it was a warm wind, and the crowd enjoyed the match. Once more, we had the phenomenon of a large section of the crowd in khaki. Johnny McMaster wasn't playing for Celtic that day, so Joe Dodds was brought forward to left-half, whilst Tom McGregor was at left-back to partner Alec McNair. In fact, it was Dodds who opened the scoring. McNair made ground on the right flank and sent over a cross ball, which eluded a few defenders, landed at the unmarked Joe Dodds, and Celtic were 1-0 up. Joe did not score many goals, but this one was a beauty.

But then towards half-time, in the words of The Sunday Post, Patsy Gallacher "got knocked and disappeared." Whilst he was off being treated, Rangers scored twice, through Tommy Cairns and Andy Cunningham. This was hard luck for Celtic, who thus went off at half time 1-2 down, but they came out with the wind behind them, and with Patsy Gallacher restored to fitness, battle was renewed. Late in the game, for all Celtic's pressing, Rangers were still ahead 2-1 on goals and 3-2 ahead on corners, meaning that one goal was not enough.

This Celtic team, however, had the priceless asset of knowing how to win football matches. Johnny Browning equalised in the 82nd minute, and then three minutes later a McNair free-kick found the head of Jimmy McMenemy, who nodded home to give Celtic a hard-worked but nevertheless deserved win, and another Charity Cup medal for Eck, his fourth in a row. No drinking and carousing for him tonight though. It was off home to see his new baby daughter. It was a double celebration, and it was odd for him to find himself so happy on a day on which the war, already going badly in the Dardanelles, had taken such a serious and ominous turn.

The 1914/15 season did not technically finish until the next week, when Alec played for Celtic in the side that beat a Rest of the League select at Hampden in a game played for Belgian Refugees, of whom there were quite a few now in Glasgow. Celtic won 1-0, and that was a fitting end to a remarkable season. Life looked good for McNair and Celtic, in spite of the war, which was now affecting everyone. Alec, however, was happy with his wife and two children. One hopes he enjoyed as much of the nice summer weather as he could, for life was soon to turn rather tragic for Eck McNair.

CHAPTER SIX

TRAGEDY AND DEALING WITH IT (1915-1918)

Summer 1915 was hardly the best time to be alive. The weather was good, but the war was not going well. It was becoming increasingly obvious that the Dardanelles campaign was a colossal disaster. The Liberal Government did not exactly fall, but, they felt obliged to ask the Conservatives to join them in a coalition. The Conservatives agreed, but the price that had to be paid by Asquith was the sacking of the man held responsible for this catastrophe, Winston Churchill.

In late May there occurred the worst railway disaster that the country had ever known, at a place near Gretna called Quintinshill, where 227 soldiers of the Royal Scots perished when their troop train collided with a stationary train. What was most poignant for Alec McNair and people from that area was that the troop train had started its journey from Larbert.

Alec was now back working in Munitions and enjoying life, as well as one could in the circumstances, at 32 Rae Street, Stenhousemuir, with his wife and two children, especially the new baby. The children were healthy, albeit his wife wasn't keeping all that well. This was put down to the after-effects of a difficult birth. Fortunately, in the close-knit and supportive community that Stenhousemuir was, Mary was well looked after by their family and friends and Eck was able to go to his very vital job in the Munitions industry

But Mary did not seem to be getting over it, permanently tired and not eating well. The doctor thought it might be a heart problem, and indeed it was. On the morning of Monday, 9 August 1915, just after midnight, Mary Niven McNair died of Cardiac Valve Disease. She was only 28 years old.

One can hardly begin to imagine what this did to Alec. The tragedy involving his baby daughter Helen in 1911 was enough for anyone to cope with. It could be argued that this was a million times worse. If there was any comfort to be got in 1915, it was that he was not alone in his suffering. There was no monopoly in anguish. Many others were suffering the same in Stenhousemuir, Glasgow and elsewhere. It was normally a young woman mourning a husband or boyfriend in 1915, or a mother grieving for a son. With the McNair family, things were the other way round.

There is no easy way of dealing with these things. The only real way forward is to take it on the chin for a while, then slowly and gradually fight back. It was a very dark period of Eck's life. McNair, however, was better equipped than most to deal with this, and he was lucky in that he had maximum support from his family. There would be no problem with looking after the two children. He had his mother and sisters. He would be able to continue working, and also to continue playing football. His family supported him in all of that, knowing that football and Celtic were both part of his identity.

And there was also his other family, the Celtic family. Willie Maley is often accused of being insensitive, tactless and lacking in grace. This is not true, at least not at this time. He was kindness and support personified. He came to Stenhousemuir to see Alec, as indeed did men like Joe Dodds, Jimmy McMenemy, Charlie Shaw, Sunny Jim Young, and quite a few players from other teams. Maley said that McNair could take as long as he needed, and that he was welcome back at any time.

Not unnaturally, Eck did indeed take a few weeks off. He played his first game of the season on the Holiday Monday, 27 September 1915 in a 5-0 defeat of Clyde at Celtic Park. The Daily Record says it was an "auspicious re-entry" for McNair. Celtic then beat Hibernian 4-0 at Easter Road on the following Saturday, but other things were happening in the world as well, and they had an impact on Celtic.

The Glasgow Cup final between Celtic and Rangers was due to be played seven days later, on Saturday, 9 October 1915. This was the time of the Battle of Loos. It is a sad cliché of the Great War to say that this involved heavy casualties, and it so happened that both Joe Dodds and Jimmy McMenemy lost a brother in this battle in the week leading up to the final. This meant that Celtic had now three men in mourning for someone dear to them that they had lost. Willie Maley, assiduous as ever in attending to the needs of his men, offered them all the opportunity to stand down if they wished. All three of them said "No," and affirmed that they would rather play in the game.

This was clearly the right decision. Life has to go on and playing in a match against Rangers does at least take one's mind for a spell off the horrors that are going on around one. There was also the wider consideration. There was hardly a family in the land unaffected by this war. The supporters needed to see their stars to cheer them up. All three men found that their decision was supported by all the families concerned, and their courage was rewarded with a 2-1 victory at Hampden, Celtic's first Glasgow Cup success since 1909, and their 10th overall.

Reports vary. The outrageously pro-Celtic The Glasgow Observer says that "one goal did not represent the disparity," and talks about thousands of Rangers fans leaving in disgust early in the second half. The Sunday Post tells us that "McNair was the best back on the field. He showed admirable restraint and judgement." Restraint was necessary, for several players, notably Jimmy Gordon of Rangers and Jimmy McMenemy of Celtic, were seen to "exchange words." The Daily Record did not think that it was a great cup final, as there was rather too much arguing among the players, and not enough football. But Patsy Gallacher and Johnny Browning got Celtic's goals (all three goals were scored in the first half) and the Celtic fans in the crowd – some 80,000 of them, with many in khaki and not a few in blue, not because they supported Rangers necessarily, but more because 'hospital blue' was now the recognised uniform of a wounded soldier – had a good afternoon. Both teams had been unbeaten up to this point.

Life, however, was far from normal for Eck McNair. How could it be? In addition to his own personal grief, he was working on shifts at his Munitions factory from 5.00am to 5.00pm, according to some accounts. In some ways, that was a good thing in that it took his mind away from his own situation, and it meant that he would be earning quite a lot of money – workers are always valued in wartime! – but it left him very little time to himself. He certainly had no time to train for football, especially in the winter months.

On the other hand, everyone was in the same boat. Life was not easy for anyone, and one often wonders just what the standard of football was really like in those distant, wartime days. Celtic were lucky, in that they had loads of players to call upon, but even so, there was no guarantee of a player's availability on any given Saturday, and many are the stories of some of the smaller teams making loudspeaker appeals for someone who "had played Junior and was not registered for another Senior team" to have a go. There were often problems with referees not being able to get to the ground in time, and sometimes an official of the home team had to do the job with the away team relying on his honesty!

Yet in spite of football being such a haphazard activity, it never lost its attraction for the public. Rather, it became even more an opiate of the masses who looked forward to a Saturday afternoon to see their team with even more relish. And, of course, as everyone was employed and there weren't always a lot of luxury goods to spend one's money on, there was enough money around for people to attend and pay their 'sickie' (sixpence). Football, like the infant cinema and indeed the more traditional music hall, did not make the mistake of pricing itself out of the market.

The life of Alec McNair in season 1915/16 was hardly a bed of roses, and soon after the winning of the Glasgow Cup (a great event for him in 1915, in spite of all the attendant grief), both McNair and Celtic hit a bad patch. A surprise 0-2 defeat to St Mirren on Saturday, 23 October 1915 at Parkhead (McNair was short with a pass for one of the goals and Joe Dodds missed a penalty) was followed the next week by a 3-0 reverse at Ibrox, as Rangers thus got revenge for their Hampden defeat. And yet it was not so bad as it seemed, for Celtic had tough luck with the crucial second goal looking like a handball. McNair was to be blamed because he stopped and claimed it, ignoring the cardinal rule of "play to the whistle." Then Patsy Gallacher missed a penalty!

There was a better game seven days later, when Aberdeen came to Celtic Park, although Alec was again criticised for failing to clear Dons' consolation goal in an otherwise competent performance as Celtic won 3-1, the goals coming late in the game in typical Celtic fashion. In other circumstances, Willie Maley might have decided to give McNair a rest, as the man was clearly suffering physically and emotionally, but he had faith in him and kept him in the team even when Celtic lost their next game 0-2 to Hearts at Tynecastle. Even without Sunny Jim Young, this was a disappointing result, and it meant that Celtic, Hearts and Rangers all had 18 points, but Celtic had played 12 games, two more than Rangers and two less than Hearts!

Things were looking bad and Celtic supporters were becoming panicky about their team. Their depression was mirrored in the general atmosphere of the war situation, which had gone from bad to worse. The Battle of Loos, which was meant to produce a breakthrough, had failed to do so, and it had turned out to be a tragically expensive loss of life. The optimists talked about "an indecisive draw," the cynics called it "a heavy defeat for both sides," and the heavy loss of life meant that, although the Government talked about "successful" recruiting schemes like that of Lord Derby, everyone knew that in 1916 there would have to be conscription.

McNair was, at least, spared that. Being in the munitions industry was considered to be a vital job, plus being a sole parent in charge of two young children meant that he was exempt from being enlisted, save in the most desperate of situations. But others in the Celtic team might yet be conscripted. It was a blessing in Eck's case that he would not be enlisted, for he would have been no soldier.

At this time in late 1915, a certain amount of depression settled over the country. The war which was meant to have finished last Christmas was quite clearly going to see another one with no end in sight. Both powers were well balanced, and if it had been a football match, it would have been a draw. But there was no referee in this war, and it went on and on, as cynical politicians, generals and (crucially) industrialists kept it going for their own ends.

McNair plodded on at his job. His children were well cared for, and he at least had his football. As yet, there was no serious problem with the food supply, although he was aware that certain exotic, foreign foods were not always easy to come by. He cannot but have been affected by the news of the casualties, and no doubt he was aware of certain undercurrents at his work asking questions about what was the point of this war, and where were all the profits going? These undercurrents, he knew, would get a lot worse if conscription was introduced, but, at the moment, things were quiet, and indeed masked by the sheer amount of patriotic jargon and emotional blackmail about 'duty.' Alec

McNair, a sensible man, must have wondered about that.

But things on the football field took a decided and permanent turn for the better. Celtic, as we have seen, lost to Hearts at Tynecastle on Saturday, 13 November 1915. They would not lose again until Saturday, 21 April 1917. This meant that the team went the entire calendar year of 1916 without losing a game. It should be said that 1916 was a dreadful year in many ways for many people and many nations. There were compensations, however, if you were a Celtic supporter!

Two Celtic wins in the latter part of November 1915 were followed by a purple patch in December when 20 goals were scored in four games, with only two conceded. The goals absolutely flowed from the scintillating play of Jimmy McMenemy, Patsy Gallacher and Andy McAtee up front while Charlie Shaw, Alec McNair and Joe Dodds (occasionally Tom McGregor, if Dodds was playing in the half-back line) mopped everything up at the back. This was just the stuff to give the troops, and if ever there was a time in world history when people needed a boost, it was December 1915. Those who had survived Loos or Gallipoli (the Dardonelles) and were currently enjoying some well-deserved leave now felt that there were some things in life that were worth working for. Similarly, one feels, McNair himself might have felt that way. He had been through the mill in 1915, but he was now beginning to come through the other side. Nothing would bring his beloved wife Mary back, but life was not without its small compensations. His children were thriving, and so was his football career.

Rangers had lost a couple of games but were still more or less on level terms with Celtic when they came to Parkhead for the 1916 New Year Day derby. A crowd of 40,000 turned up to see a very even and fair game, albeit Celtic would have won had Alec McNair not scored one of his rare own goals in one of his even rarer misunderstandings with Charlie Shaw. He seems to have been panicked by a shout from Sunny Jim Young - "Ahent ye, Eleck" - which made him think that a Rangers forward was closer than he was. Eck was embarrassed by that, and no doubt apologised profusely...but it would have been his last apology for some time.

Rangers, thus, stayed on level terms with Celtic, but Celtic did not drop another point until the first day of April. The Ibrox side, on the other hand, fell away. Willie Maley's men simply kept winning, and in Jimmy McColl they seemed to have found another great centre-forward in the mould of Sandy McMahon (who sadly died on January 25 of this year) and Jimmy Quinn. McNair had now stabilised. He was reported to have had one bad game this spring. This was on Saturday, 19 February 1916 at Hampden, where he made very little of a diminutive youngster called Alan Morton, of whom the world would hear more in the future. But Queen's Park did not score and Celtic still won that game, thanks to a goal from Patsy Gallacher.

It was a great pity that there was no Scottish Cup or Internationals that 1915/16 season, but, regulations did not permit that. The weather was generally good, but on Saturday, 25 March, Celtic's game against Motherwell at Fir Park was snowed off. This caused a problem. When could it be played? The Scottish League programme had to be finished by the end of April. Midweek football was not allowed, except for the Holiday Monday, and that was already catered for with a game against Third Lanark. Sunday football in 1916 was absolutely a no-go. Indeed, it was believed that God would make the Germans win the war if anyone even thought about it! So, it had to be two games played on the one day. This was not entirely unprecedented in the circumstances, albeit unusual, and this time there was the added twist that if Celtic won both games, against Raith Rovers at Celtic Park, and Motherwell at Fir Park on Saturday, 15 April 1916, they would win the League.

Celtic's game against Raith Rovers kicked off at 3.15pm, and against an admittedly very weakened Kirkcaldy side, they won 6-0, thereby beating Falkirk's goalscoring record of 103 from 1908. Then it was immediately into a charabanc and straight to Fir Park. Motherwell had lost 0-3 to Ayr United in the afternoon, and tonight, with the moon out by full-time, they lost 1-3 to Celtic. Maley's only line-up change between the two games had been to introduce Joe Cassidy for Joe O'Kane. Celtic thus won their 13th Scottish League title, McNair collected his ninth League-winner's medal and the team had now scored 107 goals in the League season. They would eventually reach 116 goals scored, whilst losing only 23. The 38-game schedule produced 32 wins, 3 defeats and 3 draws. It was a record that spoke for itself.

A few games still had to be played. The match against Third Lanark on the Easter Holiday Monday was played whilst historic events were going on in Dublin. Alec McNair paid little attention to such things, which were in any case played down and reported in a pejorative way in the British Press, but he was aware that some people, notably Patsy Gallacher, were quite interested in how the struggle was developing. By the time that the final League game of the season (a 5-0 win over Partick Thistle at Celtic Park) was played on Saturday, 29 April 1916, the rebels were on the point of surrendering. In historical terms, it mattered little. "A point had been made and a terrible beauty had been born," as WB Yates famously put it.

By the time that Celtic played their two Glasgow Charity Cup games in May, the executions in Dublin were in full swing. It would be some time before the incredible but true story of James Connolly, the Scotsman from Edinburgh, who was badly injured and brought in from a military hospital to be shot in a chair at the city's Kilmainham Gaol, was actually believed, but, it happened the day before Celtic won the Glasgow Charity Cup final by beating Partick Thistle 2-0 at Hampden on Saturday, 13 May. Maley's side had beaten Rangers 3-0 at Celtic Park in the semi-final the week before. Celtic had thus emulated 1907/08 by winning every competition for which they entered, and the Charity Cup medal was another addition to McNair's vast collection.

But then, seven days later on 20 May 1916, something extraordinary happened. Celtic actually lost a game! Fortunately, it was a light-hearted friendly at Hampden against the Rest of the League in aid of War Relief for Belgian Refugees and other worthy causes, but it was still vexatious to lose.

At last, this mighty season ended for both Celtic and Alec McNair. The war was continuing in all its ferocity and this summer would see two dreadful battles, one at sea and one on land. The naval battle was the Battle of Jutland, at the end of May, and the land battle was the Battle of the Somme, in early July, the much anticipated 'push.' Naturally, British propaganda would claim victory in both these battles. Those who fought in them would have to disagree, and the war had another 'two-and-a-bit' years of slaughter to go yet. McNair did well to avoid such events, although he did not have his own sorrows to seek.

By the time that the football season started again in August 1916, the penny was beginning to drop that the Battle of the Somme had not been a success. On the first day of July, when it all started, newspapers had talked about "Hitting Huns All Round," "Pouring Forward" and ridiculous stuff like "Next Stop Berlin." Yet the casualties and the telegrams with the bad news kept coming back, and slowly and reluctantly, generals and politicians began to admit that progress was not as rapid as they had hoped for, that in some areas progress had stalled and that in others, there hadn't been any progress at all! Yet the battle kept going on, and incredibly the British people kept, to a large extent, supporting the war. In other parts of the world, support was beginning to weaken. Russia was already beginning to show a few signs of cracking.

Ireland had settled. The words of the Roman author Tacitus, put into the mouth of a British chieftain nearly two millennia previously, came to mind, "Where they create a desert, they call it peace." But the problem had not gone away. It would come back. Similarly, with the labour problems on the Clyde and elsewhere. They flared up now and again.

But some things remained the same. Celtic, although having lost a few men to conscription, opened the season with eight straight wins, and by Saturday, 7 October 1916, Eck McNair had won another Glasgow Cup medal. In the semi-final against Rangers, two weeks earlier, Celtic had won 3-0, thanks, to a large extent, to soldiers Peter Johnstone and Johnny McMaster managing to get leave to play in the game. Indeed, Johnstone had travelled all night from the south of England to play. Jimmy McMenemy and Patsy Gallacher both worked in the shipyards, whilst Andy McAtee was in the mines, so all three were safe from conscription, at least for the moment. And at the back, there was still Shaw, McNair & Dodds.

Around 50,000 spectators had been at Celtic Park for the semi-final, played on Saturday, 23 September 1916, and they witnessed a rather one-sided match, with Celtic in command throughout and battering the Rangers goal with no luck until the last quarter of an hour, when Johnny Browning, Joe O'Kane and Private Peter Johnstone did the needful. The final against Clyde at the same venue a fortnight later was actually a better game, although the eventual 3-2 scoreline was deceptive, in that the Shawfield men scored first and then again in the last minute, with The Glasgow Herald remarking that between times, "it was a case of marking time, so far as the winners were concerned."

It was another cup, another medal, but, a familiar face was missing from Celtic Park that day, for Sunny Jim Young had played his last game for the club. Young had suffered a bad knee injury the week before, in a 1-0 home win over Hearts, and hard though he tried to get back to fitness, his knee had gone. An unsuccessful operation followed, and he had to announce his reluctant retirement at the end of the season. Sonny had not given up on the team, though! His famous war cries, "Face the ball, Celts," "Tak a man apiece," and simply, "Intae them, Celtic," would resound from the pavilion gallery of Celtic Park for some time.

All this meant an opportunity for Alec McNair to be the Celtic captain. He was reluctant in some ways, but he was the obvious choice. He did the job, and the team kept winning, even though they suffered a further blow in mid-winter, when Patsy Gallacher was suspended by the Scottish League from Tuesday, 19 December 1916 until Saturday, 27 January 1917, whilst Celtic were fined £25 for impeding the war effort! This was because Patsy was accused of 'bad timekeeping' in his job in the shipyards! Celtic fans were appalled at this because the offence seemed to have nothing to do with football, and the feeling that Celtic were being victimised because of last April's Irish rebellion was a difficult one to dislodge from the minds of the supporters.

It was a curious business. The Daily Record, whilst clearly sympathetic to Patsy, is limited by censorship on what it can say, but talks obliquely about him being the best player around and what a loss he will be to the game. Celtic's fault seems to have been that they played him in a couple of games in December, in the knowledge that he was being 'done' for the less than heinous offence of being late for his work. Perhaps there was a little more to it than that, but, sensible Celtic men like Willie Maley and Alec McNair held their tongue and got on with the job in hand.

Even without Young and Gallacher, Celtic still took on all comers. There was the occasional draw, for example the 0-0 match at Ibrox on New Year's Day 1917, and to a certain extent the forward play, without Patsy, suffered with a comparative dearth of goals, but, on the other hand, the defence conceded just one goal between

Saturday, 2 December 1916 and Saturday, 24 February 1917. And why was that? "Shaw, McNair & Dodds!" What was the best defence that the British Army could have if the Germans made an assault on the Channel Ports? "Shaw, McNair & Dodds!" Who should be in Russia at the moment to protect the Czar from his advancing hordes? "Shaw, McNair & Dodds!"

The Russian Czar was indeed tottering in early 1917, but there had also been a less violent, although equally treacherous, removal from power of the British Prime Minister in December 1916. Herbert Asquith, a well-meaning Premier who had been good in peace time, was unceremoniously removed in a coup organised by David Lloyd George, a far more decisive and ruthless character who would prosecute the war with more vigour.

German peace proposals were rejected – the British could have at least discussed them, one feels – and by March 1917, the Russians, although still in the war under their provisional moderately left-wing Government, were crippled and half-hearted. But there was a big development in early April, and one which eventually won the day for the Allies. The USA, fed up with the constant harassment of their shipping and loss of life (they also recalled the Lusitania of two years ago), decided that enough was enough, and entered the war on the side of the Allies. It did not bring instant success, for logistically the Americans could not be in Europe in sufficient strength until 1918. However the feeling now grew that there might be some sort of an end to it. But there was an awful lot of slaughter still to come in 1917 and 1918.

Saturday, 7 April 1917, the day after the American announcement, saw Maley's unbeaten Celtic side win the Scottish League for the fourth year in a row and the 14th time overall. The game at Boghead Park, Dumbarton had an odd start, in that the home team scored first! By half-time, however, Celtic had fought back, and their 3-1 win was enough to win the title, although it was not until the supporters got back to Glasgow and read in the evening newspapers that Third Lanark had beaten Rangers that they realised it! A huge crowd of 20,000 turned up at Parkhead on the Holiday Monday for the 5.30pm kick off to welcome the Champions once again. "Jimmy McMenemy was the star, as always," according to The Daily Record, and Alec McNair and Joe Dodds were as "safe as the proverbial houses" in the 2-0 win over Third Lanark, who were greeted warmly by the home crowd for their win over Rangers on Saturday.

Three League games remained, and in one of them, the penultimate match of the campaign, the unthinkable happened, in that Celtic actually lost! Kilmarnock did the honours, winning 2-0 at Celtic Park on Saturday, 21 April 1917, to end a 62-game unbeaten run of League games for Willie Maley's team which had commenced with a victory over the Ayrshire side by the same scoreline and at the same venue back on Saturday, 20 November 1915, some 17 months earlier! That British record would stand until it was superseded more than a century later, once again by a Celtic team, this time the 'Invincibles' under Brendan Rodgers in November 2017.

The loss to Kilmarnock had prevented Celtic achieving an undefeated League campaign, thus repeating their feat of the 1897/98 season. However, in terms of winning trophies, it did not really matter. What did matter was the Glasgow Charity Cup, and it is no surprise to record that Celtic duly won it again, this time beating Rangers 2-0, and then Queen's Park 1-0, with Parkhead chairman James Kelly making the surprising statement that he had actually been supporting the Spiders in the final, on the grounds that it would have been good for Scottish football! Such was Celtic's dominance in 1917! It was even said that the wind did not get past Alec McNair!

But Celtic got a sudden jolt and realisation about what the war was really all about in late May. Shortly after the last game of the season, the now annual game between Celtic and the Rest of the League, rumours reached the city of Glasgow that Peter Johnstone was missing, believed killed in an attempt to capture a chemical factory in what became known as the Battle of Arras. It would be some time before this was confirmed, but, everyone knew that "missing, believed killed" was almost always and inevitably bad news.

Alec McNair was distraught, not only because Young, Johnstone & McMaster had been a brilliant half-back line, but because Peter was a genuinely nice guy. He was a Fifer and a tough miner, and there was something very genuine about him. He might have stayed at home, for he had a newsagent's business, but when called upon to enlist, he did so, and his loss was all the more poignant for that reason.

Stenhousemuir, meanwhile, saw its casualties appear in The Falkirk Herald, many of them people whom Alec knew, even a few who he worked with and who had insisted on joining up, needled perhaps by ignorant jibes from women and Church people about "cowardice." The world seemed to be going crazy. McNair's own personal problems seemed to be almost trivial in comparison with those of some people. He certainly was not the only person suffering, and in some ways, he drew comfort from that. He also took comfort from his two children, his extended family and, of course, his football at the club that he loved and with whom he was enjoying almost unlimited success. But was there ever to be any end to this madness?

Season 1917/18 was not a particularly good season for anyone. It is all every well for us, 100 and more years later, to say that it was the last year of the war, as indeed it was, but no-one knew that at the time. For all anyone knew, the war could go on for a long time yet. Field Marshall Sir Douglas Haig, one of the greatest unprosecuted war criminals of them all, said that if the killing continued, the

Allies, Great Britain, the Empire, France and now the USA would eventually out-populate the Germans! It was hardly the news that the war-weary wanted to hear.

This season was also the one in which Rangers struck back. Celtic had now lost Peter Johnstone in the war, Sunny Jim Young to injury and several others to possible recruitment for the war, yet even though some were in khaki, they were still doing basic training somewhere in Scotland and able to turn out for Celtic now and again.

Eck McNair, now approaching his 35th birthday, kept turning out, but it was becoming obvious that a little sparkle had gone, and that a certain weariness had slipped in, not just with McNair himself but with the rest of the team. It would hardly be surprising that McNair was slowing up (he had never been the fastest of players), for he was still working 12-hour shifts, and his children were now quite a handful to come home to. Yet he was still fit enough, in spite of not having a great deal of time to train properly.

The first sign that something was wrong was at Hampden on Saturday, 8 September 1917, when Queen's Park took Celtic to extra-time in the first round of the Glasgow Cup, and even then, it needed an own goal to see Maley's side through. Then, against Rangers in the semi-final at Celtic Park two weeks later, the half-back line of Watson, Cringan & Brown simply collapsed and Celtic lost 0-3. They did gain a certain amount of revenge, beating Rangers 2-1 in a League match at Ibrox on Saturday, 20 October 1917, but, that advantage was all thrown away a fortnight later, when Celtic lost 2-0 to Airdrieonians at Broomfield. It was that topsy-turvy sort of form.

Alec McNair and Celtic had heard more bad news in October. This was the death of Donnie McLeod, The Slasher, who had in some ways introduced Eck to Celtic. Gunner McLeod had been wounded during the Third Battle of Ypres, in Passchendaele in northern Belgium, and succumbed to his injuries on Saturday, 6 October 1917. He too came from the Stenhousemuir area. McLeod had been too good for McNair to displace at right-back and it was only when he went off to Middlesbrough that Alec became the natural choice there. He had been a good friend to most of the team and remained popular with the Celtic supporters, who were naturally distraught to hear it.

In November 1917 came the news that the regime that had toppled the Czarist dynasty in Russia had itself been overthrown by the Bolsheviks, under a man called Lenin. In some ways, people in Britain were glad to see this victory for the common man - the great 'Red Clydesider' John McLean famously wept for joy - but there were reports of violence, as was likely to happen after centuries of repression. There was also a certain amount of hypocrisy from Buckingham Palace about what was happening to "our relatives," yet the British King George V had refused them political asylum last spring and would do so again next spring!

What it meant for Great Britain and the war was that Russia was, effectively, now out of it. Germany had effectively won the war in the east and would now have more men and resources to throw at the western allies in the spring. And there was still very little sign of the Americans!

It was not often that trains let Alec McNair down on his many journeys from Larbert to games, but, he failed to appear in time for the League match at Motherwell on Saturday, 15 December 1917. Celtic played with 10 men for a spell to give him a chance to appear, but eventually put on a reserve in Arthur McInally as they lost 4-3, something that perhaps said quite a lot about how much Celtic needed Eck McNair.

New Year 1918 was reached with Celtic still at the top of the table, in spite of some dreadful results. Form from every club was haywire, as it was now more and more difficult to create any kind of team. Youngsters had to be deployed, old unfit veterans had to be brought back, a soldier who just happened to be stationed nearby or happened to be home on leave would, not uncommonly, appear on a club's doorstep an hour before kick-off and be selected for the game! We also had the phenomenon of Willie Cringan playing for Celtic against Dumbarton, and then being arrested at full-time for desertion from the Army! It was crazy stuff, but no crazier than the rest of the world.

Conscription was clearly having its effect, in that there were fewer young men around, yet the funny thing was that enthusiasm for the game did not weaken. A crowd of 50,000, for example, was at Celtic Park on New Year's Day 1918 to see a goalless draw with Rangers, in which Johnny Browning missed a penalty. There was also, early in the New Year, one melancholy, yet, in some ways, happy occasion when 20,000 appeared to see Celtic v Scottish League for Sunny Jim Young's Benefit game. How sad it was to see Sunny, now crippled and looking so vulnerable, hobble out in civvies with a walking stick to have his photograph taken with the players! He used to be so commanding and imperious, but he still was the ever-lovable Sunny Jim!

No-one really found life easy in 1918. Food was still in reasonable supply, but there was no guarantee of any particular commodity being available at any given time, and some things had to be rationed. There was a certain "let's get on with it" attitude among many of the population, but, it was becoming clear that the Clyde (and even perhaps the Tyne and the Mersey) was not going to let this go on for ever. They now had the example of what had happened in Russia, and who knew just what could happen here?

Celtic and Rangers continued their private battle for the League Championship. Celtic still had Alec McNair, Jimmy McMenemy and Patsy Gallacher, and, although form was unpredictable, tended to have their noses in front throughout winter and looked as if they might just yet pull off their fifth Scottish League flag success in a row. Attendances still remained high and the battle between the two Glasgow giants was much discussed. It was as if the ostriches were collectively digging their heads into the sand to avoid worrying too much about what was soon going to happen in the bigger and more tragic struggle.

Everyone knew that it would all happen in the spring, and it duly did as Ludendorff launched his offensive on Thursday, 21 March 1918. Curiously, it was at that precise point that Celtic's fortunes took a turn for the worse, and it was an old Celt who came back to bite them. Davie McLean, who had left Celtic in 1909 (largely because he did not like the dictatorship of Willie Maley, but also because he could not displace Jimmy Quinn), had been a soldier of fortune with various clubs since then, and now found himself playing for Third Lanark. On Saturday, 23 March, Joe Dodds, now enlisted, was in England and playing for Fulham, Alec McNair and Charlie Shaw both had an off day, and McLean scored a hat-trick in a rare 3-1 win for Third Lanark before a 15,000 crowd at Celtic Park. He scored these goals by being prepared to shoot from a distance, as distinct from Patsy Gallacher's great individual effort.

McLean, known as 'Dyke,' may well have enjoyed making his point to Maley, but it meant that with three games left, title-chasing Celtic and Rangers were equal. Goal average had now been introduced to settle matters in the event of a points tie, and the Ibrox club were marginally ahead in that respect. But then Celtic won their next two games, difficult away fixtures at Kilmarnock and Hibernian, whilst Rangers beat Clydebank and Motherwell. It now all depended on the last League Saturday of the season, 13 April 1918.

Both the Scottish League Championship and the war itself were on a knife edge. No amount of propaganda in the newspapers could hide the fact that the Germans were doing rather well in Europe in their push to the sea. Much was the talk of an "orderly retreat" of the British and the French and "everyone was rallying for a counter-attack." People were able to read between the lines. One soldier confessed to me, some 70 years later that in the 'march back,' there was actually some happiness in the ranks, especially when one day someone claimed to have seen the sea! Field Marshall Sir Douglas Haig, still (incredibly) a hero and even a cult figure in this country, was issuing speeches talking about "backs to the wall," and it was easily seen that another German successful push would see Britain in real trouble.

But it was the Motherwell "backs to the wall" at Celtic Park on 13 April which did for Celtic. Patsy Gallacher had scored in the first half, then Motherwell equalised just before half-time from a corner-kick on the left. The second half was all Celtic, with even Alec McNair up in the attack trying to get the vital goal which would win the game for Celtic. It was 2-1 for Rangers against Clyde at Ibrox, and that was how it stayed, but Celtic simply could not get the vital goal. Full-time came at around 5.10pm that evening (the game kicked off at 3.30pm), and an era had come to an end. Willie Maley had the melancholy job of sending telegrams to the War Office to tell the troops, and also to send a congratulatory telegram to his old friend William Wilton, the manager of Rangers. Wilton had played second fiddle to Celtic all through the war, but, he now had his brief moment of happiness.

The season was not yet completely over. Celtic defeated Morton 1-0 at Hampden with a Patsy Gallacher goal on Saturday, 4 May 1918 to win the War Fund Shield, a one-off tournament, and then lifted the Glasgow Charity Cup for the seventh year in a row at the same venue, with a 2-0 victory over Partick Thistle on Saturday, 25 May. This meant that although 1917/18 had not been the best of seasons for Celtic, they had at least won silverware at the end of it. There had been 30,000 spectators at Hampden to see Celtic beat Thistle, with Eck's direct opponent being Stanley Seymour, a man who would become a legend for Newcastle United, but who at that time was based on the Clyde and had also turned out for both Morton and Rangers.

On the broader front as well, things now seemed to be taking a turn for the better. The British lines seemed to have stabilised and the German breakthrough to the sea had still not happened. Not only that, but we were beginning, at last, to see some Americans! Alec McNair may have worried about what was called the 'comb-out,' where every last man was being hunted out by the military. However, he was still safe due to his reserved occupation and his family situation. But he was also aware as he looked around at the sheer volume of casualties, that this could not go on for ever. There had to be an end sometime! Eck's last three years had been some kind of hell for him...but he was not the only one! Hell was universal in 1918.

Celtic Park, as it would have looked when Alec McNair joined the club in April 1904. The stand on the left, adjacent to the corner pavilion, burned down within 10 days of McNair signing for the club!

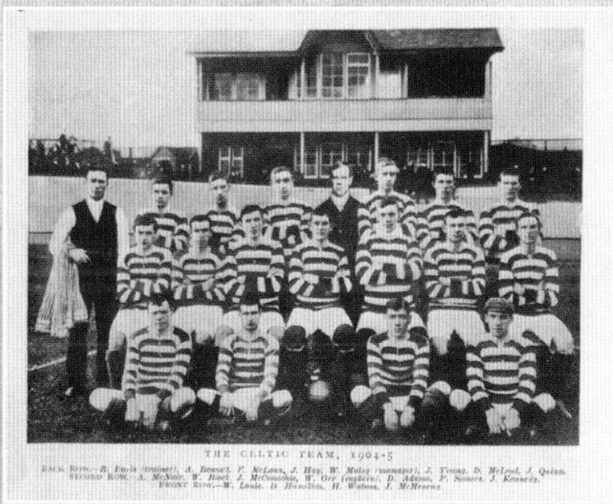

Perhaps the first photo of Alec McNair at Celtic Park, as the players line-up in his inaugural season.

A young Alec McNair in the Hoops.

The Celtic squad who won the 1904/05 Scottish League title after a 'winner takes all' play-off against Rangers at Hampden on Saturday, 6 May 1905. This was Alec McNair's first trophy success as a Celt.

Willie Loney and Alec McNair having a break from training. Photo courtesy of @celticcurio.

Alec McNair first played for his country on Saturday, 3 March 1906, against Wales at Tynecastle, albeit the Scottish national team would not change back from the Roseberry colours to navy until 1910.

The team lined up at the Leipzig game: Ned Garry, Don McLeod, Alex McNair, Jimmy Quinn, Peter Somers, Davie Adams, Willie Maley (Manager), James Young, Jimmy Hay, James Bauchop, David Hamilton, Bobby Templeton.

Leipzig. Thursday, 24 May 1906. The Celtic team line-up in an unusual 'goalmouth' pose before the opening match of their continental tour. Willie Maley's side beat VfB Leipzig 9-1 that afternoon.

The Celtic squad of 1906/07.

The changing face of Celtic Park. Following the May 1904 fire, which destroyed the original stand on the north side of the ground, the new enclosure on Janefield Street was ready for the 1907/08 season.

Alec in a match v Aberdeen in February 1910. Photo courtesy of @celticcurio.

Portrait of Alec McNair from 1907. Photo courtesy of @celticcurio.

Alec McNair with Aberdeen's Charles O'Hagan. The Irishman was the first Pittodrie player to be capped at international level. The two men came face to face at Celtic Park on Saturday, 16 March 1907, St Patrick's weekend appropriately, as Scotland beat Ireland 3-0. Photo courtesy of @celticcurio.

Wonderful image of Alec McNair – Celtic's Icicle

The Celtic team pose with three cups they won in season 1907-08, the Glasgow Charity Cup, Scottish Cup and Glasgow Cup. Celtic also won the Scottish League title that season for an unprecedented Grand Slam. Back row: Directors Tom White, James Kelly, Tom Colgan, John McKillop, James Grant & Michael Dunbar; Middle Row: Willie Maley (Manager), Jim Young, Peter Somers, Jimmy McMenemy, Davie Adams, John Mitchell, Jamie Weir & Rab Davis (Trainer); Front row: Davie Hamilton, Donnie McLeod, Willie Loney, James Hay, Jimmy Quinn & Alec McNair.

Historic images of Scotland (in Earl Roseberry hoops) facing Wales at Dens Park, Dundee on Saturday, 7 March 1908. The Scots won 2-1 in what was Alec McNair's third International appearance.

Alec McNair represented the Scottish League on 15 occasions. This medal reflects his third appearance, against the Irish League at Firhill on Monday, 25 October 1909. Alec's name is inscribed on the reverse.'

Saturday, 4 January 1913. Charles Lowrie is the Partick Thistle forward. Celts won 1-0. Photo courtesy of @celticcurio

An image of Alec in action from 1912. Photo courtesy of @celticcurio

The Scottish League Shield, which was presented to Celtic by the other members of the Scottish League in recognition of the club's having won the league championship in six successive years from 1905 to 1910.

Photo taken on Saturday, 21 January 1911, when Celtic drew 0-0 with Falkirk at Celtic Park. On that occasion, Alec and Jimmy Hay were paired at full-back, with normal partner Joe Dodds at left-half.

The Celtic Scottish Cup-winning squad from 1911/12.
Back Row: Directors Michael Dunbar, Joseph Shaughnessy, John McKillop, Tom Colgan;
Middle Row: Willie Quinn (Trainer), Willie Loney, Jimmy McMenemy, Joe Dodds, Jimmy Quinn, Peter Johnstone, Jim Young, Willie Maley (Manager);
Front Row: John Brown, Andy McAtee, Paddy Travers, James Kelly (Chairman), Patsy Gallacher, John Mulrooney, Alec McNair.

Saturday, 21 October 1911. Alec McNair and referee R T Murray at Ibrox, with the 'Bovril Stand' in the background. Both men hailed from Stenhousemuir. Photo courtesy of @celticcurio.

The Scotland cap awarded to skipper Alec McNair for 'The International' against England at Hampden, played on Saturday, 23 March 1912. The match ended 1-1 before a crowd of 127,307.

1912. Photo courtesy of @celticcurio. Note the myth of him being born in Bo'ness.

No 86—ALEXANDER M'NAIR, Celtic F.C.

In the long and brilliant list of past and present Scottish players, there is none worthier than the able, manly, and modest artist. Great men as a rule rise from humble surroundings, and Captain M'Nair, of this season's International team v. England, is one of those. Born in Bo'ness, like the late Bernard Battles, he migrated to the Midlands, and saw service with President A. M. Robertson's club, Stenhousemuir, hence this gentleman takes a just pride in the play and personality of his protege. M'Nair joined Celtic in May, 1904, and he is due in regard to his work on their behalf since that year to be bracketed with James Young, James Quinn, James M'Menemy, and William Loney, a quintette of players who have built up their club's and their own personal reputations. When you have, as is happily the case with M'Nair, ability of the first degree as a player, allied to a most likeable personality, you have a duality of power that makes for popularity. As a player, he is a gentleman and an artist, scorning low methods, and earning as much respect from his foes as he does from his friends. To the old and to the young in the sport, we can point to no finer exemplar or model on or off the field of play than Alexander M'Nair.

In the same match against Aston Villa the famous Celtic full-back partnership of Alec McNair (left) and Joe Dodds watch anxiously while the well-dressed referee awaits developments.

Two wonderful images from the Celtic v Aston Villa match played on Saturday, 27 April 1912. The Villa player looks like Harry 'Happy' Hampton, the West Midlands club's all-time leading League goal scorer.

Celtic 1913/14.
Back Row: Willie McStay, Tom McGregor, Joe Dodds, Henry Jarvis;
Second Row: Willie Quinn (trainer), Alec McNair, Willie Loney, Jim Young, Andrew Davidson, Jimmy Quinn, Peter Johnstone, Willie Maley (manager);
Front Row: Johnny Hill, Johnny McMaster, Charlie Shaw, Joe Cassidy, Jimmy McMenemy;
Ground: Andy McAtee, Patsy Gallagher, Johnny Browning, Barney Connolly.

1912. Photo courtesy of @celticcurio.

Celtic's legendary 'Holy Trinity', Charlie Shaw, Alec McNair & Joe Dodds, established 1913.

Alec lines up with his Scottish League teammates at Turf Moor, Burnley before the match against the English League on Saturday, 21 March 1914. The Scots fought back from 0-2 down to win 3-2. McNair is second left on the back row between Jimmy McMenemy and Charlie Shaw. Immediately in front of McMenemy is the third member of the 'Holy Trinity', Joe Dodds, beside a fifth Celt, Andy McAtee.

Saturday, 18 April 1914. Celtic's victorious Scottish Cup-winning team parade the trophy, ahead of the home League clash with Hibernian, who they had defeated in the final two days earlier. Back row; Willie Maley (Manager), John McMaster, Joe Dodds, Charlie Shaw, Alec McNair, Peter Johnstone, Jimmy McColl, Willie Quinn (Trainer). Front row; Andy McAtee, Patsy Gallacher, Jim Young (Captain), Jimmy McMenemy, Johnny Browning. The Scottish Cup would then go into cold storage following the outbreak of war. It would be 1923 before the old trophy returned to Parkhead. On that occasion, the opposition in the final would once again be Hibernian.

(Left to right)—M'Nair, Moscrop, Gordon, Thomson, Hampton, and Smith.

Scotland captain Alec McNair in action against England in 'The International' at Hampden on Saturday, 4 April 1914. On the ball is his direct opponent, Eddie Mosscrop of Burnley.

Season 1914/15. Back Row: Andy McAtee, Charlie Shaw and Johnny McMaster;
Middle Row: Jimmy McColl, Alec McNair, Johnny Browning, Jimmy McMenemy, Patsy Gallacher, Willie Quinn (Trainer);
Front Row: Willie Maley (Manager), Peter Johnstone, Tom White (Director), Jim Young, James Kelly (Chairman), Joe Dodds, Michael Dunbar (Director).

Celtic 1915/16. Alec McNair third from left in middle row.

Taken before the Celtic v Scottish League XI game at the end of season 1915/16. Alec McNair is second from left in back row.

Alec wrote a series of 'My Football Career' articles for the Sunday Post in June 1920.

THE SUNDAY POST, JUNE 6, 1920. 15

My Football Career

BY

ALEC M'NAIR, SCOTLAND'S GREAT RIGHT BACK

Alec M'Nair at Home.

The "Big Match."

Great Goalkeeping at Dundee.

A Thrilling Game.

A Dramatic Moment.

A Memorable Cup-Tie.

LAWN TENNIS.

WHIPPETING.

QUOITING.

THE NEWBURY CUP

LATEST TIPS FROM THE STABLE.

BY THE COLONEL.

SELECTIONS FOR THIS WEEK.

The Scotland shirt Alec wore whilst captaining his country to a 3-0 win over Ireland at Celtic Park on Saturday, 13 March 1920. The Irish, who featured McNair's club teammate Patsy Gallacher at inside-forward, wore blue jerseys at that time, hence the requirement for Scotland to use a change kit.

THE SUNDAY POST, JUNE 13, 1920. 15

My Football Career

BY

ALEC M'NAIR, SCOTLAND'S GREAT RIGHT BACK

MY FIRST CAP.

ALEC MACFARLANE'S CHANCE.

THE JONES FAMILY.

TOM SINCLAIR'S GREAT RECORD.

GEMS FOR ROYAL ASCOT.

FORM WEIGHED UP.

BY THE COLONEL.

YESTERDAY'S W...

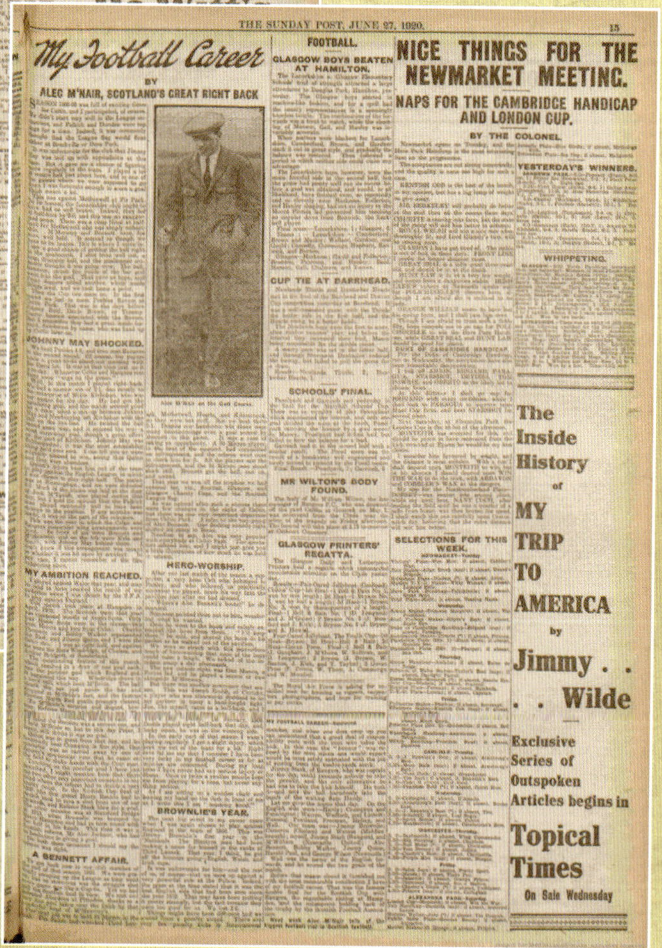

THE SUNDAY POST, JUNE 27, 1920. 15

My Football Career

BY

ALEC M'NAIR, SCOTLAND'S GREAT RIGHT BACK

Alec M'Nair at the Golf Course.

JOHNNY MAY SHOCKED.

MY AMBITION REACHED.

HERO-WORSHIP.

BROWNLIE'S YEAR.

A BENNETT AFFAIR.

FOOTBALL.

GLASGOW BOYS BEATEN AT HAMILTON.

CUP TIE AT BARRHEAD.

SCHOOLS' FINAL.

MR WILTON'S BODY FOUND.

GLASGOW PRINTERS' REGATTA.

NICE THINGS FOR THE NEWMARKET MEETING.

NAPS FOR THE CAMBRIDGE HANDICAP AND LONDON CUP.

BY THE COLONEL.

YESTERDAY'S WINNERS.

WHIPPETING.

SELECTIONS FOR THIS WEEK.

Celtic 1920/21
Back Row: Willie Cringan, Archie Longmuir, Johnny McMaster, Patsy Gallacher, John McFarlane, Willie McStay, Johnny Gilchrist;
Middle Row: Willie Quinn (trainer), Alec McNair, Tom Craig, Duggie Livingstone, Willie Lawrie, James Murphy, Johnny McKay, Charlie Watson;
Front Row: David Pratt, Tommy McInally, Andy McAtee, Hugh Brown, Charlie Shaw, James Price, Joe Cassidy, Adam McLean, Willie Maley (Manager).

Select's Victory.

A team representing Celtic and Rangers and a Scottish League Select eleven met at Celtic Park, Glasgow, yesterday in a benefit match for Alex. M'Nair, the Celtic and Scottish international right back.

There would be 25,000 spectators present when play opened. Good work by Cunningham and Morton led to Gallacher scoring the first goal. Shortly after this M'Nair had to retire owing to injuries, and his place was taken by M'Stey. The Celtic-Rangers combination were not having things all their own way. Led by M'Menemy, the Select made good progress.

M'Nab got the ball, and sent across to Craig, who had no difficulty in equalising. The young Celtic centre continued to trouble the opposing defence, and Manderson, M'Stey, and Shaw had to be on the alert. He got in several good shots, however, which Shaw ably dealt with. Morton and Cunningham gave a sparkling display, and towards the interval M'Inally had a good try, which just missed. Half-time:—One goal each.

In the concluding stages of the second half M'Farlane scored two goals for the Scottish Select

Celtic and Rangers—Shaw; M'Nair and Manderson; Gordon, Cringan, and Murphy; Donoghue, Gallacher, M'Inally, Cunningham, and Morton.

Scottish Select—Brownlie (Third Lanark); Neave (Kilmarnock) and Farrell (Clyde); M'Intyre (Morton), Townsley (Falkirk), and Marshall (Clyde); M'Nab (Morton), M'Menemy (Partick Thistle), Craig (Celtic), Allan (Clyde), and M'Farlane (Celtic).

Referee—Mr R. Murray, Stenhousemuir.

Tuesday, 4 January 1921. The players line-up before a well-deserved Benefit game for Alec McNair.

Celtic 1921/22
Back Row: John Connor, David Pratt, Willie McKnight, Charlie Shaw, Joe Cassidy;
Middle Row: Willie Quinn (Trainer), Hugh Hilley, Alec McNair, Jimmy McStay, Joe Dodds, Willie McStay, Tommy McInally, Sam Glasgow, Johnny Gilchrist;
Front Row: John McFarlane, Frank Collins, Johnny McMaster, Andy McAtee. Johnny McKay, Patsy Gallacher, Willie Cringan, James Murphy, Adam McLean, Willie Maley (Manager).

Caricature of Alec McNair published in October 1922, just two months before his 40th birthday.

Celtic 1922/23
Back Row: Hugh Hilley, Willie McStay, Patsy Gallacher, Johnny Gilchrist, James B. Murphy;
Middle Row: Willie Quinn (Trainer), Johnny McMaster, Alec McNair, John McFarlane, Sam Glasgow, Adam McLean, Willie Cringan;
Front Row: Andy McAtee, Jimmy McStay, James F. Murphy, Charlie Shaw, Joe Cassidy, Willie Crilley, Paddy Connolly.

Saturday, 31 March 1923. Scottish Cup final between Celtic and Hibernian. In the top picture, Willie Cringan leads the team out followed by Adam McLean, Paddy Connolly, John 'Jean' McFarlane and Joe Cassidy. In the lower picture, the Celtic players are Adam McLean and Patsy Gallacher.

Celtic – Scottish Cup winners 1923
Back Row: Eddie McGarvie (trainer), Alec McNair, Willie McStay, Charlie Shaw, Hugh Hilley, Willie Maley (manager), Jimmy McStay, John McFarlane, Willie Quinn (trainer);
Front Row: Andy McAtee, Joe Cassidy, Adam McLean, Willie Cringan, Patsy Gallacher, Paddy Connolly.

Alec McNair, manager of Dundee FC 1925/27.

CONVENER

The Late Mr Alec M'Nair

FORMER CELTIC AND SCOTLAND FOOTBALLER

A wide circle of friends, particularly throughout the Scottish football world, heard with regret on Monday of the death of Mr Alec M'Nair, one-time famous Celtic and Scottish international player.

Mr M'Nair, who had been seriously ill for the last six months, returned to his home in Rae Street, Stenhousemuir, from a Glasgow nursing home a week previous to his death, which took place on Sunday morning.

In his 69th year, deceased was a native of Stenhousemuir, and was educated at Larbert Central School, from which he went to the Larbert Foundry (Messrs Dobbie Forbes & Co., Ltd.) to serve his apprenticeship as a grate fitter. He started his football career in his 'teens with Stenhouse Thistle and Stenhouse

Hearts, two Stenhousemuir Juvenile combinations which in their day produced several notable exponents of the game. Later, he gave his services to Stenhousemuir F.C. as a half-back, and from Ochilview graduated to Parkhead in 1904. There, with Celtic F.C., he gained many international honours as a right full-back and became known to countless followers of football as "The Icicle," so cool and imperturbable was he in the most exciting match.

FOOTBALL HONOURS

He gained his first International "cap" within two years. Between 1906 and 1920 he played fifteen times for Scotland — the first World War denied him of several more "caps" — and fourteen times for the Scottish League. He retired from the game in 1924, having won all the honours possible for a footballer.

Mr M'Nair was a member of the team which Mr Wm. Maley, the former Celtic manager, considers the best ever to have represented the Parkhead club:—Adams; M'Leod (or M'Nair) and Orr; Young, Loney and Hay; Bennett and M'Menemy, Quinn, Somers and Hamilton.

Mr M'Nair latterly took the place of M'Leod in a side who finished at the top of the first division of the Scottish League in six successive seasons — from 1905 (when they shared the championship with Rangers and won a play-off) to 1910. The feat has never been equalled. With the passing of Alec M'Nair, only Willie Loney and Jimmy M'Menemy of that great eleven are alive.

Following his retiral from the game, Mr M'Nair entered the business world and became a stockbroker, in which profession he enjoyed the confidence of a large large clientele of friends in Larbert, Falkirk, and Glasgow. Predeceased by Mrs M'Nair many years ago, Mr M'Nair is survived by a daughter and son. The latter, Mr James M'Nair, now resident in Helensburgh, followed in his father's footsteps and played football, first with the Larbert Central School, then with Larbert Amateurs and later with Falkirk and Stenhousemuir.

THE FUNERAL

Among the many floral tributes to arrive at the home of the deceased prior to the funeral, which took place to Larbert Cemetery on Tuesday afternoon, was a handsome wreath from the directors of Rangers Football Club. Other wreaths came from the directors of Celtic F.C., Stenhousemuir F.C., the Scottish Football League, Falkirk Tryst Golf Club, Lodge Carron No. 139, the Regal (Falkirk) Cafe Coffee Club and Mr William Maley.

The service at the house and place of interment was conducted by the Rev. Peter M'Phail, B.D., Larbert East, and the pall bearers comprised Mr James M'Nair, Helensburgh (son); Mr Archibald Donaldson, Glasgow (son-in-law); Mr James M'Nair, senior, Larbert (brother); Mr James Niven, Falkirk (brother-in-law); Mr James M'Nair junr, Greenock (nephew); Mr James M'Nair, Stenhousemuir (nephew); Mr David M'Nair, Larbert (nephew) and Mr William M'Nair, Stenhousemuir (nephew).

There was a large attendance of mourners including Mr Robert Kelly, chairman, Mr James M'Grory, manager, Mr Desmond White, secretary, Mr Tom Devlin, director and several playing members of the Celtic F.C.; Mr Fred Denovan, Scottish League secretary; Mr T. G. Colquhoun, Clyde F.C. director; representatives of Stenhousemuir F.C. and Patsy Gallacher, Jimmy Brownlie, Willie Loney, Joe Dodds, Jimmy M'Oustra, Jim M'Coll (now Hibs trainer) and George Jarvis, all former team mates of the deceased. Mr Willie Maley was represented by his son Mr William Maley, junr.

Falkirk Burglaries

A series of burglaries, only one of which is regarded by the police as serious, took place in Falkirk during the past week.

A number of houses in the south side of the town were broken into and ransacked. The thieves did not succeed in getting any substantial reward from their depredations in dwelling houses. In one case, however, two gold watches were stolen, and in another a sum of £30 was taken.

The serious offence occurred late on Thursday evening when the premises of Messrs A. & R. Turnbull, drapers and outfitters, 74 High Street, Falkirk, were entered. Goods to the value of about £100 were stolen. The thieves gained entrance by going through the Parish Churchyard and climbing on to the roof of the building. They forced open a window and dropped down into the premises.

It is thought that in getting away the goods, the thieves had used a motor car. Before leaving, the burglars locked most of the doors from the inside, and in the morning the staff could not get the full use of several departments.

Alec McNair's obituary, following his sad passing in November 1951.

Celtic 1924/25. Alec McNair's last season at Celtic Park.

Final resting place and memorial to Alec McNair and his beloved family, erected in Larbert Cemetery.

CHAPTER SEVEN

THE WAR ENDS (1918-1920)

By the time that the football season started again in August 1918, it was impossible not to detect a certain optimism about the war. Everyone was talking about a place called Amiens. No-one could pronounce it properly, but it seemed to be a place where the British Army had rallied and were now, with the help of their Allies, driving the Germans back. ("Drive them back? Drive? I would make the buggers walk!" said an old lady when told the news). But although it was desirable to cheer up the public, it would not do to give out false hope. There was still a long way to go, and a lot of lives to be lost. Nevertheless, the position was an improvement, although there had been so much fake news and false hope given out in the past that people read their newspapers with a very large pinch of salt.

But August was also a time of sadness for the honest Alexander McNair. Three years now he had been widowed. It never got any easier. Some 130 years previously, Robert Burns had penned this verse;

"Thou lingering star with lessening ray

That loves to greet the early morn

Once more thou usherest in the day

My Mary from my soul was torn!"

For Eck, the start of the football season was a permanent reminder of his loss. But he was never a morbid, maudlin character and realised that in 1918, he was far from the only person suffering. A new factor had entered the equation, in a deadly illness which was affecting both armies in the field and the civilian sector as well. For most people, it was mild, or at least it would have been in normal circumstances, but, these were far from normal circumstances. Wounds, malnutrition with not enough vitamins and general demoralisation of everyone played its part. Those who believe that "mental health plays its part in physical health" had a great deal to work on here! As indeed did those who studied their Bible and realised that War and Pestilence were two of the four horsemen of the apocalypse, the other two being Famine and Death.

Football still continued, albeit in even more straitened circumstances than before. Jimmy McMenemy had said he was retiring in 1918, then changed his mind (he had a 'good few years' to go yet, as it turned out!) and there was still Patsy Gallacher, but Celtic like everyone else were struggling to get together a team, or at least a settled team. Andy McAtee was now in the army, as was Joe Dodds, and Alec McNair's left-back partner was now Dougie Livingstone or Tom McGregor, depending on availability.

Results were generally good, but whether that was because Celtic were good or because other teams were in an even worse state than Celtic is hard to say. The Glasgow Cup final was reached again, but, sadly, this would prove an unhappy experience for McNair and Celtic, as a patchwork side went down 0-2 to Rangers on Saturday, 5 October 1918 before an astonishing Hampden crowd of over 60,000. The Sunday Post of the following day tells on its front page of the great British advance at Cambrai, another German retreat, and how Prince Max of Baden had spoken to the Reichstag, suggesting peace which included the giving up of Belgium.

Clearly things were beginning to happen, but in the Glasgow Cup final the rivalry was no less intense. The huge crowd saw Peter Pursell of Rangers and Jimmy McColl of Celtic sent off for fighting, with Tommy Cairns of Rangers and Patsy Gallacher of Celtic lucky to avoid the same fate. Rangers won 2-0 with a goal at the start and the end of the second half. And yet some things stayed the same. "McNair was the best back afield. Time and time again, friend and foes voiced their appreciation of his tactics, and his picking up of forward passes was one of the features of his final."

But things continued to be difficult for Celtic. Two weeks later, on Saturday, 19 October 1918, Rangers came to Celtic Park and won 3-0, and then the following week, although Celtic would eventually win 5-0 at Dumbarton, the game had to be delayed by half an hour to allow both teams time to get a team together. Such were the challenges created by transport problems and players calling off through 'illness' – the influenza pandemic which would later be known as the Spanish Flu.

It was clear that football was becoming farcical, but, everyone kept going as best they could. Celtic beat St Mirren 1-0 at home on Saturday, 2 November 1918, and by the following week, it was becoming apparent that a qualified optimism was justified about the war. The Kaiser had abdicated and was on his way to exile in Holland, as his country collapsed all around him. An Armistice was being negotiated at that time, apparently, but men were still being killed. Nevertheless, Celtic and Hearts played out a 1-1 draw at Parkhead on Saturday, 9 November 1918, the Hearts goal being scored by a wounded ex-serviceman by the name of Andrew Wilson, who would become a prolific star for Dunfermline Athletic and Scotland after the war. For some reason, he played under his middle name, and thus it was 'Andrew Nisbet' who equalised Patsy Gallacher's opening goal.

The Armistice was agreed (or more correctly, dictated to the Germans) in the early hours of Monday, 11 November 1918 and came into effect at 11.00am – the three elevens of the 11th hour of the 11th day of the 11th month. It did not bring any immediate relief, however. The fighting stopped, but that did not prevent there being more casualties, for there were still many men dying of wounds sustained in the last awful months of the war. In addition, there was the flu, the deprivation and the sheer unhappiness caused by the unnecessary loss of so many lives. Armistice celebrations did take place, but for so many people, including decent, honest men like Eck McNair, the dominant emotion was relief rather than triumph.

For Celtic, very little happened in November 1918 after the signing of the Armistice. Games against both Clydebank and Airdrieonians were fogged off, and the match at Firhill on Saturday, 23 November (a 1-0 win for a barely recognisable Celtic team against Partick Thistle) was dominated by conversation about Jimmy McMenemy, reported to be very ill with the Spanish Flu.

In early December, Celtic travelled to Motherwell and lost 1-3. Willie Maley's side were at their lowest point of the season. The Sunday Post states, quite openly, that Celtic were outclassed. They were now fourth in the League table and, but for Alec McNair, the score would have been a lot worse. There was some qualified good news on other fronts. Jimmy McMenemy was recovering and even hoping to play again for Celtic one day, having apparently decided against retirement, and things in western Europe had now settled down a little, although the flu was still present, and Russia was still in the throes of internecine fighting, as well as the pandemic and even, in some areas, famine.

In Great Britain itself, there was to be a General Election on Saturday, 14 December 1918. It was a classic piece of Lloyd George being at his most opportunistic. He was the "hero of the hour," the "man who won the war," as he himself put it, and he arranged the Election whilst his Coalition was still holding together and before the Labour opposition could organise or even get home from the war! Even the much-trumpeted historical advance of women having the vote was not what it seemed. Women had to be aged 30, and either be a householder or own property. It did not take a genius to work out that such women were likely to vote for the Coalition, rather than the Labour opposition!

The wily Welshman's plan worked, but that afternoon of Saturday, 14 December 1918 was also significant for Celtic, in that it turned their season. A crowd of 10,000 turned out for the visit of Dumbarton to Celtic Park, and they all rose as one to applaud the Celtic team as it came out of the pavilion, for it included Willie McStay (released early from the forces because he was needed to work in the mines) and Jimmy McMenemy, now recovered from his illness and looking as fit as ever in spite of his 38 years. McStay now partnered Alec McNair at left-back, but, in any case Joe Dodds was soon back as well, and Celtic's season now took off. They beat Dumbarton 2-0 that day, then Hamilton Academical and Hibernian before the turn of the year, and then, crucially, earned a draw against Rangers at Ibrox on New Year's Day 1919.

Indeed, Celtic were unlucky not to win, scoring first through Jimmy McMenemy and giving Rangers as good as they got before a massive crowd of 70,000. Celts were still behind in the table at the New Year, but they never lost another League game that season. Andy McAtee was back by the beginning of February, he and McMenemy making all the difference in the forward line, whilst Alec McNair kept everything tight at the back. Twice they slipped up with draws, and some of the wins were tight. However, just as happened in 1915, for example, good form will make your opponent crack, even when you are not playing them directly. Rangers eventually crumbled in the face of Celtic's consistent play.

Times remained hard. The last day of January 1919 saw the George Square riots, when a panicky Government had troops in readiness, thinking that a peaceful demonstration about working conditions and rents was the first step to a Bolshevik Revolution. The troops were still in evidence in the background on Saturday, 1 February 1919, as the crowd assembled at Celtic Park to see Celtic beat Kilmarnock 2-1. The police were barracked that day for their perceived part in the George Square disorder of the day before.

This was bad enough, but Ireland had now attempted to secede from Great Britain after the General Election of 1918. It had been a great triumph for Sinn Fein, but, the British would not let Ireland go, and an Irish Republican Army ambush at Soloheadbeg, in County Tipperary, on Tuesday, 21 January 1919 was generally regarded as the opening shot in the Irish War of Independence, causing British Prime Minister Lloyd George to recruit his brutal force of Auxiliaries from bitter ex-soldiers and prisoners from Dartmoor and Peterhead Prisons. They became known as the infamous Black and Tans.

In such circumstances, the fans need someone calm and solid. They found one such person in Alec McNair, who managed to keep cool in the face of everything, a perfect role model for everyone in the most desperate of circumstances. World war, pandemic, civil war, poverty, labour problems – all these things affected Alec as well, but, he had the ability to cope with them and to teach others how to do the same. If there was any doubt, it was always said, he "could pass it back to Chairlie!" This phrase became current. If anyone had a problem of any kind – be it to do with a wife, a job, a child, lack of money – and asked someone for advice, the advice could well be "Och, just pass it back to Chairlie." Shaw, McNair & Dodds remained a symbol of stability in a world which was the very opposite!

There had not been time to organise a Scottish Cup this year, as the season was well advanced by the time Armistice was reached on 11 November 1918, but, there was a Victory Cup. Celtic were the favourites, after they beat Vale of Leven and Albion Rovers (by no means negligible opposition, for Albion Rovers would reach the final of the Scottish Cup in 1920), but then, surprisingly, they went out to St Mirren in one of their very few poor games of spring 1919. Patsy Gallacher missed a penalty, Willie Maley's side were up against a goalkeeper called Billy O'Hagan, who simply had a great game, and Celtic were without Jimmy McMenemy. St Mirren went on to win the Victory Cup.

International football also made its welcome reappearance in 1919, albeit they were all declared Victory Internationals and made unofficial. Alec McNair played in the 3-1 win for the Scottish League against the English League at Birmingham City's St Andrew's ground on Saturday, 22 February, and then he played for Scotland against Ireland at Ibrox, four weeks later, on Saturday, 22 March 1919, although he very nearly didn't! Railway transport (still working under wartime conditions and bedevilled by labour disputes) let both McNair and Jimmy McMullen of Partick Thistle down, and the Scots had to start the game with nine men, as they had no reserves available. The train eventually did arrive, and a taxi was sent to Buchanan Street Station. The two men ran on late (although the kick-off had been slightly delayed) to a great cheer and Scotland won 2-1. The Sunday Post, whose reporter was perhaps a little annoyed at being kept waiting, damns Eck with faint praise, reporting that "McNair did many brainy things but was slow and occasionally rather easily beaten."

Alec also played in the two Victory Internationals against England, a 2-2 draw at Goodison Park, Liverpool on Saturday, 26 April 1919 then a defeat for Scotland by the odd goal in seven at Hampden one week later before 85,000 people, the highest attendance anywhere in the world since 1912. Scotland had a shocking first half in the latter match, and were deservedly 0-3 down at half-time, with Eck McNair getting the blame for the second goal, but they rallied in the second half and were unlucky to go down 3-4. The important thing was that football was back. It had dominated British cultural life before the war; it would continue to do so after it.

If McNair was disappointed by his performance in the Scotland game, he would have every right to feel happy about what he did for Celtic, particularly in the run-in to the League Championship. In the second last game, against Hearts at Tynecastle, for example, Celtic were 3-0 up with a goal from Andy McAtee and two from Jimmy McColl and looking comfortable, but suddenly they tired, and Andy Wilson scored twice for Hearts within the last 10 minutes. Hearts pressed for an equaliser, but Eck was on top of the situation reassuring Willie Cringan and Willie McStay and making sure that Celtic remained that vital one point ahead of Rangers.

The title was won at Somerset Park, Ayr in sweltering conditions on Saturday, 10 May 1919 with a comfortable 2-0 win, thanks to goals from Andy McAtee and Adam McLean. Patsy Gallacher was undeniably the star, however. The Sunday Post adds "with less effective backs than McNair and Dodds, it is conceivable that Ayr United might have scored in the second half, but this pair gave nothing away." Celtic had now won the Scottish League Championship 15 times (out of 29 starts!), and Alec McNair had now amassed an astonishing amount of 11 Scottish League-winner's medals.

It is a great shame to record that the Celtic team failed to maintain its excellent record in the Glasgow Charity Cup. The club had won the trophy every year since 1912, but this year went down to Queen's Park in the semi-final. It was the first time the Spiders had beaten Celtic since Halloween 1903, on the day they opened their third Hampden. 1918/19 was a strange kind of a season.

Alec McNair might now have been justified in asking himself just how long he could go on. He had already played for Celtic for 15 seasons and was now nearly 37 years old. He had never been the speediest of players, but now he was aware that he was slowing down even more. Yet that was the only thing that was wrong with his game. Eck was as tactically aware as anyone, his passes were accurate, and his tackling was as clean as a whistle. He was a good leader, albeit a reluctant captain at times, but he had a great relationship with everyone, not least Charlie Shaw and Joe Dodds. The other veteran, Jimmy McMenemy was also beginning to be 'asked questions about,' but, he and McNair got on well. Patsy Gallacher, prodigiously talented, and not always amenable to discipline, had a great respect for his captain McNair, and then there was Andy McAtee. What a difference he had made to the team since coming back from his military service in the Italian Alps in February 1919!

And then there was Willie Maley, Mr Celtic himself. The Boss. Occasionally abrupt and abrasive, and certainly not of 'the icicle temperament' like McNair, Maley would on occasion consult Eck about things. The manager's marriage had broken down, and it was perhaps natural that he would want to talk to Alec, a widower, about the team that they both loved. The war was now over, a new era was beginning, the world was changing dramatically and in ways that affected Celtic and their supporters intimately. How would they cope with the new post-war world, where the very parameters of life itself, let alone the game of football, were changing beyond recognition?

The war was now officially over when the Treaty of Versailles (the indisputable cause of the next war, according to many historians) was signed in June 1919. That did not, of course, mean the end of the misery, because the folly of war was obvious to anyone who walked along any street in any town and saw the number of young men with one leg, one arm, hideous facial disfigurements or with the less immediately obvious mental wounds of shell shock. Buchanan Street Station, every morning and night, was the haunt of beggars, often with the pathetic placard of "Woonded (sic) at Somme" hanging round their neck. Eck, himself no stranger to loss and bereavement but now with the comfortable, although not lavish, income of a professional football player, would often stop, talk kindly to the distressed man and drop a penny in his box, leaving the wounded ex-Serviceman wondering if that was really the great Alec McNair?

There were places where war was still going on. Large wars usually beget smaller ones. An attempted counter revolution was going on in Russia, a struggle in which the British government gave some limited if misguided help to the 'Whites,' who were trying to dislodge Lenin and the 'Reds. And there was also Ireland. McNair would have had to be blind, deaf and dumb not to be aware of this, not only from the passionate Patsy Gallacher and young Tommy McInally in the dressing-room, but also in the songs being sung with increasing fervour from the terracing. And in summer 1919, the Irish troubles were only just starting. They would become a lot worse in 1920 and 1921.

The new season of 1919/1920 began with a bang, Celtic winning their first 12 games in a row, usually very comfortably. Joe Dodds was injured and out for the first part of the season, but, the team was hardly weakened by the rapid development of Willie McStay, the first member of the family dynasty to appear for Celtic. But he was not the main attraction. That was a young man whose goalscoring ability soon had everyone calling him 'The Boy Wonder.' This was a man called Tommy McInally.

The McInally cult among the supporters grew and grew rapidly. The young man found it quite hard to deal with, and emotional problems soon began to surface – problems that taxed Alec McNair on the field and Willie Maley off it. The advantage was that there was nothing nasty about Tommy. He was also Celtic through and through. The trouble was that (as they sometimes said about Jimmy Johnstone, a not dissimilar figure in many ways) although Tommy "was not daft, there were times when he did daft things!" The Glasgow word 'gallus' springs to mind as well.

And yet he was such a talented player that they could not be too strict with him. He was also a great social asset (at least in the time that Eck McNair played with him) for the team and had a real impish sense of humour. Many was the time that Willie Maley called him into his office to 'have a word with him' about some misdemeanour at training, or to reproach him for bad timekeeping, only to have his anger dissolved by a witty remark made by Tommy, and his frown dissolved into a smile. In the long term, 'the boy' was going to give Maley and Celtic an incredible amount of grief, but for the moment, in the early part of the 1919/20 campaign, there was little that McInally could do wrong in the eyes of his teammates and supporters. It is hardly surprising that in later years, the Celtic manager would confess that "I always had a soft spot for the boy."

It would be difficult to imagine two more dissimilar characters than Tommy McInally and Eck McNair. Yet opposites attract sometimes, and McNair, who was almost twice the age of McInally, went out of his way to befriend him. Eck had been in the game for long enough and had lived through enough of all sorts of strange and difficult times to realise that a great deal of McInally's clowning actually hid a somewhat vulnerable and insecure character. He was just exactly the man to deal with such a character. The 'quiet word' was as valuable as anything.

Celtic's barnstorming start to the season included another capture of the Glasgow Cup for Alec McNair. The first round saw 63,000 roll up at Celtic Park on Saturday, 6 September 1918 to see Celtic v Rangers. It was only a 1-0 victory, albeit Celtic were well on top with the 'Five Macs' – McNair, McStay, McMenemy, McInally and McLean – outstanding. The goal came from a piece of Tommy McInally magic, as he beat a couple of men, then lobbed the ball over goalkeeper Herbert Lock for the waiting Adam McLean to score. Rangers' Jimmy Walls (inevitably called 'Derry's Walls' by his fans!) lost his cool and kicked Patsy Gallacher. It was the long walk for that one, of course, and the only chance that Rangers got came to Tommy Cairns, but his drive was tipped over the bar by Charlie Shaw.

McInally scored a hat trick in the 3-1 semi-final win against Queen's Park, a fortnight later, before Partick Thistle put up a far better show in the final, again played at Parkhead, on Saturday, 4 October 1918, Celts winning 1-0. Eck McNair had to leave Larbert early in the morning to get to Celtic Park in time because there was a rail strike on, and very few trains were running. But rail strike or no rail strike, 40,000 still turned up to see Celtic win their first Glasgow Cup final since 1916/17, the only goal of the game coming from Tommy McInally in the second half, after he had feinted to pass then lobbed the ball over the goalkeeper's head. The Sunday Post talks about a great Cup-tie atmosphere, with bands, bugles and whistles and a large contingent of Celtic supporters from all over the country, from as far afield as Dundee, who had defied the lack of trains and had got there, somehow.

This was the start of the trend of the 1920s, with massive crowds in spite of occasionally indifferent performances. Enthusiasm had reached a new peak, and it was almost as if those who had survived the war and the flu (now, in the latter part of 1919, still there but definitely in retreat) were convinced that they must now enjoy life to the utmost, lest the bad days return once more. Full-time in this Glasgow Cup final was greeted by a full-throated roar from the green-and-white bedecked supporters, and Alec McNair must have realised that as long as he could eke out some more days of playing football for this crowd, then retirement could have no attractions.

Celtic's winning run of 12 games in a row came to an abrupt halt on Saturday, 18 October 1919 when they went down 0-3 to Rangers at Ibrox before a vast crowd of 73,000, some of them wearing captured German helmets painted blue-and-white or green-and-white, according to the preference of the wearer. The defeat was not as bad as it sounded, but it was a significant win for Rangers, nevertheless. The report of the game in The Sunday Post was written by Albert Shepherd, one-time centre-forward of Newcastle United before the war (he had scored twice in the 1910 English FA Cup Final, including the first ever penalty kick in a final) and he had met and played against Eck McNair on one or two occasions. He has this to say about his old adversary. "McNair showed what the old brain can do by cleverly intercepting a pass by Paterson. Under all the Rangers' pressure, McNair never turned a hair – and I noted that he has not as many to turn as of yore – showing what a brilliant defender he is."

Celtic's problem in this game lay in the inability of the forwards to get going, and, in particular, the failure of Tommy McInally and Patsy Gallacher to work together. They were, of course, two of a kind, both in playing style and in character, and perhaps two mercurial, talismanic characters in the one side was one too many.

Certainly, the evidence would back this up, for there seemed little problem with the Celtic defence but sometimes goals would simply not come for the forwards. New Year 1920 was reached with Celtic only once defeated (in that Ibrox game) but having drawn on five occasions, (including three draws in a row against Falkirk, Ayr United and Partick Thistle in November), whereas Rangers tended to win. Nevertheless, it was very close and Celtic's 2-1 home win over Third Lanark on Saturday, 27 December 1919 saw them six points behind Rangers but with two games in hand.

The 1920s opened at Celtic Park before a crowd of 75,905 in lovely weather to see Celtic and Rangers draw 1-1 in what was described as a "rousing game," which Celtic were possibly unlucky not to win. The draw, of course, favoured Rangers. Alec McNair was injured in that game – the ground was still hard after some rather severe frost – and he then missed a couple of games.

It was at the end of January 1920, with two successive away defeats, that Celtic lost their chance of retaining the League championship. They lost, incredibly, 2-0 to Clydebank, at Clydeholm, and then by 2-1 to Dundee at Dens Park. Celtic would always be behind Rangers after those stumbles. On occasion, they narrowed the gap, but, two draws, away to Motherwell then at home to St Mirren in the second half of April sealed their fate.

The events of Monday, 26 April 1920 did not show Celtic or their supporters in the best light, but they owe their genesis to the two games against Dundee at Dens Park at the end of January and in early February, and to the rather complex relationship between the two clubs in that strange city called Dundee. Celtic, as we have already said, lost to Dundee in the League, on Saturday, 31 January 1920, but immediately got revenge the following week in the Scottish Cup, by winning 3-1 at the same ground. The games had both been hard-fought, with quite a few vendettas between individual players. A positive feature of the game had been the jousts between the two Ecks – McNair of Celtic and his direct opponent Troup of Dundee. The spoils were equally divided between the two of them, and unlike some other encounters between players over the two games, it was totally sporting.

Dundee had enjoyed a large Irish population since the days of the Potato Famine, An Gorta Mor. They worked in the jute factories, tended to live in the Lochee area of town, and were generally accepted by the population. But as Dundee in 1920 lacked an Irish team other than the poor Second Division Dundee Hibernian, the Irish in the city supported Celtic. It was often said that the Dundee Irish only went to support the Dundee Hibs at Tannadice Park when they couldn't afford the train fare to Glasgow to see Celtic. There was, therefore, keen rivalry between the supporters of Dundee and the Dundee-based supporters of Celtic.

On Saturday, 24 April 1920, Celtic had still not entirely given up on catching Rangers, although their hopes were fast evaporating.

They played a good game to defeat Ayr United 4-0 at Celtic Park on a windy day, whilst hoping that Dundee could do them a favour by beating Rangers at Ibrox. The score, however, was Rangers 6 Dundee 1 and when some Dundee players foolishly allowed themselves to be quoted as saying that Rangers would be "worthy champions," some Celtic supporters began to smell a rather large rat. Had Dundee lain down to Rangers? (In 2003 the same was believed of Dunfermline Athletic in similar circumstances). The Dundee Press, The Courier and The Advertiser, were a little puzzled by Dundee's lack of fight, it has to be said, and it was a somewhat unfortunate quirk of the fixtures that Dundee now came to Celtic Park on the Holiday Monday of 26 April 1920.

In fact, it was a small crowd – only 7,000 – but this time Dundee fought well – a lot harder than they had fought at Ibrox. The score was 1-1 as the game reached its closing stages when, after a few other meaty challenges involving other players, Bert McIntosh of Dundee and Adam McLean of Celtic clashed. With breathtaking suddenness, some of the younger members of the Celtic crowd invaded the park, (the railings had been taken away for the war effort and had not yet been replaced) attacked McIntosh, the referee Mr McMillan of Hamilton and any other Dundee played who happened to be in sight.

Conspicuous, even heroic in all this, was Alec McNair, who was seen to protect as many Dundee players as possible, in particular his direct opponent, the diminutive Alec Troup, whom he ushered into the old pavilion, then turned to stay the crowd, appealing with his hands in the air to stop the hurling of stones at the Dundee players. He was, naturally, very embarrassed by all this, and knew that although the game was abandoned, the result would in all probability now stand as a 1-1 draw. Indeed, there was a danger that Celtic might have some points deducted for the hooliganism of their crowd. Celtic's League campaign was effectively over. He was sad at all this but was wise enough to spot the real problem of poverty, ignorance and the war, which had deprived so many vulnerable youngsters of a father figure. A week later, when Celtic came to Dundee to play in a friendly match for the St Patrick War Memorial, Eck McNair was given a cheer whenever he touched the ball, as an acknowledgement for what he had done at Parkhead that day.

The Scottish Cup had also brought disappointment in 1920. After Dundee had been defeated at Dens Park and then Partick Thistle at Celtic Park, Celtic were drawn against Rangers at Ibrox on Saturday, 6 March 1920. It was a tough but enjoyable game of football before a crowd of about 85,000 with Celtic distinctly unlucky to go down 0-1 to a Muirhead goal just after half-time. Andy Aitken, The Daddler,' one-time of Newcastle United, writing in The Sunday Post, is of the opinion that Celtic were worthy of a draw, even though the deployment of Patsy Gallacher in the centre-forward position was clearly a mistake, as indeed was the omission of Tommy McInally. Alec McNair, however, "played a very sound game," but what he would have made of the attempted invasion of the park by some so-called Celtic supporters we do not know. Fortunately, he and other Celtic players, aided by the Glasgow Police, pushed the "potential miscreants" back. As we have seen, an unruly support would cause Celtic further embarrassment later in the season.

There was some sort of revenge for the disappointments of the season in the Glasgow Charity Cup, which Celtic won again. The semi-final was against Rangers at Ibrox on Saturday, 8 May 1920. Due respect was paid to the memory of William Wilton, the Rangers manager, who had perished in a drowning accident on the Clyde the previous weekend, before Celtic proceeded, albeit with a weakened team, to beat Rangers 2-1. This time, Tommy McInally was in the centre and he made all the difference, even though he did not score, whereas "for the Celts, Shaw, McNair and Cringan were heroes in the strife." Two men, one from each side, Charlie Watson of Celtic and Jimmy Gordon of Rangers, were sent off for fighting.

The final took place the following week, and this time Eck McNair had the difficult job of taming Queen's Park's talented left-winger Alan Morton, who, rumour had it, was interesting Rangers. A crowd of 50,000 on a fine sunny day saw McNair get the better of Morton, and Celtic won the Glasgow Charity Cup once again, with Adam McLean scoring the only goal of the game.

It was, however, a disappointing season for Celtic after it promised so much. But there was one area in which there was no problem, and that was right-back, where Alec McNair was consistently described in newspapers as "the best back afield" and "sound in judgement" or "brainy in tactics." Clearly, the Scotland selectors shared this opinion, choosing Eck for all three Internationals and making him captain against Ireland and England.

The first post-war International was played, eccentrically, on a Thursday, 26 February 1920 at Ninian Park, Cardiff and was a creditable 1-1 draw. Then Ireland were comfortably despatched 3-0 at Celtic Park on Saturday, 13 March, before Alec McNair had the misfortune to captain Scotland in one of the craziest Scotland v England games of them all. It was played on an absolute quagmire of a pitch on Saturday, 10 April 1920 at Hillsborough, Sheffield. There seems to be little doubt that had this game not been an International, with a crowd of 40,000 inside the ground, it would have been called off. Conditions were absolutely atrocious, with players barely able to keep their footing. England won this pantomime 5-4.

Some people thought that this was the most exciting International of all time, but, those who played in it would not agree. It was "downright dangerous," according to some. Scotland probably deserved a draw, but it was England who scored more goals. It was a shame that this would turn out to be Eck McNair's last International match for Scotland. The contrast between this farce and the great game at Hampden in 1914 could hardly have been greater.

CHAPTER EIGHT

THE ROARING TWENTIES (1920-1925)

In the summer of 1920, Celtic shed two players, both of them mistakes. In the case of Joe Dodds, it was due to a temporary falling-out with the management, possibly over money, and Joe duly came back a year later, after a spell with Cowdenbeath (If it was money, then we are faced with the horrendous fact that Cowdenbeath were more generous to Joe Dodds than Celtic!). The other man who departed was Jimmy McMenemy, Celtic apparently being of the opinion that the ageing 'Napoleon' was past his sell-by date. McMenemy duly proved them wrong, when he won another Scottish Cup medal that season for Partick Thistle, and against Rangers at Celtic Park of all places!

One of the reasons for not doing more grovelling to keep Joe Dodds was that Willie Maley believed he had a ready-made replacement waiting in the shape of Willie McStay. In that he was correct, for McStay became a great full-back, deservedly earning caps for Scotland. One suspects, however, that Alec McNair would have preferred the club to keep Dodds, for it took him a while to adjust to McStay, good though he was. McNair was himself injured after New Year 1921 and was out of the side for a long time (something that happened to him very rarely), and it was during that time that the team lost key games. He was now no longer the captain either, although that means very little, because he was always there as an elder statesman to help out.

In some ways, this was still a great Celtic side. In their goal, Charlie Shaw was now the captain and was so good that when other teams scored against him, opposition supporters sung songs about how "Oh, Chairlie Shaw, he never saw whaur Alan Morton/Willie Hillhouse/Oor Wee Troupie/Tokey Duncan pit the baw," depending on whether one supported Rangers, Albion Rovers, Dundee or Raith Rovers, whilst Celtic supporters retaliated with "Oh, Chairlie Shaw, he built a wa', tae stop them scorin' wi' the ba'." It is interesting to note, en passant, that this song has the same tune as "The Red Flag," the song that was terrorising the middle classes in 1921 with their fear of Bolshevism!

The half-back line was Johnny Gilchrist, Willie Cringan & Johnny McMaster, three great players but none of them good at toeing Maley's increasingly dictatorial line and there would be trouble in store. The Parkhead forward-line was the one that could guarantee to bring tears to the eyes of Celtic supporters 70 years later. It was Andy McAtee, Patsy Gallacher, Tommy McInally, Joe Cassidy & Adam McLean. It was a great combination, yet everyone was surprised that they only repeated what they did the previous season by winning both Glasgow trophies but not the Scottish ones. It was a distinct under-performance for a team of such prodigious talent.

The reason has been hinted at earlier. A certain amount of temperamental instability in some players and Willie Maley's inconsistent approach to it. Some players got away with murder. Tommy McInally, for example, was indulged endlessly on the grounds that "I always had a soft spot for the boy," whereas the Celtic manager was far tougher with Johnny Gilchrist and Willie Cringan when a more relaxed approach might have paid benefits. Neither of these two was easy to deal with, it has to be said, but neither was impossible either.

When Alec McNair was injured and out of the side from January to April 1921, the team was still a good one but lacked consistency, losing the Scottish League by going down to teams like Ayr United, Kilmarnock and Raith Rovers and, tragically, to Hearts in the quarter-final of the Scottish Cup. It is difficult to resist the conclusion that they missed McNair. He was now in his late 30s, and even his greatest admirers in the Press and on the terracing agreed that he was now a bit on the slow side, but he still had the football brain and, equally important, he had the temperament and the ability to calm things down both on and off the field. Not for nothing was he called The Icicle.

Alec had his great games as well this season. Having defeated Third Lanark in the first round of the Glasgow Cup, Celtic played Rangers in the semi-final at Celtic Park on Saturday, 18 September 1920. Rangers, at this point, had a 100% record, and were really looking good, with Alan Morton on the left wing looking particularly impressive, but, Maley's Celtic, with McNair in inspirational form, stopped them in their tracks. Once again, Andy Aitken, 'The Daddler' of Newcastle United fame, cannot hide his admiration for Eck in The Sunday Post. "Really I am astonished to find Alec McNair stick it so well. His clearances, sometimes from within a few feet of the goal were perfect and his intercepting work masterly. I thought Alec had complete mastery of Alan Morton..."

Celtic had scored through Tommy McInally just before half-time and then Adam McLean in the second half. Rangers did pull one back through Alan Morton late in the game, but, Shaw, McNair and McStay organised the defences in the last frantic few minutes when Rangers pressed for the equaliser in a pulsating game which had the crowd of 65,282 "gasping."

Clyde was the opposition in the final, played at Celtic Park on Saturday, 2 October 1920. After the semi-final, it was a bit of an anti-climax. Andy McAtee scored the only goal of the game, and hard though Clyde tried to delight their fans in the 45,000 crowd, Celtic's defence held good, although we are told that on one occasion that "McNair foozled (sic) a kick quite near goal, though his recovery was a bit of the old-time skill." Full-time came and Alec McNair had won another Glasgow Cup medal – his seventh.

For the rest of 1920, it was Rangers who had the upper hand in the Scottish League race. It was the period when the troubles in Ireland were at their height, with daily massacres and reprisals. It was also the time of the execution of Kevin Barry and the death through hunger strike of the Lord Mayor of Cork, Terence MacSwiney – both well-commemorated in song at Celtic Park in later years – and sometimes, one felt that this had its effect on Celtic players. Certainly, when they did beat Rangers 2-0 at Ibrox on New Year's Day 1921 – the famous Joe Cassidy game – the Celtic Brake Clubs on their way home had little compunction about commemorating this game as a victory for the rebels and Sinn Fein against the forces of the crown.

Alec McNair played in that Ibrox game, of course, and also in the match against Clyde at Celtic Park, two days later. That would end up a 1-0 win for Celtic, with Cassidy again on target, but, McNair injured his ankle. This was particularly badly timed, for he had been granted a benefit game the following day, Tuesday, 4 January 1921, by a grateful Celtic management for all his years with them. McNair may have been embarrassed at this. But, 30,000 spectators turned up at Parkhead to see a Celtic and Rangers select play against a Scottish League XI. Naturally Eck had to make at least an appearance in this game, but he was obviously still injured from the previous day, and after just 10 minutes, he hobbled off to a loud cheer to be replaced by Willie McStay.

It was light-hearted stuff, of course, and the supporters enjoyed seeing Rangers players like Bert Manderson, Jimmy Gordon (reputed to be an uncompromising Orangeman) and Alan Morton in the green-and-white of Celtic. The fact that they did so showed their high regard for Alec McNair, but it was perhaps unwise for Eck to appear and try to run about even for a few minutes. He might have been better to allow McStay to take his place and perhaps lead the teams out in 'civvies.' As it was, after a brief and none too successful attempt at a comeback against Motherwell at Fir Park on Saturday, 22 January 1921, McNair was out until April, by which time, to his distress, the team had lost both the Scottish League and the Scottish Cup.

Alec did not play in the Glasgow Charity Cup that month (Celtic won it again!), although he did go on the tour of France in May, which included a visit to the battlefields and the laying of a few wreaths in honour of Donnie McLeod, Peter Johnstone, Leigh Roose and others. It was, however, widely believed that, now not far off his 39th birthday and suffering from a bad ankle, this might be the swansong of Alec McNair.

Those who thought that, however, did not know Alec McNair. He had a long time to go yet! In fact, there is good reason to believe that 1921/22 was one of his better seasons – and there are a lot to choose from in his case! Joe Dodds was back from his odd decision to go to Cowdenbeath for a year, and apart from a spell in the autumn when Joe was injured, Celtic had Shaw, McNair & Dodds at the back, and then we had Gilchrist, Cringan & McMaster in the middle, with McAtee, Gallacher, McInally, Cassidy & McLean up front. There was really little wrong with the playing ability of that team, and we are really not surprised to hear that they won the Scottish League that year. But there were problems.

There was one in particular, called Tommy McInally. Prodigiously talented, but prone to temperamental disturbances, so severe on occasion that he is prevented from being looked upon as the best player in Celtic's history (aye, maybe even better than Patsy Gallacher!) and considered a comparative failure, even though the support raised him to heroic status.

Therein perhaps lay the problem. He had started his Celtic career with a bang and had been christened "The Boy Wonder" and other things by the Press. The supporters believed that, Willie Maley believed that and worst of all, Tommy McInally himself believed that. As he grew older and more confident in the ways of the world (he had never lacked confidence in his playing ability), he became less and less of a team man, upsetting his colleagues by his unpredictable and quixotic behaviour.

Older and wiser members of the team, like Alec McNair, now no longer captain but more of a wise counsellor to whom the current skipper Willie Cringan and others would turn, tried to understand what made Tommy tick, but failed. Maley would always try to indulge McInally, for he had great faith in Tommy's ability, when there were times that a sterner line had to be taken. McNair felt that there were situations when love need not exclude a firm putdown, and even punishment on occasion. Always, however, a great believer in the 'quiet word first' idea, Eck kept trying to bring out the consistent best in Tommy but once again he was unsuccessful. Eventually, Tommy McInally had to be dropped, Joe Cassidy moved to the centre and the earnest John 'Jean' McFarlane brought into the inside-left position. That decision, taken by Willie Maley in consultation with men like Charlie Shaw and Alec McNair, eventually won Celtic the League in 1922.

Alec McNair missed the first couple of games that 1921/22 season through injury, but he was back in his usual place by September. He, personally, still played well, but the team was often unreliable and inconsistent, drawing games that they ought to have won and losing one to Hibernian at Easter Road, in spite of a scarcely believable individual goal scored by Patsy Gallacher. This took place on the Edinburgh Holiday Monday of 19 September 1921, when immediately after Hibs scored, Tommy McInally kicked off and tapped the ball to Patsy, who simply ran up and scored, weaving his way past about six defenders and rounding the goalkeeper to net a truly remarkable goal. Gallacher then picked the ball out of the net and presented it to a Hibs defender! And yet Celtic lost the game!

The first real indication that something was wrong came in the Glasgow Cup final defeat to Rangers at Hampden on the opening day of October. The score was only 1-0, but, it could and should have been more. Rangers scored early through Davie Meiklejohn and Celtic never really got into the game. Maley's side were without Andy McAtee, and the lack of the earnest Crojan played its part in the defeat, but then again Rangers were without Alan Morton. There was little wrong with Shaw, McNair and McStay (Joe Dodds was injured) but there was little doubt whom the Celtic support blamed for it all – Tommy McInally.

He had been the subject of transfer speculation all week, with every club in the country, apparently - but in particular Liverpool and Partick Thistle - expressing interest. McInally had done little to discourage all this, naturally enjoying being the centre of attention, but did himself few favours in this Glasgow Cup final, with The Sunday Post putting things tactfully but nevertheless directly and pointedly by talking about his "tendency to play the man first instead of the ball... a blemish that contributed to the failure of more than one player in his own team." As centre-forward, Tommy ought to have been leading the line, but failed to do so. The following Tuesday, in a League game against St Mirren before an angry Celtic Park crowd, a 2-0 win restored some credibility, but, McInally was barracked, then faked a run to the Pavilion in a vain attempt to clown his way back into favour but merely exacerbated the situation. He ended up sulking on the left wing, whilst Patsy Gallacher and Joe Cassidy scored the Celtic goals.

This clearly could not go on, and possibly Eck McNair had one of his famous 'quiet words' with the boy. Things did take a turn for the better after that, albeit not completely. Tommy McInally did score in the creditable 1-1 League draw against Rangers at Ibrox three weeks later and seemed to win back some credibility in the eyes of the fans, but, the team still failed to sparkle with a fair sprinkling of goalless draws. Such results, of course, say little for the forward-line, but they also tell us that there was little wrong with the veteran McNair. Remarkably, often in newspaper reports about games, we find sentences like "Celtic's best players were Gilchrist, McAtee, Gallacher and, naturally, McNair," as if there was something wrong in the world order if Eck ever had a bad game.

The New Year game at Parkhead, played on Monday, 2 January 1922, was a thrilling affair, albeit a 0-0 draw spoiled, to a certain extent, by a high wind. Nevertheless, however much this says about the effectiveness of Alec McNair, the draw was a good result for Rangers, who were still three points ahead of Celtic, and playing well enough not to seem likely to drop any more. It meant that Celtic really had to win every game from now on in and hope that two other teams could beat Rangers.

It was the Scottish Cup that brought matters to a head about Tommy McInally. Little bother was experienced with the overawed Montrose, Maley's men winning 4-0 at Parkhead on Saturday, 28 January 1922, but then after a more difficult game in the next round against Third Lanark at Cathkin two weeks later, which Celtic scraped through 1-0, they found themselves playing at home against Hamilton Academical, a team in the lower half of the First Division, on Saturday, 25 February 1922. It was a game that Celtic, tough opponents though the visitors had been in the past, should have won with a degree of ease. What actually happened that afternoon rocked Celtic and amazed the world.

The shock 3-1 defeat cannot really be explained away by Hamilton Academical winning the toss. The visitors scored three goals in the first half, and by the time Joe Dodds converted a penalty kick in the 87th minute, the 20,000 crowd had departed in angry silence. It may be that the Accies had a good day and Celtic had a bad day, but the home fans now demanded the head of Tommy McInally. He played on the Wednesday after the game, ironically against that same Hamilton side in the League, and equally ironically, he scored in the 4-0 win, but he effectively disappears from the scene after that, eventually being transferred to Third Lanark in the summer. The McInally 'self-destruct' button had been pressed.

But another, more helpful, switch or button had been pressed as well, and a new reinvigorated Celtic appeared. They had been helped to a certain extent because Rangers too, embroiled in the Scottish Cup, which caused them all sorts of psychological problems in the 1920s, were struggling, but the bottom line was that if Celtic won their games, they would win the title. Celtic drew 0-0 with Third Lanark at Cathkin on the day that Patsy Gallacher was playing at Parkhead for Ireland against Scotland, Saturday, 4 March 1922, and they drew 1-1 at Falkirk, a fortnight later. Apart from that, they kept winning, sometimes in tight corners, but, of course, that is what winning Championships is all about.

It is in circumstances like this that the experience of men like Alec McNair is invaluable. He had simply been on too many football fields by now, had so much experience of life, on and off the field, and was just so valuable to the team. Eck could read situations. He could get to a ball quicker than most attackers, just by being a split-second ahead in his thinking. He could clear a ball, pass a ball both forward and back and generally had enough 'brain' to avoid trouble for himself and to keep his teammates out of trouble. That is why he was called The Icicle, and why men like Joe Cassidy, Patsy Gallacher and Andy McAtee talked so highly of him.

Cassidy, in particular, started scoring the goals, doing so from a confidence that he was in a settled, productive and harmonious team. The defence was always well marshalled by McNair, and the forward-line orchestrated by Gallacher. Potential banana skins like Hearts at Tynecastle and Queen's Park at Hampden were well negotiated, and on Saturday, 8 April 1922, Celtic really turned it on to beat Dundee 4-0 at Parkhead. They played "delightful football" throughout and it was all the more creditable for the team because Johnny Gilchrist and Willie Cringan were away playing for Scotland in the 1-0 win over England at Villa Park. Alec may have regretted his advancing years, in that they kept him out of contention for the Scotland team, but he was happy enough with Celtic for whom he was still doing a grand job.

McNair was in fine fettle the next Saturday, when Celtic took the short trip to Coatbridge to beat Albion Rovers 2-0, the day made even better by the news that Morton had won the Scottish Cup for the first time ever by beating Rangers 1-0 in what The Dundee Courier describes candidly as the "roughest Cup final on record."

Celtic now had 64 points and two games to play, Rangers having 59 with four to play. Willie Maley's Bhoys simply had to win both those games, against Partick Thistle at home 48 hours later and Morton away on the last Saturday of the month. Thistle, even with Jimmy McColl now playing for them, could make little impression on Shaw, McNair & Dodds, as Celtic won 3-0, but, Rangers also won their game that day and their two matches in hand. Thus, we approached the last day of the season with Celtic, one point ahead, going to Morton and Rangers playing at Clyde. Saturday, 29 April 1922 would turn out to be one of the most dramatic days of Alec McNair's lengthy career, but once again it brought out the best in him.

Eck needed to be at his calmest and coolest that afternoon for several reasons. One was the sheer size of the crowd – 23,500 packed inside Cappielow, a record which stands to this day. Cappielow is a ground where the crowd is almost on top of the players. Another factor was the sheer passion of Morton and their fans, now on a high after their Scottish Cup victory two weeks previously, and yet another was the fanaticism of the Celtic crowd desperate to win the Scottish League flag. There were several disruptions to the play, some caused by overcrowding but others caused by missiles - including rivets stolen from the shipyard - being thrown from one section of the crowd to the other. The situation was not helped by what was going on in Ireland at this time, nor by the ongoing Labour unrest in shipyards, mines and railways.

If ever there was a time for Rudyard Kipling's quotation "If you can keep your head when all about you are losing theirs and blaming it on you..." this was it for Alec McNair. With several of the players clearly overawed by all this, and showing every sign of 'losing it,' Eck had to remain calm. He had to be The Icicle today, and he was. Morton, for long spells in the game, were on top, with their midfield predominant. The Greenock side scored through Alf Brown before half-time, and things looked grim for Celtic, for it was still 0-0 at Shawfield, and that combination of results would have given Rangers the title on goal average.

Celtic had to score, but it was difficult to concentrate on the job in hand with the constant babble of noise and the very real fear that at any point the crowd might erupt into serious violence. Nor was there any real way of knowing what was happening at Shawfield. People shouted "1-0 for Rangers," or "1-0 for Clyde," but, Alec McNair would know that was rubbish. In 1922, the only people who had any chance of knowing the score would be the men from the Press, who had a telephone link to their newspaper offices, but they were at the moment far too intent on watching this game, in which Morton were pressing for a second goal.

"McNair was the epitome of coolness, allowing nothing to disturb him. The uproar of the crowd on the terracing or their proximity on the track, the speed of his opponents the realisation that a Championship was at stake...he continued to play his normal game, totally alert, utterly competent." Rhapsody in Green, (Tom Campbell and Pat Woods, 1990).

More than once, Eck saved Celtic from going further behind, but, the need was now for a goal, as time was slipping away. Celtic did not really look like scoring, but eventually with six minutes to go, a high aimless cross was sent into the penalty box by Johnny Gilchrist and goalkeeper Edwards rose to collect it. Unaccountably, when under no pressure, Edwards dropped it and Andy McAtee, lurking more in hope than expectation, managed to get an undignified head on the ball (it was more like his face!) and Celtic equalised to the accompaniment of mayhem on the terracing.

Now, as often happens, Celtic took command and for the last few minutes came close to getting the goal which would have definitely given them the League title. But full-time came, and as Eck McNair shook hands with his opponents (the game itself had been a good clean one in spite of all that was going on in the surrounds), he would not have been human if he had not looked up into the Press Box to see if there were any indication of what had happened between Clyde and Rangers at Shawfield. The absence of any animation led Alec to believe that that game had indeed finished 0-0 and that, therefore, Celtic had won their 16th League flag and he personally had now won 12 League-winner's medals. A smiling Willie Maley duly confirmed that as being the full-time result at Shawfield.

The day did not, however, end there. Outside the ground were scenes of reckless disorder, with windows smashed, ongoing fights, broken windows and many injuries, proving perhaps that so many young men had, sadly, learned only too well how to be violent from their years in khaki, or worse still, were seeking a return to it. McNair was sad at all that, of course, although by the time that the Celtic charabanc departed, the crowd had begun to disperse. It was, in spite of all that had happened, a proud moment for the club and for her seemingly immortal Alec McNair, who had played such a large part in the triumph.

The Glasgow Charity Cup was an anti-climax that season, Celtic losing to Rangers in the semi-final on corner kicks, having beaten Partick Thistle by the same method in a game in which Alec McNair was not playing. There followed a dreadful tour of the new country called Czechoslovakia and Germany – a tour which McNair might have been better off missing out on. Three defeats in Prague, corrupt referees, and several players crocked was what happened in Czechoslovakia, and then Celtic were criticised for playing in the still disapproved of country called Germany. Willie Maley rightly decided that such criticism was rubbish, and played a game against a Prussian Select, in what would have been the 1916 Olympic Stadium in Berlin (Alec McNair and Charlie Shaw between them perpetrating a hideous own goal in a 1-1 draw), and then they finished the tour on a high note by taking on the British Army on the Rhine in Cologne and beating them 5-0. The Army then, presumably in all sincerity and not making a political point, presented Celtic with a Union Jack to fly over Parkhead the next season!

Eck McNair was probably beginning to lose count of how many seasons he had been in first-class football when the 1922/23 season kicked off. His early season adventures took him to Alloa Athletic, who had won the Second Division Championship the previous spring, but, it was probably true to say that the weekend of 2-4 September 1922 was not a happy one in the life of either McNair himself or of Celtic.

In the first place, Celtic went out of the Glasgow Cup, at the first time of asking, to Queen's Park at Hampden. It was one of those games that the Press, the neutrals and the winning team talk about it being a classic with "great entertainment," but, if you are on the wrong side of a 4-3 scoreline, then your main feeling is crushing disappointment. There had been a great goal from Patsy Gallacher, but no Celtic team should lose four goals and McNair felt that he had not done himself justice. Joe Dodds was off on his travels again, this time permanently, and he had been replaced by Hugh Hilley, an honest journeyman but not in the class of Joe Dodds at his best.

The second blow was the transfer of Tommy McInally, on Monday, 4 September 1922, to Third Lanark.

One wonders how Eck felt about this. McInally had, indeed, let the team down badly last season, and Celtic had only begun to pick up once he was dropped. On the other hand, there was a supreme talent there, and it was such a shame to lose such a clearly able player. If only Tommy had had a better temperament, things might have been so much different, McNair felt. Third Lanark's manager at this time was ex-Celt and ex-Ranger, Alec Bennett. No doubt, McNair and Bennett, still friends for Eck did not very often have enemies, had talked to each other about Tommy McInally. It would have been interesting to know what they said to each other!

But these two blows paled into insignificance in comparison with the news that reached Glasgow that Monday night. Sunny Jim Young had been killed in a motorcycle accident in Ayrshire at the age of 40. Alec McNair, naturally, was devastated, as was all of the Celtic family, and it took a long time for Willie Maley, in particular, to recover. Young had typified Celtic in their great years. Never the most elegant of football players, and often inclined to get himself into scrapes that he would have been better out of, Sunny, with his loud stentorian war cry of "Face the ball, Celts" or his sound, but simple, advice about how to defend a corner kick - "Tak a man apiece" - would be much missed. McNair was at the cemetery in Kilmarnock on the Wednesday, to pay his respects to a man to whom he owed much and with whom he had so much in common. Temperamentally, they were poles apart – Sunny was anything but an 'Icicle'– yet they had so much in common. Neither was from a traditional Celtic background, in that neither was a Roman Catholic, but, they both drove a horse and cart through the façade of bigotry, for they both grew pari passu to love the Celtic.

Eck McNair was now out of the first team for a spell. Because he was getting a little older, injuries came more often and were a little harder to heal. He returned on Saturday, 7 October 1922 for a home game against Partick Thistle. Celtic won 4-3, but, The Glasgow Observer, always in the past a great admirer of McNair was compelled to say that he was "getting slower," but that, nevertheless, he displayed his best touches.

Alec was far from a regular this season, as Celtic struggled. A 1-3 defeat to Rangers at Celtic Park on Saturday, 28 October was described as "tame," and before the New Year, Celtic had also lost to Ayr United, Airdrie and Kilmarnock. It was very clear that there would be no realistic title challenge. Manager Willie Maley himself was struggling. He never coped well with grief, nor was he much good at dealing with temperamental players who, frankly, refused to accept the bullying dictatorship that he tried to impose on them. "The war changed all that," was a familiar cliché in the 1920s.

McNair kept playing when he was asked to do so, but probably realised now, as he approached his 40th birthday on Christmas Eve 1922, that his best days were behind him. Yet he also saw for himself a role as an unofficial coach and mentor for the youngsters who were beginning to appear at Celtic Park. Celtic had made the questionable decision to dispense with their reserve team, so young players very often appeared straight from the junior ranks into the first team. That was a big leap, albeit Eck was always there to give them a hand, and was always secure enough in himself and his own achievements not to patronise or to begin sentences with "in my day…" He realised that the world had changed and that he would inevitably have to change with it.

Autumn 1922 saw changes in the world outside football as well. Lloyd George's Coalition, which had been in power since the dark days of the war, eventually collapsed and broke up. The Election in mid-November saw the return of the Conservatives under a new Prime Minister called Andrew Bonar Law, who, poor man, would not last long, for he was already suffering from the illness that would kill him. The 1922 General Election also saw the permanent split of the Liberal Party and the inexorable rise of the Labour Party under that charismatic Scotsman from Lossiemouth called Ramsay MacDonald. So, things were changing, but, there was one funny aside as well, when that egocentric blowbag Winston Churchill was defeated in Dundee by a Prohibitionist, who seemed to have persuaded all the alcoholics and drunkards in Dundee (and there were loads of them!) to come out of the pubs for a moment to vote against Churchill!

The New Year of 1923 arrived with Eck McNair out of the Celtic team. The match against Rangers at Ibrox, a dreadful performance resulting in a 0-2 defeat, was shrouded with fog, and it might have been better if the game had been called off. But there was, as always, the Scottish Cup. Celtic, with nine trophy wins, were now just one behind Queen's Park's record of 10 successes, and if they could win the cup, it would salvage something out of a very poor season indeed. Alec was also personally focused on the Scottish Cup. He had already won five winner's medals and would have loved another just to finish off his career on the right note.

The Scottish Cup triumph of 1923 was, of course, all about Joe Cassidy, who scored in five out of the six games played. Three out of those six games were played against Fife teams, and it was only Raith Rovers against whom Joe failed to score. Nevertheless, he scored two against Lochgelly United, four against Hurlford (he also missed a penalty that day), another brace against East Fife, one against Motherwell in the semi-final and the only goal of the game against Hibernian in the final.

Alec McNair, who was now playing sporadically in League games, was sensibly deployed by Willie Maley in the latter stages of the tournament, his experience, knowledge of the game and ability to calm everyone down being a tremendous benefit for the side. In the semi-final, for example, against Motherwell at Ibrox on Saturday, 10

March 1923, Celtic found themselves up against a prolific centre-forward called Hugh Ferguson. Between them, Willie Cringan and Alec McNair tamed this great man, while Eck's "coolness" also dealt with the "strong and skilful wingers Reid and Ferrier." It was, in fact, one of Celtic's better performances of the season, with the 2-0 victory leading the supporters in the 71,506 crowd to believe that the corner had perhaps been turned.

The opponents in the final were Hibernian, now managed by Alec Maley, brother of Willie. These two teams, as Eck well recalled, had last met in the Scottish Cup final of 1914, and how the world had changed since then! He, Charlie Shaw, Andy McAtee and Patsy Gallacher had survived from that last final, and were determined to repeat the success, realising that, in McNair's case in particular, there might not be very many more Scottish Cup finals.

The teams who lined up at Hampden on Saturday, 31 March 1923 were as follows:

Celtic: Shaw, McNair & W McStay; J McStay, Cringan & McFarlane; McAtee, Gallacher, Cassidy, McLean & Connolly

Hibs: Harper, McGinnigle & Dornan; Kerr, Miller & Shaw; Ritchie, Dunn, McColl, Halligan & Walker

Referee. Mr T Dougray, Bellshill

It was a dry but very dull day in Mount Florida and, as often happens between Celtic and Hibernian, there was not a great deal of good football played. Alec McNair would say later that it reminded him of that previous Scottish Cup final (first game) in 1914. However, the difference here was that Celtic scored. It was a poor goal as well, a long ball from defence finding the head of Joe Cassidy who placed it over Hibs goalkeeper Harper, who was caught in no man's land. The cheering from the Celtic fans was not necessarily in appreciation of a great goal, but more through sheer relief that their team was ahead in a dour struggle for their first post-war Scottish Cup.

Some 25 minutes still remained at that point, and, naturally, Hibernian pressed. They had a fine side, which included Jimmy McColl, who had played in 1914 (but for Celtic, not Hibs) and Jimmy Dunn, who would become a Wembley Wizard in five years' time, and Celtic were compelled to bring a few men back to help repel the desperate Hibernian surge. It was in moments like this that one saw once again the value of Eck McNair. Perpetually on the move (he was still a remarkably slim and fit man for someone who was now 40), he tackled intelligently, knowing how exactly to do so without conceding a foul. McNair had the anticipation to break up moves and, if necessary, was prepared to concede a corner kick if he was not able to "pass it back to Chairlie." He also had the ability to "take the dog for a walk," as the technical term was for taking the ball to the opposition corner flag and keeping it there, whilst inviting the tackle or giving the opposition the opportunity to put the ball out of play. If a free-kick or throw-in was awarded, Eck would immediately retire back to his own half and await the next onslaught.

But it was very much a team effort. McNair was aware that other players, like the two McStay brothers (Jimmy had now joined Willie), were anxious in pursuit of their first Scottish Cup medal, as indeed was the young Fifer, Jean McFarlane. They needed to be encouraged and reassured. Time was running out, and the last five minutes were particularly tense until referee Tom Dougray of Bellshill pointed to the pavilion. Celtic had now won 10 Scottish Cups and McNair had won six of them. His collection of medals now equalled the Celtic record of Jimmy McMenemy, although Napoleon had also won a seventh with Partick Thistle in 1921.

The Sunday Post, a long-time admirer of Eck says, "It was certainly a personal triumph for Alec McNair. In the closing period of his career, he achieved a distinction that could not fail to give him great satisfaction. It was in the second half, particularly, that his coolness, resource and illimitable strategy served to outwit the Hibs' fight for an equaliser and not to put too fine a point upon it, to extricate his side from at least a couple of tight corners. There were several efforts of his, quiet enough, but undeniably effective that will rank as classics in the history of Scottish Cup finals."

Tom Campbell and Pat Woods, writing in The Glory and the Dream, described his performance in the 1923 Scottish Cup final thus. "Celtic had been shaky at the season's end and McNair was no longer a regular in the side because of recurring injuries, but in the emergency, he was recalled, to steady the defence. His performance that day, composed and efficient as always, was compared to that of a veteran actor summoning up reserves of strength and character, responding to the demands of the audience, relying on his craft, experience and authority to compensate for any physical shortcomings. He could have chosen no more fitting finale to a magnificent career."

Thus, McNair went home that night on his train to Larbert Station, possibly wondering how much longer he could go on. He felt fit, he was well, and it would be a shame to retire, would it not? Not that this season was necessarily finished yet, of course. He played a few of the irrelevant League games and was decidedly unlucky not to win another Glasgow Charity Cup medal, when Rangers beat Celtic in extra-time in the semi-final in May. Not that it really mattered of course. The Scottish Cup was back at Parkhead, Celtic had equalled Queen's Park's record and Alec had another winner's medal. "Och, no, Eck, let's not retire. We have a wee bit left yet," he may have said to himself.

It might have been better if he had bowed out gracefully in 1923, albeit he had no desire to, and Willie Maley wanted him to stay, possibly even as an unofficial assistant manager. McNair's religion at that time of history was possibly a factor in Celtic's thinking to prevent him officially becoming the assistant manager. He was certainly always available to give advice. Eck still wanted to play, however, and Maley was very keen to deploy him, not least because it allowed the Celtic manager to experiment with Willie McStay, who although naturally a right-back and a very talented one, could also play on the other side.

But season 1923/24 was not a great season for Celtic. It had started with serious player unrest about bonuses, and although that issue was smoothed over for a while, the form of the team never really reached great heights after a depressing exit (without McNair) from the Glasgow Cup to Rangers at Ibrox in September 1923, then the departure of centre-half and captain Willie Cringan to play for Third Lanark the following month. Goalkeeper Charlie Shaw would now be the new skipper of Celtic.

The team did not really play badly, and there was an abundance of talent there, but, there was a depressing tendency to draw games that should have been won. By the New Year, it was clear that there would be no Scottish League challenge in 1924. A close study of newspaper reports on Eck McNair's performances reveals a common theme, namely that a fast speedy winger will often get the better of the 40-year-old, yet there was always the feeling that McNair's tenacity, his technical ability and his general knowledge of the game was such that he was an asset to the team.

Annoyingly, a late goal conceded to Rangers at Celtic Park on New Year's Day 1924 gave the Ibrox men a point that they hardly deserved. Celtic had really needed to win that one, in which The Dundee Courier states that "McNair showed all his old craft at back, making intuition serve for speed that he now lacks."

There was a temporary return to form over the following three weeks, Celtic enjoying some good wins against Hamilton Academical,

Third Lanark and Aberdeen, before the whole thing collapsed on Saturday, 26 January at Kilmarnock, when the side went down 0-2 to exit the Scottish Cup. The Sunday Post, normally sympathetic to Celtic, described them as "a feckless lot who got their deserts," with McNair "degrees and degrees" below form. Effectively, this ended Celtic's season, and there were more horrors to behold as the League season fizzled out.

But there were two things that cheered up the fans. One was the arrival of the first Labour Government, admittedly a minority one, but enough to scare the establishment. Celtic-supporting John Wheatley, MP for Shettleston, was appointed the Minister of Health (which in 1924 included Housing) and he was one of the very few successes of Ramsay MacDonald's short-lived Government. Wheatley did a great deal to encourage the building of council houses with indoor toilets. He was also a regular attender at Celtic Park.

The other thing about the 1923/24 season was that there was still sting in the tail as Celtic won the Glasgow Charity Cup by beating Rangers 2-1 in the final on Saturday, 10 May 1924. The comparatively inexperienced Paddy Connolly and Jimmy McGrory made their mark, but behind them was the veteran Alec McNair, who after a slow start, gained ascendancy over Alan Morton and won what proved to be his last winner's medal for the club. It was a sweet moment for Celtic and their supporters in the 30,000 crowd, enjoying the pleasant sunshine which "improved tempers" after some recent performances. It reminded historians of 1903, when Sunny Jim Young was introduced in a Glasgow Cup final, and of 1913 when it was Charlie Shaw. In 1924, it was the turn of Jimmy McGrory.

Surely now, it was time for Eck to retire? He might well have, if any other club like Falkirk or his own Stenhousemuir, for example, had made him an offer as Player Manager. McNair's knowledge of the game was unsurpassable, as indeed was his love of the game. He had played football with or against the best players of his day, had countless Scottish caps and medals, and he was still very fit, something that he worked at in his determination to keep going. Yet no-one, as far as we can ascertain, made any offer and there was a reluctance on the part of either Alec McNair or Willie Maley to cut the knot, and so he remained at Celtic for another year.

Alec played just 12 games in season 1924/25, usually only as cover for injuries, because the right-back was now definitely Willie McStay, a man who was very prepared to acknowledge all that he had learned from McNair. The season was, in some ways, a typical Celtic campaign of that era, with inconsistency the order of the day in the League but redeemed (and how!) by a magnificent Scottish Cup run which included the 5-0 semi-final victory against Rangers and a great 2-1 win over Dundee in the final, to secure a record 11th success. All that is largely due, as we know, to Patsy Gallacher and Jimmy McGrory, but, it would be a fool who would not acknowledge the unseen contribution of Eck McNair, providing his own calm and reassuring words of comfort and wisdom in the dressing-room and the training sessions.

Saturday, 18 April 1925, one week after the Scottish Cup triumph, seems to have seen Eck play his last game for Celtic, in a 1-1 draw against Queen's Park at Parkhead, his 584rd League match for the club, a record which stands to this day, almost a century later. Indeed, it may never be equalled. Born on the Christmas Eve of 1882, McNair was now well into his 43rd year as he finally bowed out as a first-team player at Celtic. Again, no Celt who followed him has surpassed that achievement, indeed, we can "leave it to Chairlie" to become the only other man to have played for Celtic in his fifth decade, the great goalkeeper and now club captain Shaw being 33 days beyond his 40th birthday when he turned out at Cappielow six months after Eck's last game, on Saturday, 24 October 1925. There must have been something in the Parkhead water at that time, as three of the next four names on that 'Oldest Celt' list are McNair's contemporaries, Jimmy McMenemy, Jimmy McStay and his older brother, Willie.

Retirement was now not far away, and Eck McNair may have decided that he would go back to work in the iron works in Falkirk. He was by no means a wealthy man, albeit he had earned enough from football to mean that his lifestyle for himself and his two children was adequate and comfortable at a time when few people would have been able to say that. His savings may have also allowed him a certain amount of leeway to decide when he was going to retire.

"Relentless Anno Domini," as it was called, may now have caught up with Alec and called time on his playing career, after well over 20 years with his beloved Celtic FC, but, he was not yet completely finished with football. Eck still loved the game, and in the spring of 1925, a bid was made for his services. It was from Dundee, the team so recently beaten by Celtic in the Scottish Cup final. They were looking for a manager.

CHAPTER NINE

MANAGER OF DUNDEE (1925-1927)

On Friday, 5 June 1925, Alec McNair became the new manager of Dundee. His appointment had followed a period of negotiation, with McNair wondering whether this was the job for him. He realised that his playing career, lengthy and impressive, was now over and a part of him wanted to go back to Stenhousemuir and return to the job that he had done before joining Celtic – a grate fitter.

But he loved football. It was often felt that he would have done a good job as assistant manager to Willie Maley at Celtic, with a view to taking over some day, but, no offer ever came. This may have been because the traditionally parsimonious Celtic board felt that they couldn't afford an assistant, or possibly because it was felt that McNair's religion might have been a problem, or possibly just because the increasingly curmudgeonly Willie Maley simply didn't want anyone, even Eck who had always been one of his favourites.

McNair was now prepared to listen to offers. There may have been others, but, the one he chose was Dundee. Apparently, they had been keen on Alec as a player in the days of 1906 and 1907, when there was no obvious slot for him in the Celtic team, yet he was far too good a player not to play for someone. But Dundee's polite and discreet enquiries at that point had been quietly refused.

Dundee is a strange city, with a very right-wing newspaper which sells to almost every house in town whilst most of its readers vote in the other direction! That was true in 1925, and it remains true almost 100 years later. The good thing for a historian about this is that the fortunes of both Dundee and Dundee Hibernian/United are well chronicled. The games are reported in a stable of newspapers - The Courier, The Evening Telegraph and The Sporting Post on a Saturday night, and The Sunday Post. Naturally, one has to allow for a certain amount of local bias, but there is also, from time to time, a pro-Celtic bias (rare in a Tory newspaper) because, of course, they had to allow for Dundee's vast Irish population. When Tommy Gallacher - Patsy's son - wrote in The Courier in the 1950s and 1960s, that bias was quite pronounced!

Today, Dundee has two teams with a yoyo relationship to the Premier Division. In 1925, there was one good team and one poor team. Dundee were respectable, having won the Scottish Cup in 1910 and, as McNair well knew, reached the final this very April. They were well supported, always tough to beat, particularly at Dens Park, and since the War, they had had some fine players, whom Eck had played against. Their Directors had a fatal flaw – since then melancholically maintained – that of selling their best players when they didn't really have to. In 1923, for example, Dundee had sold their wonderfully talented left-winger Alec Troup on to Everton. In the 1960's, they would dismantle their 1962 League Championship-winning team by selling Ian Ure, Alan Gilzean and Andy Penman. Even when the prodigious Charlie Cooke arrived from Aberdeen, he lasted only a short time at Dens Park before he was moved on to Chelsea.

Dundee United, on the other hand, were a poor and poorly supported Second Division team. Until 1923, they had been Dundee Hibernian, but in a conscious and deliberate attempt to distance themselves from the Dundee Irish (who normally supported Celtic in any case!) they had changed their name to Dundee United. Some 50 years later, they distanced themselves even further from their Irish roots by deciding to wear orange strips – something that seemed to be going rather too far to the other extreme! In season 1924/25, however, they had excelled themselves and earned promotion to the First Division, so Alec McNair would have a rare couple of fixtures - Dundee derbies – to enjoy.

Dundee was sometimes called 'Juteopolis.' The manufacturing of jute bags for the GPO and industry was the order of the day and there were many jute factories (usually called 'the mills') in the city. The funny thing was that the 'jute barons' were numerous and there was no one huge factory or employer of labour. There were many smallish factories, but that meant there were loads of chimneys belching out smoke. The term "Bonnie Dundee" could only really apply to that 18th century Scottish historical character - Lord Graham of Claverhouse, Viscount Dundee - who did not, incidentally, like the Orangeman any more than the Celtic supporters did; it could not really apply to the city in the 1920s. Dundee was far from bonnie.

In one respect, however, Dundee was ahead of most of Scotland and the United Kingdom. This was in the employment of female workers. It is commonly supposed that women only started working in factories after the Great War. Not so, in Dundee. The nature of the work in jute factories was such that women could be employed (and paid much more cheaply by rascally employers), for there was no heavy lifting, for example, and women with their smaller fingers were more suited to weaving, in any case. Children too, particularly girls, were employed in an era of history which no-one had any right to feel proud about.

Dundonians, like the rest of Scotland, were passionate about their football. Alec McNair started with one great advantage, in that they already knew him and respected him for the gentlemanly and almost scholarly way in which he played the game. He was also well remembered for his 15 caps for Scotland and for the way that he had rescued Alec Troup and other Dundee players from the baying mob at Celtic Park in the riot of April 1920. He was already a well-known figure, a legend (to employ a slightly overused modern phrase), and the fact that McNair accepted the job said a great deal about the status that Dundee currently enjoyed in Scottish football.

It is a truism that a good player does not always make a good manager. The best managers are usually those who were 'good enough' but not great players – one thinks of Willie Maley, Jock Stein and Sir Alex Ferguson. None of these three was felt to be a brilliant football player, but, each one excelled in the management of his club and consequently won loads of honours.

The other thing that all of those three shared was the ability, when necessary, to turn nasty and ruthless. Each man could be charming, encouraging, polite, pleasant, humorous, knowledgeable and communicative. A football manager must be all these things, particularly to the fans and the Press. He must also be hard, unpleasant and ruthless. Bill Struth of Rangers had the nickname 'Ruthless Struth,' simply because there were times when he had to be. There is, for example, perhaps a place for sentiment in football on occasion. It must not, however, cloud a manager's judgement. A job has to be done, and the job consists of nothing more and nothing less than winning football matches.

Alec McNair ticked many boxes for being a manager. He was a diplomat, a communicator and a man who could cope well with the Press (a particular issue in Dundee, where the local Press was so strong and influential). He certainly knew the game and could assess a player. He also knew Scotland, in the sense that he was aware of which pitch was a good one and which could be unpredictable. He knew the referees, the crowds and the other managers. There seemed no reason why he could not be a success for the currently middle-ranking Dundee. His problem may well have been that he was not enough of a brute. Eck lacked the nastiness that was required. He was a gentleman, and gentlemen seldom make good managers.

Alec's first season was 1925/26 and Dundee finished exactly halfway up (or down) the Scottish League table with 37 points from 38 games. The club had sold its best goalscorer, Davie Halliday, to Sunderland for £4,000 – a decision apparently taken before McNair arrived as manager, and, thus, they were handicapped from the start. They still had, however, an old colleague of Eck's in Davie McLean, who had played for Celtic between 1907 and 1909, and who had enjoyed a long and varied career in the meantime. McLean was still a capable goalscorer, indeed, it had been he who had scored Dundee's goal in that April's Scottish Cup final against Celtic.

Form was patchy in the first part of the season. There was, for example, an astonishingly bad 0-5 defeat to Cowdenbeath, but on the other hand, on Saturday, 24 October 1925, Dundee managed to beat Rangers 2-1 at Ibrox, their first victory there since 1913. The following week, as luck would have it, saw Dundee at Celtic Park, and what a feather that would have been if McNair had managed to put one over Willie Maley and his old mates. But "You never were properly thrilled", was the verdict of The Dundee Courier of this 0-0 draw, which was as dull as it sounded. Nevertheless, it was a good result for Dundee to earn a point at Parkhead on the back of the victory at Ibrox, and Alec was well received by both the Celtic support and his old friends. There was also no scoring in a rather anti-climactic Dundee derby three weeks later, although when the teams met again at the primitive Tannadice Park early in the New Year of 1926, Davie McLean scored the only goal of the game.

Hopes might have been high for another Scottish Cup run after reaching the final the previous season. After a competent win over Highland League outfit Inverness Caledonian, Dundee were drawn against their traditional rivals Aberdeen and managed a 0-0 draw at Pittodrie. Some 9,681 spectators were able to persuade their employers that they were ill on the Wednesday afternoon for the replay at Dens Park, but most of them would be very disappointed to see their team go down 3-0. This had followed a heavy snowfall in the morning then heroic efforts to clear the pitch of snow (with manager Alec McNair joining in) in order to get the game on. Sadly, for Dundee, it was all in vain.

Celtic came to Dens Park on Wednesday, 17 March 1926. (The game was postponed from the previous Saturday). Dundee actually scored first, but, Celtic chasing the League title and with the now returned Tommy McInally on song, won 2-1. The Courier did its best to say that Dundee deserved a draw, and in truth they were handicapped by an injury to 'Napper' Thomson, but Celtic showed that they were genuine League Championship contenders by winning without playing particularly well. Paddy Connolly and Jean McFarlane were singled out for praise in the other newspapers. Celtic did, in fact, win the title that year, but lost the Scottish Cup to St Mirren in the final. Alec McNair's Dundee, as mentioned earlier, finished halfway up the League table, 10th in the 20-club division.

For season 1926/27, Davie McLean had gone back to his native Forfar, and McNair turned to another ex-Celt to replace him, this time of more recent vintage. It was Joe Cassidy, who had scored the only goal of the game against Hibernian in the 1923 Scottish Cup final but had then gone to Bolton Wanderers. Joe was one of those players who "left home when he left Celtic," but, for a spell at least, he shone for Dundee. Indeed, it was one of the Dens Park club's better seasons, as they finished fifth, six points and two places behind Willie Maley's Celtic. City rivals Dundee United finished bottom and were relegated back to the Second Division, together with Morton.

Dundee enjoyed some good results this season, winning 17 of their 38 matches. The game at Celtic Park on the opening Saturday of October finished goalless, but Celtic then came to Dens Park two weeks in succession in February 1927 and won both matches, the first in the League and the other in the Scottish Cup. The League game was memorable as being the debut of a young goalkeeper from Fife called John Thomson. The nervous youth started well but was at least partly to blame for Dundee's goal in the latter stages of the first half. He recovered well to defy Joe Cassidy on several occasions, as Celtic scored twice at the other end through Alec Thomson and Jimmy McGrory to win 2-1.

The following week in the Scottish Cup, Celtic "with the three Macs in the Celtic van" – Jimmy McGrory, Tommy McInally and Adam McLean outstanding - won 4-2. Poor Joe Cassidy hardly got a kick of the ball, against the mighty half-back line of Peter Wilson, Willie McStay & Jean McFarlane, and the Celtic fans sang the Negro slave song "Poor Old Joe." He was, however, given a cheer at the end, as indeed was Alec McNair. It was rare for opposition players to get such a reception from Celtic supporters, albeit they were hardly, to Celtic eyes, your normal opposition players or manager!

After their exit from the Scottish Cup, Dundee rallied. Alec McNair had developed two very good players in forward Andy Campbell and wing-half Colin McNab and finishing in a respectable position such as fifth kept the club's supporters (and more importantly) The Courier happy. Eck was aware, though, that there was a distinct lack of ambition among the Dundee directors, who often gave the impression that they were only interested in selling on their best players, rather than maintaining any realistic challenge to the Glasgow Two.

Alec also found that he was not really enjoying the job of being a football manager, and after a very poor start to the 1927/28 season, he resigned on Friday, 7 October 1927. Perhaps, ironically, his last match in charge had been a home defeat to Willie Maley's Celtic, six days earlier. The whole thing was conducted with a certain amount of quiet dignity and a distinct absence of any vitriol or spite, but, even so it was a shock to the footballing world. A fan calling himself 'Carolina Port' (the name of Dundee's original ground before they moved to Dens Park) wrote a letter to The Courier deploring this decision, calling McNair "a loss to the city," adding that "he is one of the biggest monuments (sic) in Scottish football." He then sums it up by saying that "his situation may be filled but his place will be vacant."

McNair, now nearing his 45th birthday, was unhappy about all this, but it was in some ways a voyage of self-discovery. As in everything else in his life, he was cool and calm with a distinct lack of bitterness or rancour. He may have had his own feelings and views on certain things, but, he kept everything to himself.

Alec now retired from the game, but he certainly did not give it up. He was frequently seen at Brockville, Ochilview and Celtic Park, always willing to talk to everyone, always willing to give a quote to a journalist about a game, and always prepared to write the odd piece himself for a newspaper. He would remain a respected and much-loved character.

CHAPTER TEN

SUBSEQUENT LIFE AND ASSESSMENT (1927-1951)

Having left the manager's post at Dundee, Alec McNair now retired to a private life in Stenhousemuir. Little, in fact, is really known about what he did, other than that he was a stockbroker, and there were not many former football players who turn to that profession! Nor is it a profession that lends itself to banner headlines in newspapers for historians to hunt out. He set up business at 2 Bank Street, Falkirk in April 1928, with 'Celtic' the address for telegrams.

Between 1949 and 1951, until he had to give it up because of bad health, he was a Referee Supervisor. Now that was an excellent job for him! Referees and Alec McNair always had a great respect for each other. Eck was never in trouble on the field – it is difficult even to find any indication that a referee 'had a word' with him – nor was he ever quoted as saying that a referee had a bad game. He was intelligent enough to realise that referees had a difficult, even an impossible, job. Nor would he have had any truck with any bogus thinking that referees are institutionally against Celtic.

Eck's job as Referee Supervisor would have suited him down to the ground. He still loved the game, and this gave him the opportunity to travel to various grounds, sitting unobtrusively in the stand at Queen of the South, Forfar Athletic, Morton or Kilmarnock, noting how the referee performed, then, after the game, talking to the referee himself, offering constructive advice. Occasionally, he would have been recognised, but he would never have gone out of his way to be recognised. If someone had said, "Excuse me, if you don't mind me asking, but are you Alec McNair?" he would have acknowledged it and talked in a kindly fashion to the enquirer. No doubt, as sadly often happens in Scottish football, he would occasionally have been subject to boorish abuse from the intellectually challenged.

Alec McNair died in the early hours of Sunday, 18 November 1951 at his home at 5 Rae Street, Stenhousemuir of bronchial carcinoma, with an (unspecified) secondary carcinoma. He was 68 years old and had been ill for some time, latterly in a coma. The death certificate was signed by his son James, then living in Helensburgh, and Alec's occupation is given as stockbroker's clerk. McNair had been in a Glasgow nursing home but had returned home to Stenhousemuir about a week previously.

In his later years, Eck had been looked after by his family. They had always been very supportive, particular his two maiden sisters, Mary and Janet, who are now buried alongside him, together with his wife Mary and baby daughter Helen.

Alec was a well-known and well-loved local character in Stenhousemuir. His funeral was held at the beautiful Larbert Cemetery, and was well-attended, with wreaths from Celtic, Stenhousemuir FC, Rangers FC, the Scottish Football League, Falkirk Tryst Golf Club, Lodge Carron no 139, the Regal Falkirk Café Coffee Club and Willie Maley, who at 83 years old was now too ill to attend but sent his son, William junior (The wreath from Lodge Carron no 139 may raise an eyebrow or two from those who worry about such things!). A number of McNair's old friends from his playing days were at the cemetery to pay their last respects on the day. Those included his old full-back colleague Joe Dodds, Patsy Gallacher, Willie Loney, Jimmy McColl, Jimmy McOustra and George Jarvis and his International goalkeeper, Third Lanark's Jimmy Brownlie.

Celtic were represented by chairman Bob Kelly, manager Jimmy McGrory, plus directors Desmond White and Tom Devlin and several of the current players.

Tributes poured in for McNair, as they had done even when he was still playing. Almost every Scottish newspaper had something to say about him, all of it laudatory. It was hard to find anyone with a bad word to say about him, and tribute was paid to him at many grounds before the next game.

Such respect had been forthcoming for years. Willie Maley, in particular, had been very active in singing the praise of Alec McNair for a long time. "Shaw, McNair and Dodds understood one another so well that they developed the pass-back into a scientific move, of which there have been many imitators but none to equal the originators. It was indeed a spectacle to see either McNair or Dodds passing the ball, with unerring accuracy and cheeky coolness, to Shaw two yards away, with the opposing forwards almost on top of them. That was their method of getting out of a corner, which in all probability would otherwise have been fatal." (Weekly News, 25 July 1936)

On other occasions, usually in a column that he wrote in The Evening Times on a Saturday night, Maley (whose memory could sometimes be described as selective or even inaccurate, but never about McNair) wrote such things as; "The coolest, most intelligent player I have ever seen." "He had an obvious sincerity and the straight look." "Cool and calm." "Prosaic and practical." "Effective and methodical." "Dignified and judicious." "He was a treasure and a gentleman in every sense of the word. In his 20 years' service, I never once had reason to alter my first impression of him. Alec was the coolest and most intelligent and thoughtful player I have ever seen." "Nothing disturbed him and in our keenest tussles and most exciting experiences he maintained and unruffled demeanour. A most popular fellow in every company." "Alec McNair would have distinguished himself in any position, even in goal with that calm cool head and the sharp eyes."

Jock Bell, the referee, said that, "It was a delight to see him wait for his man, pounce just when the moment was right and clear with such crispness and confidence."

Bobby Archibald, a man of many clubs but particularly Raith Rovers, said, "I could never beat him...superb judgement...well-built but he seldom used his weight...a yielding back inviting you to come on, try it, turn back, sprint up the wing, cut in...it was all the same to Alec."

And the great Hughie Gallagher, who was younger than Alec McNair but played against him once or twice for Airdrieonians, said, "Brains with a minimum of bash...the greatest back I ever played against."

James E Handley, who saw McNair as a young man and was the writer of The Celtic Story, written in 1960, said, "As for McNair – well, he would have been the perfect subject for a 'time and motion' study if they had troubled about such things in those days. No footballer was his peer in the science of achieving the maximum result with the minimum of effort. The most dashing forward seemed to be mesmerised in his presence. He was gentled along until he had unprofitably crossed the bye-line or, alternatively, the ball was withdrawn from him, almost apologetically. Then McNair might elect to do something with it that shot up the blood pressure of the spectators but left him stone cold. His back-passing and dribbling in the goalmouth had the fascination for onlookers that the tightrope walker in the circus exercises on the audience, who know in their hearts that he is not going to fall but nevertheless await the unexpected. His distribution was uncannily economical, for he was supreme in the art of making the ball do the work."

So how good was he? No-one is now left who saw him play, but those of us with fathers, grandfathers and great-grandfathers who saw him will, no doubt, recall being told about how good he was. He was 'The Icicle' because he was so cool and because he was one of the best players around. Possibly the closest parallel in living memory was Danny McGrain. Those of us who saw Danny at his best saw how the normally unspectacular position of right-back could be made to look entertaining and thrilling. Those who saw Eck McNair would have felt likewise.

In his memoirs in The Sunday Post in 1920 (when he still had a few years of his career still to go), McNair says that he never had any "prepared programme of how to outwit an opponent." He felt that it was necessary to see the team formation, to make allowances for weather conditions, to assess how his colleagues were coping with their direct opponent, to have a look at the referee to see if he was going to be tough or lenient, the demeanour of the crowd and all sort of other things.

He gives a list of all the opponents that he found difficult – Sandy MacFarlane and Jack Fraser - and later Alec Troup - of Dundee, Bobby Templeton, not without cause called the 'Blue Streak' when he played for Kilmarnock after leaving Celtic, Willie Smith of Hibernian, Willie Wilson of Hearts, Alex Smith of Rangers and Alan Morton of Queen's Park. On the International front, Alec enjoyed his jousts with Arthur Bridgett of Sunderland and England, and Ted Vizard of Bolton Wanderers and Wales.

Of the men he played with for Celtic, Eck McNair clearly loved them all, on a personal level singling out Peter Somers for his ability to entertain on and off the field and to play practical jokes on everyone. Alec could never bring himself to say, "James Young," or "Jimmy Young." It was always "Sunny Jim," or even just "Sunny." Jimmy McMenemy was clearly a class act, and Jimmy Quinn was simply Jimmy Quinn. Adjectives fail the writer when Patsy Gallacher is described. It was great to play alongside such men, and under Willie Maley, the man who made Celtic. McNair enjoyed playing for them. He never really wanted to play for anyone else and enjoyed the camaraderie of the dressing-room and Seamill Hydro and other places. He was one of the many men who was not born into Celtic, but came to love them for the intangible, indescribable thing that Celtic is.

Alec remained a great character beyond his football career. At a golf tournament one time, he was being followed by a crowd and was stuck in a bunker, clearly in doubt what to do with the ball. Someone in the crowd suggested that he "Pass it back to Chairlie," and Eck himself laughed. On another occasion, Celtic were playing Partick Thistle at cricket at Hamilton Crescent. As befitted a man from Stenhousemuir, he was quite good at cricket, and on this occasion, he scored 20, but admitted that he was upstaged by a great catch taken by Bobby Templeton.

For his beloved Celtic, Alec McNair played a total of 584 Scottish League games, 57 Scottish Cup games, 45 Glasgow Cup games, 30 Glasgow Charity Cup games and numerous friendlies and tour matches. Those would make up an incredible total of 716 appearances.

He won 12 Scottish League medals (assuming he was given one for playing in the Play-off in 1905), in 1904/05, 1905/06, 1906/07, 1907/08, 1908/09, 1909/10, 1913/14, 1914/15, 1915/16, 1916/17, 1918/1919 and 1921/22.

He won six Scottish Cup medals, in 1906/07, 1907/08, 1910/11, 1911/12, 1913/14 and 1922/23.

He won seven Glasgow Cup medals, in 1906/07, 1907/08, 1909/10, 1915/16, 1916/17, 1919/20 and 1920/21.

He won nine Glasgow Charity Cup medals, in 1911/12, 1912/13, 1913/14, 1914/15, 1915/16, 1916/17, 1917/18, 1919/20 and 1923/24.

He played 15 times in Full Internationals for Scotland and made a further 15 appearances for the Scottish League.

That was quite a haul! And it doesn't even begin to tell you how great a player he was!

CHAPTER ELEVEN

FIFTEEN CONTEMPORARIES OF ALEC McNAIR

WILLIE MALEY (1868-1958) is commonly referred to as 'The Man Who Made Celtic.' Maley played in Celtic's very first game in May 1888 and was a good, although not outstanding, right-half. He did excel at administration and became a committee member, sometimes called Match Secretary until 1897, when he was officially appointed Celtic's Secretary/Manager on a professional basis. His first few years in that role were not particularly successful, but, by 1904 a great Celtic team had emerged, and the club won six successive League titles between 1905 and 1910, including the famous season of 1907/08, when Celtic won every competition for which they had entered. During the Great War of 1914-18, Celtic also dominated Scottish football but Maley was then less consistently successful in the 1920s, even though he had many fine players, such as Patsy Gallacher, Jimmy McGrory and John Thomson.

In the last few seasons of the 1930s, after a period in the doldrums, Willie Maley's team were back amongst the domestic honours, winning two League titles, the Scottish Cup of 1937, then the all-British Empire Exhibition Trophy of June 1938. He retired in unhappy circumstances in February 1940, replaced by his old captain, Jimmy McStay, and was persona non grata at Celtic Park for a spell until making his peace with the club in the early 1950s. Maley's death on 2 April 1958, just three weeks or so before his 90th birthday, was a source of great sadness for Celtic supporters all over the world.

JIMMY QUINN (1878-1945) was the darling of all Celtic supporters, and a much-loved and well-known character in Edwardian Britain. A shy, retiring miner from Croy in Dunbartonshire, Jimmy first played for Celtic at the turn of the century, albeit it was not until April 1904 that he really made his mark with a hat-trick in the Scottish Cup final victory over Rangers. Quinn was never really a rough player, but he knew how to 'bump' or shoulder-charge goalkeepers. He was twice suspended after being sent off in games against Rangers, unjustly in both cases. However, he returned to play a great part in Celtic's sustained success until injuries caught up with him in the latter part of 1913.

Jimmy played his last game for the club in January 1915, but he was never keen to leave Celtic Park, coming in to help Willie Maley (without being paid for it) with coaching and advice, and he was never too proud to be seen doing menial tasks like carrying the hamper off the train at away games. Quinn lived in Croy all his life until his passing in November 1945, Jimmy never really getting over the death of his son John, an Argyll and Sutherland Highlander, a year earlier, whilst in action in Holland. The great Billy Meredith, of Manchester City, Manchester United and Wales, appeared at his funeral in Kilsyth, freely admitting that "Jimmy Quinn was the best goalscorer of them all."

JIMMY YOUNG (1882-1922) was commonly known as Sunny Jim or Sunny and was generally regarded as being one of the best Celtic players of them all. A Kilmarnock man, Young joined Celtic in 1903 from Bristol Rovers and within a year had settled down as right-half of a great Celtic team. Fiercely loyal and much-loved by the supporters and manager Willie Maley, Sunny played for Celtic until September 1916, when injury compelled his retirement.

Perhaps lacking the elegance of a Peter Wilson or a Pat Crerand (which perhaps explains why he did not play more often for Scotland), Young was, nevertheless, a determined, gritty and rugged defender, even, on one occasion, playing in goal, in his native Kilmarnock in a League fixture at New Year 1909, when goalkeeper Davie Adams had been injured the day before! Sunny Jim Young became captain of Celtic in 1911 and led the great 1914 side with his two famous war cries of “Face the ball, Celts” or, at a corner or free-kick, “Tak a man apiece.” He enjoyed winding up the opposition support, but, there was no better-loved man in all of Scottish football than Sunny Jim. His sudden death in September 1922 was a tragic one, the former Celtic captain involved in a motorcycle accident near Darvel, in Ayrshire, at the age of just 40.

WILLIE LONEY (1879-1956) was a great centre-half in a club which has been rich in such players and is well worthy of a mention in the same breath as Jimmy McStay, Willie Lyon, Bobby Evans and Billy McNeill. He was born in Denny in Stirlingshire, and a feature of Loney was the large number of nicknames he was given, like ‘The Denier,’ ‘The Obliterator,’ ‘The Gobbler’ or ‘No Road This Way.’ He was a hard tackler, good in the air and had a great positional sense with the ability to read a game.

Never known as a speedy player, Willie, nevertheless, had a good turn of pace when required. He was an unlucky player as far as injuries were concerned, suffering a broken arm in 1907 and various leg injuries at other points. He played, of course, as an attacking centre-half, often interchanging position during a game with his great friend, Jimmy Quinn, and it is a mystery why he never got more of an opportunity to play for Scotland. He had two great wing-halves beside him, in Sunny Jim Young and Jimmy Hay. However, he was a worthy member of that great troika of astonishing proficiency, versatility and cohesion. Loney's attacking forays up the field yielded him a career total of 33 goals.

JAMES HAY (1881-1940) was a fine left-half and an outstanding Celtic captain, taking over when Willie Orr disappeared from the scene in 1907. An Ayrshireman, Jimmy Dun Hay was not necessarily the best player in that fine side, but, he was the man who kept it all together and brought out the best in the others, being Willie Maley's mouthpiece on the field, geeing up Jimmy Quinn and keeping Sunny Jim Young quiet in order to produce a team, the likes of which one is unlikely to see ever again. Hay had his health problems as well, not least in January 1908 when he fell dangerously ill with appendicitis. He recovered well though, and by the spring of that year captained the side to their grand slam.

In 1911, for reasons never well explained, Jimmy moved to Newcastle United to take over the role of Peter McWilliam, who had been injured whilst playing for Scotland. Hay fitted in well there, but, his best football was played for Celtic. A man of the utmost integrity, he became manager of Ayr United after the war and resigned from that post after reporting a director of that club, who had tried to bribe a referee. Jimmy died in April 1940, a much loved and respected figure in the game.

JIMMY McMENEMY (1880-1965) hailed from Rutherglen. Known as Napoleon, he was one of the best football players to ever play for the club, being an outstanding inside-right and then seamlessly moving to inside-left to accommodate Patsy Gallacher. McMenemy was a very complete player, both a maker of goals and a scorer of them, notably his famous strike at Celtic Park against Rangers on New Year's Day 1914.

It was often said that football was like a chess board to McMenemy, for he could more or less move wherever he wanted, a feature of his play being his ability to know exactly what weight to put on a pass. He was a very calm individual whose catch phrase was "Keep the heid, Celtic." Jimmy played for Celtic from 1902 until 1920, surviving a serious dose of Spanish Flu a few days after the Great War ended, from which he recovered to play an important part in the winning of the 1919 League Championship. After he left Celtic in 1920, he won a Scottish Cup medal in 1921 with Partick Thistle, to add to the six he had won at Parkhead. Then, from the mid 1930s onwards, he returned to be trainer and de facto manager of the Celtic team which won the Empire Exhibition Trophy of 1938.

ALEC BENNETT (1880-1940) came from Rutherglen around the same time as Jimmy McMenemy. The Artful Dodger was one of the best right-wingers in Celtic's history, but, for reasons of ethnicity (which existed in his own mind rather than anywhere else, for it was never a problem with men like Sunny Jim Young and indeed Eck McNair), Alec was never truly happy at Celtic Park, claiming that Rangers wanted him and that he wanted to go there. And all this was in spite of the efforts of Willie Maley and Alec's great friend, Jimmy McMenemy. Bennett's attitude was even more surprising in view of the outstanding success that he enjoyed at Celtic Park and the warm affection in which he was held by the supporters.

He eventually got his wish in 1908, but not before he had shown the world what a great right-winger he was. Alec's best years were those he spent with Celtic. He was speedy, had "intelligent feet," could cross a ball and take a goal (he had been a centre-forward at one stage of his career) and played well when he got the opportunity for Scotland. His departure from Celtic to Rangers lacked the venom and the treachery of Maurice Johnston's similar decision in 1989, but, it was equally wrong-headed. After the Great War, Bennett became the manager of Third Lanark.

PETER SOMERS (1878-1914) was from Strathaven, and with his small figure he became known as the 'Powder Monkey,' in a very appropriate image for the man who supplied the ammunition for men like Jimmy Quinn. Peter's contribution to Celtic has sometimes been undervalued by historians, but certainly not by the supporters of the time who adored him. Somers was also much-loved by his teammates, not least for the fact that he was very sociable, had a great sense of humour and could play the piano. This was a valuable asset on the European tours or the trips to Rothesay and Highland hotels to prepare for big games.

His regular position in the team was at inside-left and he was a forager of the old-fashioned type, whose role was to go and find the ball. This occasionally involved helping out the defence, but Peter was able to do exactly that, his best game possibly being the 1907 Scottish Cup final against Hearts, in which he scored twice. Somers arrived at Celtic Park before the majority of that great team and left in 1910 to play for Hamilton Academical for a spell. His death, at the age of just 36 in November 1914, was a premature and a sudden one, following gangrene in his leg and an amputation.

CHARLIE SHAW (1885-1938) was possibly one of the most loved Celtic players of all time, certainly as great a goalkeeper as John Thomson or Ronnie Simpson, and it was said that the only reason he never won a Scotland Cap was because the 10 outfield Celts were so good that he never got enough practice!

Charlie was born in Twechar, played for Port Glasgow Athletic and then moved to London and Queen's Park Rangers before joining Celtic in 1913. It was his performances in his first season which showed what a great goalkeeper he was, with his long list of shutouts along with Alec McNair and Joe Dodds.

Shaw became the captain of Celtic in 1923 when Willie Cringan moved to Third Lanark, and was an inspiring figure, about whom very few people ever had a bad word to say, even the opposition supporters, who sang songs about him in a way that one could almost describe as affectionate. He had the advantage of looking like everyone's favourite uncle, but behind that pleasant exterior, there existed a stern firmness, particularly in his views on the way that professional football players were treated. When Charlie lost his Celtic place to Peter Shevlin in 1925, he emigrated to the USA, where he died in 1938.

PATSY GALLACHER (1891-1953) is regarded by many as the greatest football player of them all, and certainly his trickery, ball-winning skills and ability to take a goal were second to none, acknowledged as such in the Press reports of the time. Gallacher was born in Donegal and his family were living in Clydebank when he joined the club in 1911. Although slightly built and the butt of a few jokes from people who should have known better, Patsy soon impressed with his play and the success of the Celtic team in that outstanding 1913/14 season owed a great deal to the magnificent inside-forward play of himself and Jimmy McMenemy.

When war came, he acquired almost legendary status among the soldiers in the trenches, as Celtic enjoyed more or less of a monopoly of honours back home, and his success continued into the 1920s, culminating in his famous 'somersault' goal in the 1925 Scottish Cup final win over Dundee. A few months after that, Patsy moved to Falkirk, but his heart was always at Parkhead, and on one famous occasion the Celtic fans sang "Will Ye No Come Back Again?" for one of their favourite Celts of all time. To have witnessed Patsy in his prime was a treat and an honour, many an old-timer silencing an argument on football players by saying, "Look! I saw Patsy Gallacher!"

TOMMY McINALLY (1899-1955) from Barrhead might well have been Celtic's best-ever player, if he had been able to suppress his self-destruct instincts. Tommy remained a hero with the Celtic crowd, not least because he was one of them, in spite of the comparative lack of achievement when his early years betokened so much. He played for Celtic in two spells, 1919-1922 and 1925-1928.

He began as the 'Boy Wonder' in 1919, with magnificent ball control, speed and a devastating shot. But he lacked self-control, and in 1922, his clowning when Celtic were going out of the Scottish Cup at home to Hamilton Academical meant that he was dropped then transferred to Third Lanark. McInally's second spell at Parkhead was remarkably similar to his first, with a great first season in which he and Jimmy McGrory led the team to the Scottish League Championship. But this fine form was not maintained, and in 1928 Tommy was off once again, this time to Sunderland, for whom he was no great success. He wasn't always a great team man, but, for some reason, Willie Maley repeatedly made excuses for his wild and erratic behaviour, which included walking out on the team on several occasions. And yet Tommy McInally remained a cult hero. What a pity he couldn't behave himself!

JOE DODDS (1887-1965) came from Carluke and joined the club in 1908. He was a left-sided player who could play at both left-half or left-back, but it was at full-back that he excelled himself, particularly in the 1913/14 season, when Shaw, McNair & Dodds gave nothing away. In April 1914, Joe also had an outstanding game in Scotland's 3-1 win over England at Hampden. Solid and dependable, slightly more of an attacking full-back than normal for the times, Dodds was a great team man, never thinking that he was in any way better than anyone else.

The Great War came at a bad time for his career. Joe's brother was killed at the Battle of Loos in 1915, and he himself served as a driver in the Royal Field Artillery. He returned from the conflict to win the League in 1919. However, in 1920, he fell out with Willie Maley and went to play at Cowdenbeath for a season. He subsequently played for Queen of the South, before returning to Celtic Park in the late 1930s as a backroom man, alongside his old friend Jimmy McMenemy. Unlike many players of that era, Joe Dodds lived a long life, eventually dying at the age of 78 in October 1965.

JIMMY GORDON (1888-1954) from Saltcoats was probably RANGERS' best player in Alec's era and is often unfairly portrayed as a 'hard man.' He was actually a very fine wing-half, possibly the Rangers equivalent of Sunny Jim Young of Celtic, whose enthusiasm caused him to do and say the occasional unwise thing. Gordon joined Rangers in 1907, where he proved his versatility by playing in several positions before settling down in the right-half position. He won three Scottish League medals in 1911, 1912 and 1913, and 14 Scotland caps, playing alongside McNair on several occasions.

During the war, Jimmy was a Sergeant in the Highland Light Infantry and was able to 'guest' for several other clubs, most notably Hearts and Fulham. Much-loved by the Ibrox support, he was tough and competitive but basically very fair, and he became a great friend of many of the Celtic players, including Alec McNair. Indeed, Gordon was happy to don the green-and-white to play in Alec's Benefit match in January 1921. In 1920, he had left Rangers to play for Dunfermline Athletic for a spell before finally retiring and opening a set of billiard halls in Glasgow, together with his former Ibrox colleague, Jimmy Galt.

ALEC TROUP (1895-1952) played for his hometown team Forfar Athletic, then moved to DUNDEE, Everton and Dundee again. Alec was a tricky little player, standing not much taller than 5 feet, a man with the ball-playing ability of Jimmy Johnstone but perhaps lacking the 'devil' that 'Jinky' had.

The way that McNair and Troup treated each other when Celtic faced Dundee drew much comment in newspapers as being the way that football should be played. (There were other players on both sides who were a great deal less gentlemanly in their approach to the game) The men were, of course, International colleagues and McNair is given a great deal of credit for rescuing Troup and other Dundee players from the baying crowd on that disgraceful day of the Parkhead riot in April 1920.

Troup joined Everton in 1923 and played a big part in the Goodison club winning the English First Division title in 1928, famously taking the corner-kick from which Dixie Dean broke the goalscoring record on the last day of the season. After he retired, Troup returned to his native Forfar and his gentlemen's outfitters shop, where he died in early 1952, a much-loved and admired figure, only a few weeks after his old friend Alec McNair.

JESSE PENNINGTON (1883-1970) It was often considered an honour to have played on the same field, even in opposition, as 'Peerless Pennington,' and, of course, Alec McNair had that honour on several occasions when Scotland played England. The feeling was reciprocated, for Pennington held McNair in equally high esteem. A left-back, and generally reckoned to be the best defender in England, Jesse played for WEST BROMWICH ALBION from 1903 to 1922, more or less the same period that Eck played for Celtic!

His greatest moment was captaining the Baggies to the English title in the first post-war season of 1919/20. Renowned for his gentlemanly behaviour, Pennington might have prevented Barnsley's winning goal, but this might have involved a foul and he refused to do this. And on another occasion, when his team were offered a bribe to throw a game, he reported the matter to the police, after seeming to go along with it so that the culprits could be arrested. He played 25 times for England, and in domestic football, Jesse appeared for no-one other than his beloved West Bromwich Albion.

CHAPTER TWELVE

INTERNATIONAL & REPRESENTATIVE CAREER

Alec McNair played in 15 full Scotland Internationals. In his time, Scotland only played three Internationals per season, against the other three British or 'Home' nations.

It was generally recognised that the teams who played against Wales and Ireland did not necessarily reflect the best players available (for example, Anglo-Scots - men who played for English clubs - were frequently not considered), for the games against these countries were often seen as merely trial matches for what was referred to as 'The International' between Scotland and England. Scotland v England was, after all, the oldest International fixture in world football, dating back to 30 November 1872.

Any study of International football, particularly Scottish International football, however, will often find it difficult to give any rational explanation of team selections!

This was particularly true in McNair's day, when the team was chosen by a panel of Selectors, often club chairmen, whose knowledge of the playing side of the game was often somewhat limited!

It is probably not true (as was frequently claimed) that there was some sort of institutional bias against Celtic players. The facts simply do not support this contention, but, that does not mean that the best side was always the one chosen!

....

1. SCOTLAND 0 WALES 2; Tynecastle Park, Edinburgh; Saturday, 3 March 1906

Alec could hardly have chosen a worse start to his International career. In front of a huge 25,000 crowd at a packed Tynecastle, a Scotland team wearing the primrose and pink colours of Earl Roseberry deservedly lost to Wales for the first time on home soil. McNair was at right-half and was described by The Courier as being "somewhat feeble in his tackling, although in placing had no superior on the field." Eck himself praised the three Jones players in the Welsh side, and also the performance of Leighton 'Dick' Roose in the Welsh goal.

Scotland: Raeside, MacLeod & Richmond; McNair, Thomson & May; Stewart, MacFarlane, Quinn, Fitchie & Wilson.

Wales: Roose, Blew & Morris; Hughes, Morgan-Owen & Latham; W. Jones, Morris, J. Jones, R. Jones & Evans.

Referee - Mr Lewis, England

....

2. SCOTLAND 3 IRELAND 0; Celtic Park, Glasgow; Saturday, 16 March 1907

Unaccountably, Alec McNair was played at left-half by the Scottish selectors, and not surprisingly, his performance was not up to his usual standard. Scotland, however, still won comfortably. Shortly after Scotland scored their third goal (from the penalty spot), referee Mr Lewis blew for time five minutes early, as the conditions of wind and rain were becoming farcical.

Scotland: Muir, Jackson & Agnew; Key, Thomson & McNair;

Bennett, Walker, O'Rourke, Somers & Fraser.

Ireland: Scott, Willis & McCartney; Wright, Connor & McLure; Blair, Maxwell, McGuire, O'Hagan & Young.

Referee - Mr Lewis, England

....

3. SCOTLAND 2 WALES 1; Dens Park, Dundee; Saturday, 7 March 1908

McNair scarcely put a foot wrong for Celtic this season, and it was the same here in this entertaining game at Dens Park before 18,000 spectators, where Scotland fought back from being 0-1 down at half-time to record their first win against Wales since 1903. The hero of the hour was left-winger Willie Lennie of Aberdeen, who scored a great goal to win the game.

Scotland: Rennie, Agnew & Chaplin; McNair, Thomson & Galt; Bennett, Walker, Spiers, MacFarlane & Lennie.

Wales: Roose, Blew & Morris; Hughes, Parry & L. Davies; W.C. Davies, Jones, W. Davies, Green & Evans.

Referee - Mr Mason, England

....

4. SCOTLAND 1 ENGLAND 1; Hampden Park, Glasgow; Saturday, 4 April 1908

A record crowd, given as 121,452 but commonly believed to be more than that, saw a disappointing match, which ended in a 1-1 draw. It was all the more disappointing because Scotland were leading for so long in the game, and it was, in any case, widely believed that England's goal did not cross the line. McNair himself was not 100% sure but tends to think that the referee was correct. There were one or two break-ins caused by overcrowding. Alec had his work cut out against left-winger Arthur Bridgett of Sunderland, and a draw was generally agreed to be a fair result. Scotland might have won if Jimmy Quinn had been in the centre rather than out on the left wing.

Scotland: McBride, McNair & Sharp; Aitken, Thomson & May; Howie, Walker, Wilson, White & Quinn.

England: Hardy, Crompton & Pennington; Warren, Wedlock & Lintott; Rutherford, Woodward, Hilsdon, Windridge & Bridgett.

Referee - Mr Mason, England

....

5. ENGLAND 2 SCOTLAND 0; Crystal Palace, London; Saturday, 3 April 1909

One of Alec McNair's poorest games. Scotland never really recovered from the loss of two early goals from George Wall of Manchester United. The Scotland side, McNair included, were simply outplayed by England. McNair was once again playing at right-half, although he was now an established right-back. Jimmy Stark missed a penalty kick, after several players had refused to take it! The Crystal Palace had a reputation for intimidating players sometimes, and this was one of them!

England: Hardy, Crompton & Pennington; Warren, Wedlock & Lintott; Pentland, Fleming, Freeland, Holley & Wall.

Scotland: Brownlie, Cameron & Watson; McNair, Stark & McWilliam; Bennett, Walker, Quinn, Wilson & Paul.

Referee - Mr Stark, Scotland

....

6. SCOTLAND 1 WALES 0; Rugby Park, Kilmarnock; Saturday, 5 March 1910

Once again, Alec McNair was played out of position, but played well enough in this somewhat scrappy 1-0 victory before a record crowd for Kilmarnock of 22,000. Andrew Devine of Falkirk scored a great goal in the last five minutes to give Scotland a victory when a draw might have been a fairer result. Scotland struggled after Jimmy McMenemy suffered a bad injury. Note that the Welsh goalkeeper, the legendary Leighton Roose, played his one and only game for Celtic at Shawfield seven days later.

Scotland: Brownlie, Law & Mitchell; McNair, Loney & Hay; Bennett, McMenemy, Quinn, Devine & Robertson.

Wales: Roose, J. Jones & C. Morris; Hughes, Peake & L. Davies; Meredith, W. Davies, E. Jones, A. Morris & Evans.

Referee – Mr Bamlett, England

....

7. SCOTLAND 1 WALES 0; Tynecastle Park, Edinburgh; Saturday, 2 March 1912

Jimmy Quinn's late goal was enough to give Scotland victory. The Scots had attacked for most of the game but had been unable to break through until Quinn scored "one of these goals he is justly famous for," according to The Scotsman.

Scotland: Brownlie, McNair & J. Walker; Mercer, Thomson & Hay; Sinclair, McMenemy, Quinn, R. Walker & Robertson.

Wales: Evans, Llewelyn Davies & Lloyd Davies; J. Jones, Hughes &

Russell; Meredith, Wynn, E. Jones, Williams & Vizard.

Referee – Mr Mason, England

....

8. IRELAND 1 SCOTLAND 4; Windsor Park, Belfast; Saturday, 16 March 1912

Eck McNair was made Scotland captain for this game, (an odd decision because he was not at that time the skipper of Celtic) and clearly made a very good job of it against a poor Irish team. Belfast was, in 1912, a political hotbed and would continue to be so for many years. It was a good day for Scotland all round, because the rugby team won the Calcutta Cup that day by beating England at Inverleith.

Ireland: Hanna, Willis & Craig; Darling, O'Connell & Moran; Houston, McKnight, McAuley, Enright & Young.

Scotland: Brownlie, McNair & J. Walker; Gordon, Low & Bell; Sinclair, R. Walker, Reid, Aitkenhead & Templeton.

Referee – Mr Bamlett, England

....

9. SCOTLAND 1 ENGLAND 1; Hampden Park, Glasgow; Saturday, 23 March 1912

McNair was still team captain and led Scotland to an honourable 1-1 draw before an astonishing crowd of 127,307. Both sides scored early in the game, and from then on, they could not be separated. A draw was a fair result. Both Bobby Templeton and Jimmy Quinn were playing in the wrong position.

Scotland: Brownlie, McNair & J. Walker; Gordon, Thomson & Hay;

Templeton, R. Walker, McLean, Wilson & Quinn.

England: Williamson, Crompton & Pennington; Brittleton, Wedlock & Makepeace; Simpson, Jefferis, Freeman, Holley & Wall.

Referee – Mr Mason, England

....

10. ENGLAND 1 SCOTLAND 0; Stamford Bridge, London; Saturday, 5 April 1913

Scotland lost this game to a shoulder charge by Joe Hampton on goalkeeper Jimmy Brownlie. It was an unfortunate goal to lose, but England were possibly just the better team. A crowd of 52,000 saw this game in which Alec McNair played well throughout, and Scotland had hard luck when Andy Wilson hit the crossbar near the end.

England: Hardy, Crompton & Pennington; Brittleton, McCall & Watson; Simpson, Fleming, Hampton, Holley & Hodkinson.

Scotland: Brownlie, McNair & J. Walker; Gordon, Thomson & D. Wilson; Donnachie, R. Walker, Reid, A. Wilson & Robertson.

Referee – Mr Jackson, Scotland

....

11. IRELAND 1 SCOTLAND 1; Windsor Park, Belfast; Saturday, 14 March 1914

According to some accounts, Scotland eccentrically lined up in this game with Joe Dodds at right-back and Alec McNair at left-back! They changed to their more normal positions, however. It was a tough match played on a heavy pitch in front of a partisan crowd, with pistol shots apparently being heard. The political situation was tense, as Ireland was on the brink of civil war over the Home Rule bill! Scotland looked likely winners until Ireland equalised very late in the game. The Daily Record thinks that the Irishman was offside and that the referee was frightened to disallow the goal because of the intimidating atmosphere in the ground. The draw guaranteed Ireland the International Championship. Alec McNair was Scotland's captain.

Ireland: McKee, McConnell & Craig; Harris, O'Connell & Hamill; Houston, Nixon, Young, Lacey & Thompson.

Scotland: Brownlie, Dodds & McNair; Gordon, Thompson & Hay; Donaldson, McMenemy, Reid, Wilson & Donnachie.

Referee – Mr Bamlett, England

....

12. SCOTLAND 3 ENGLAND 1; Hampden Park, Glasgow; Saturday, 4 April 1914

Undoubtedly one of the proudest days in the life of Alec McNair, as he led Scotland to a 3-1 win over England at Hampden, in front of a crowd of 105,000. Jimmy McMenemy was the star of the show, but The Daily Record tells us that McNair "never gave Smith or Mosscrop a kick of the ball." It would be a game that would be recounted and retold many times in the trenches in the years to come. It was as well that the huge crowd did not know what was on the horizon.

Scotland: Brownlie, McNair & Dodds; Gordon, Thompson & Hay; Donaldson, McMenemy, Reid, Croal & Donnachie.

England: Hardy, Crompton & Pennington; Sturgess, McCall & McNeal; Walden, Fleming, Hampton, Smith & Mosscrop.

Referee – Mr Bamlett, England

....

13. WALES 1 SCOTLAND 1; Ninian Park, Cardiff; Thursday, 26 February 1920

In the first International after the war, played eccentrically on a Thursday afternoon before a small attendance of 16,000, Scotland looked as if they were heading for a defeat until Tommy Cairns of Rangers popped up to grab a late equaliser. A small band of Scottish supporters sang "Annie Laurie" in the stand but were drowned out by "Land of My Fathers."

Wales: Peers, Millership & Russell; Matthias, J. Jones & Jennings; Meredith, I. Jones, Davies, Richards & Evans.

Scotland: Campbell, McNair and Thompson; Gordon, Cringan & McMullan; Reid, Crosbie, Wilson, Cairns & Morton.

Referee – Mr Mason, England

....

14. SCOTLAND 3 IRELAND 0; Celtic Park, Glasgow; Saturday, 13 March 1920

Alec McNair once again captained his country for this match, in which a white-shirted Scotland side comfortably defeated a sadly outclassed Irish team, even with Patsy Gallacher in it! The highlight of the game was a great individual goal scored by Andy Wilson of Dunfermline. The crowd was a large one, just under 40,000.

Scotland: Campbell, McNair & Blair; Bowie, Low & Gordon; Donaldson, McMenemy, Wilson, Cunningham & Morton.

Ireland: Scott, Manderson & Rollo; Hamill, Lacey & Emerson; Robinson, Gallacher, Brooks, Gillespie & McCandless.

Referee - Mr Mason, England

....

15. ENGLAND 5 SCOTLAND 4; Hillsborough, Sheffield; Saturday, 10 April 1920

A crazy match, which was played on a quagmire of a pitch. Had it not been an International, with a large crowd assembling to see the first official Scotland v England game after the Great War, it is probable that the game would have been postponed. Good football was virtually impossible, and errors were frequent, as the players struggled to maintain their footing. Scotland, although 4-2 up at half-time, lost 4-5. Eck McNair was Scotland's captain, in what turned out to be his last International.

England: Hardy, Longworth & Pennington; Ducat, McCall & Grimsdell; Wallace, Kelly, Cock, Morris & Quantrill.

Scotland: Campbell, McNair & Blair; Bowie, Low & Gordon; Donaldson, Miller, Wilson, Paterson & Troup.

Referee – Mr Dougray, Scotland

....

McNair also played in 15 Scottish League Internationals. Those were often considered as 'stepping-stones' to full Internationals, the key difference being, of course, that only players currently signed with Scottish League clubs were eligible for 'caps.' The situation was complicated in England, for there were two Leagues operating there, one rather pompously calling itself the Football League (as if no-one else played the game!), consisting mainly of Midland and Northern clubs, and the second being the Southern League, containing London clubs plus south-coast based teams such as Southampton and Portsmouth. The Football League will be termed, for the sake of clarity here, the English League.

....

**1. ENGLISH LEAGUE 2 SCOTTISH LEAGUE 0; Villa Park, Birmingham;
Saturday, 29 February 1908**

A disappointing day for the Scots, even though one of the English goals was quite clearly a handball. Eck McNair played well at right-half.

English League: Hardy, Crompton & Burgess; Warren, Wedlock & Greenhalgh; Tickle, Smith, Hilsdon, West & Hall.

Scottish League: Rennie, Main & Agnew; McNair, Thomson & May; Bennett, McMenemy, McTavish, Kyle & Smith.

Referee – Mr Mason, England

....

2. IRISH LEAGUE 1 SCOTTISH LEAGUE 2; Grosvenor Park, Belfast; Wednesday, 10 February 1909

Not a great game, but a competent performance from Alec McNair, and according to The Scottish Referee, "Quinn was in great request by the Irish supporters, and every time 'Jamie' touched the ball, he was cheered. They did not seem caring about victory as long as the Celt distinguished himself."

Irish League: Edmonds, Seymour & McCartney; Darling, Connor & McClure; Hunter, Robertson, Halligan, McAuley & Sloan.

Scottish League: Brownlie, McNair & Richmond; Fairfoul, Loney & Findlay; Armour, Hunter, Quinn, Somers & Paul.

Referee – Mr Mason, England

....

3. SCOTTISH LEAGUE 2 IRISH LEAGUE 0; Firhill Park, Glasgow; Monday, 25 October 1909

A fairly easy victory for the Scottish League in front of 10,000 spectators. The Courier damns McNair with faint praise by saying that he was "all right." Star of the match was Bobby Templeton.

Scottish League: Brownlie, McNair & Chaplin; Gordon, Robertson & Hay; Kivlichan, McMenemy, Quinn, MacFarlane & Templeton.

Irish League: McKee, McCartney & Willis; Wright, Connor & Moran; Cunningham, Dodds, McDonnell, Enright & Thompson.

Referee – Mr Chadwick, England

....

4. ENGLISH LEAGUE 2 SCOTTISH LEAGUE 3; Ewood Park, Blackburn; Saturday, 26 February 1910

A fine victory for the Scottish League on a snow-covered pitch. The conditions were difficult, but the Scots were so superior that The Scottish Referee suggested playing the whole League team against England at Hampden in April!

English League: Dawson, Crompton & Hayes; Brittleton, Harrop & Makepeace; Garbutt, Holley, Parkinson, Bache & Wall.

Scottish League: Brownlie, McNair & Miller; Halley, Loney & Hay; Bennett, McMenemy, Quinn, Devine & Templeton.

Referee – Mr Campbell, England

....

5. SCOTTISH LEAGUE 1 ENGLISH LEAGUE 1; Ibrox Park, Glasgow;
Saturday, 4 March 1911

A tough game at Ibrox with the Scottish League being the better team but just unable to force a victory, in front of a huge crowd of 65,000.

Scottish League: Brownlie, McNair & Walker; Young, Raisbeck & Hay; Bennett, McMenemy, Reid, MacFarlane & Smith.

English League: Dawson, Crompton & Pennington; Veitch, Robertson & Bradshaw; Simpson, Bloomer, Shepherd, Bache & Henshall.

Referee – Mr Mason, England

....

6. SCOTTISH LEAGUE 3 IRISH LEAGUE 0; Firhill Park, Glasgow;
Monday, 30 October 1911

Bad weather restricted the attendance to 5,000. The Irish League did well to hold the Scots to a goalless draw at half-time, but were then overwhelmed in the second half with a Willie Reid hat-trick

Scottish League: Allan, McNair & Blair; Wilson, Anderson & Nellies; Rankin, Bowie, Reid, Bennett & Smith.

Irish League: Green, Lavery & McCann; Andrews, Stewart & Reid; Hunter, Napier, Walden, Ryder & McEwan.

Referee - Mr Kirkham, England

....

7. ENGLISH LEAGUE 2 SCOTTISH LEAGUE 0; Ayresome Park, Middlesbrough;
Saturday, 17 February 1912

The Scottish League were outplayed, and but for McNair and Blair at full-back, the margin of defeat might have been a great deal more. The Scottish League's cause was not helped by an injury to Jimmy Quinn.

English League: Williamson, Crompton & Pennington; Duckworth, Boyle & Fay; Wallace, Buchan, Freeman, Holley & Mordue.

Scottish League: Brownlie, McNair & Blair; Mercer, McAndrew & Galt; Bennett, McMenemy, Quinn, Cunningham & Brown.

Referee – Mr Bamlett, England

....

8. SOUTHERN LEAGUE 1 SCOTTISH LEAGUE 0; Millwall, London;
Monday, 14 October 1912

Probably Alec McNair's least memorable representative game, his own goal being the only score of the match. However, it would prove to be a significant day for Celtic. Southern League goalkeeper Charlie Shaw of Queen's Park Rangers had a great game, before approaching McNair at the end to talk about returning to Scotland. He duly signed for Celtic and the 'Holy Trinity' would soon be underway.

Southern League: Shaw, Collyer & Walker; Tout, Wilson & Wake; Walden, Shea, David, Bown & Lamb.

Scottish League: Bradford, McNair & Blair; Mercer, McAndrew & Gordon; Sinclair, King, Reid, Bennett & Smith.

Referee – Mr Baker, England

....

9. SCOTTISH LEAGUE 5 SOUTHERN LEAGUE 0; Cathkin Park, Glasgow;
Monday, 13 October 1913

A crowd of 10,000 at Third Lanark's home ground saw a very one-sided game but were rather upset at some of the rough tactics of the Southern League team. The Scotsman says that "McNair showed his usual judgement."

Scottish League: Brownlie, McNair & Dodds; Gordon, Mercer & Nellies; McAtee, Bowie, Reid, Croall & Neil.

Southern League: Webster, Collyer & Ireland; Comrie, Mitchell & Higham; Jefferson, Ingham, Davis, Bowler & Evans.

Referee – Sergeant-Major Vick, Scotland

....

10. IRISH LEAGUE 1 SCOTTISH LEAGUE 2; Celtic Park, Belfast;
Wednesday, 5 November 1913

Played in beautiful sunny weather after some heavy rain, this was one of the better games between the two League sides. The Scots just edged it, Willie Reid scoring the winner with three minutes to go. Patsy Gallacher, an Irishman, was playing for the Scottish League!

Irish League: Scott, McConnell & Dawson; Napier, Scraggs & Leddy; Smith, Crone, Hamilton, McNeill & McEwan.

Scottish League: Brownlie, McNair & Dodds; Wright, Mercer & Nellies; McAtee, Gallacher, Reid, Cunningham & McNeil.

Referee – Mr Bullimar, England

....

11. ENGLISH LEAGUE 2 SCOTTISH LEAGUE 3; Turf Moor, Burnley;
Saturday, 21 March 1914

A breathtaking win by the Scottish League team, who came back from being 0-2 down to win 3-2 before a crowd of 38.000. The north-west of England seemed to have been invaded by "Scottish excursionists wearing absurd headgears, whilst also drinking large quantities of whisky." The famous Celtic defensive trio were penetrated twice early on but then rallied and eventually dominated.

English League: Hardy, Compton & Bodcock; Barbour, Boyle & McNeal; Jephcott, Stevenson, Peart, Hodgson & Mosscrop.

Scottish League: Shaw, McNair & Dodds; Gordon, Wright & Nellies; McAtee, McMenemy, Reid, Croal & Smith.

Referee – Mr Taylor, England

....

12. IRISH LEAGUE 1 SCOTTISH LEAGUE 2; Grosvenor Park, Belfast;
Wednesday, 18 November 1914

Not everyone approved of this match being played, for the war had now been going on for over three months and did not look as if it were going to be "over by Christmas!" All the goals came in the first half and it was a good game of football in, more or less, perfect conditions for the 6,000 spectators. The Belfast Telegraph talks about Scotland's defence playing a "sound, methodical game."

Irish League: McKee, Rollo & McCann; McCracken, Scraggs & Hamill; Lyner, Nixon, McDonnell, Napier & Young.

Scottish League: Brownlie, McNair & Bulloch; Gordon, Johnstone & Nellies; Low, Gourlay, Gracie, McMenemy & Browning.

Referee – Mr Baker, England

....

13. SCOTTISH LEAGUE 1 ENGLISH LEAGUE 4; Celtic Park, Glasgow;
Saturday, 20 March 1915

The Sunday Post unequivocally describes this as the "Scottish League Team's Sorry Show," saying that "the nimble English ran rings round them." Even worse news was coming from the Dardanelles, with heavy losses sustained by the British. This would be the last representative game played until the war ended.

Scottish League: Brownlie, McNair & Dodds; Gordon, Wright & Nellies; McAtee, Bowie, Reid, McMenemy & Wilson.

English League: Smith, Longworth & English; Fleetwood, Roberts & McNeal; Chedgzoy, Buchan, Elliot, Latheron & Martin.

Referee – Mr Jackson, Scotland

....

14. ENGLISH LEAGUE 3 SCOTTISH LEAGUE 1; St Andrews, Birmingham;
Saturday, 22 February 1919

A disappointing defeat for the Scottish League in the Victory International. The crowd was reduced to 35,000, thanks to a combination of miserable weather, the Spanish Flu and the number of soldiers not yet demobbed. Nevertheless, quite a few men in khaki were seen in the crowd. Things had not settled on the labour front, nor in Ireland, where Sinn Fein had now seceded and formed their own Dail in Dublin. The English team were more direct, but The Scottish League were not disgraced, and at the end of the game, the crowd sang "Auld Lang Syne!"

English League: Hardy, Longworth & Womack; Fleetwood, Parker & Grenyer; Harrison, Whittington, Cock, Clennell & Morgan.

Scottish League: Stewart, McNair & Orr; Gordon, Cringan & Nellies; Archibald, Rankin, Culley, Gourlay & Morton.

Referee – Mr Davies, England

....

15. SCOTTISH LEAGUE 0 ENGLISH LEAGUE 4; Hampden Park, Glasgow;
Saturday, 20 March 1920

Nearly 100,000 were inside Hampden Park to see the Scottish League well-beaten by a very good English League side. McNair "came out of the ordeal very well" and impressed the visiting players by his "cool performance," but, the Scots were over-run by an excellent English team.

Scottish League: Shaw, McNair & Dodds; Gordon, Cringan & MacLachlan; McAtee, McMenemy, Ferguson, Cunningham & Morton.

English League: Hardy, Longworth & Pennington; Bamber, McCall & Grimsdell; Chedgzoy, Kelly, Cock, Morris & Smith.

Referee – Mr Bell, Scotland

....

CHAPTER THIRTEEN

CAREER MILESTONES

In a wonderful career which spanned more than two decades, Alec McNair played more than 700 games for Celtic and made 30 representative appearances for Scotland or the Scottish League select. The detail underpinning that career with club and country is covered earlier in the respective chapters. However, for ease of reference, the following is a snapshot of the some of the key moments which comprised that trophy-laden period in the life of The Icicle.

....

Saturday, 9 May 1903
– Alec's first appearance for Celtic

A 20-year-old left-half plays a trial match for Celtic against Airdrieonians at Broomfield under the name of 'Woods.' It would later transpire that the player involved was Alec McNair, at that time playing with his local side, Stenhouse Hearts. Note that Celtic would not adopt the famous hooped jerseys for a further five months, so the chances are that Alec played one match in the green-and-white vertical striped kit of the day. He would choose to play for Stenhousemuir the following season, 1903/04, developing his game under the watchful eye of Celtic manager Willie Maley and his 'network of spies.'

....

Saturday, 30 April 1904
– Alec signs for Celtic

Almost exactly one year after that trial, 21-year-old Alec McNair signs for Celtic and immediately joins his new Parkhead teammates on a short tour of the north of Scotland.

....

Monday, 2 May 1904
– Alec makes his Celtic debut

Northern League side Aberdeen FC were less than one year old when they provided the opposition to Celtic as McNair played his first match as a signed player at Pittodrie, Willie Maley's men winning 3-1. The Dons would join the Scottish League in the Second Division that summer. The Celtic line-up at the beginning of Alec's wonderful career was as follows:

Adams, McLeod & Strang; Young, Loney & McNair; McConnachie, McMenemy, Gilligan, Somers & Quinn.

....

Saturday, 10 September 1904
– Alec makes his home and competitive Celtic debut

Alec makes his first appearance of the new season, brought in as a replacement for injured left-winger Davie Hamilton, for a first-round Glasgow Cup-tie against Queen's Park at Parkhead. Celtic won 3-0 with goals from Finlay McLean, Peter Somers and Jimmy Quinn, and the team was as follows:

Adams, McLeod & Orr; Young, Loney & Hay; McLean, McMenemy, Quinn, Somers & McNair.

....

Saturday, 17 September 1904
– Alec makes his League debut

Seven days later, Eck retains his place in an unchanged team to receive his League debut at Love Street. Jimmy Quinn netted a double and captain Jimmy Hay scored the winner in a 3-2 victory over St Mirren.

Adams, McLeod & Orr; Young, Loney & Hay; McLean, McMenemy, Quinn, Somers & McNair.

....

Saturday, 4 March 1905
– Alec scores his first competitive goal for Celtic

Although Alec had found the net in friendly matches before this, notably with a double at his old stomping ground of Ochilview against Stenhousemuir, it would be at Fir Park, Motherwell where he would score his first competitive goal for Celtic, the third in a 6-2 victory in what was the club's 26th and final League match of the campaign. Rangers were six points behind at this stage with three games still to play, the winning of which would force a play-off for the League title. Jimmy Quinn grabbed a hat-trick, with Willie Loney and Peter Somers also on target before the bottom-of-the-table hosts snatched two late consolation goals. Note that some sources cite Davie Hamilton rather than Alec McNair as the scorer of this goal. The Celts line-up on this day was as follows:

Adams, McLeod & Orr; McNair, Loney & Hay; Bennett, McMenemy, Quinn, Somers & Hamilton.

....

Saturday, 6 May 1905
– Alec wins his first trophy with Celtic

With Rangers eventually winning their three games in hand to finish level with Celtic on 41 points, a play-off at Hampden was arranged to settle the destination of the League Championship. With Alec back in the side to replace the injured Sunny Jim Young, two goals in two minutes on the hour mark from Jimmy McMenemy and Davie Hamilton would see the title heading for Celtic Park, and McNair's incredible medal haul get underway. The Celtic line-up on this momentous afternoon was follows:

Adams, Watson & Orr; McNair, Loney & Hay; Bennett, McMenemy, Quinn, Somers & Hamilton.

....

Saturday, 3 March 1906
– Alec wins his first International cap for Scotland

Wales were the opposition and Tynecastle the venue as 23-year-old Alec wore the navy of Scotland for the first time. The following side would lose 2-0 to the Welsh before 25,000 spectators in Gorgie:

Raeside (Third Lanark), McLeod (Celtic) & Richmond (Queen's Park); McNair (Celtic), Thomson (Hearts) & May (Rangers); Stewart (Hibernian), MacFarlane (Dundee), Quinn (Celtic), Fitchie (Woolwich Arsenal) & Wilson (Hearts).

....

Saturday, 6 October 1906
– Alec plays and wins in his first cup final for Celtic

The 1906/07 Glasgow Cup final at Hampden against Third

Lanark, featuring legendary goalkeeper Jimmy Brownlie at one end and on-loan Ranger Tom Sinclair between the Celtic posts for the final time at the other, would see Celts come back from 1-2 to edge the match by the odd goal in five, thanks to an early penalty from captain Willie Orr and second-half goals from Sunny Jim Young and Peter Somers. The Celtic line-up as Alec won his first-ever cup final was as follows:

Sinclair, McLeod & Orr; Young, McNair & Hay; Templeton, McMenemy, Quinn, Somers & Hamilton.

....

Saturday, 20 April 1907
– Alec plays in his first Scottish Cup final for Celtic

A brace from Peter Somers and another spot kick conversion by Willie Orr saw Willie Maley's men beat Hearts 3-0 at Hampden to clinch the first-ever League and Cup Double in Scottish football history. The Celtic line-up that afternoon was follows:

Adams, McLeod & Orr; Young, McNair & Hay; Bennett, McMenemy, Quinn, Somers & Templeton.

....

Saturday, 18 January 1908
– Alec scores his final competitive goal for Celtic

Almost three years after opening his account at Fir Park, Motherwell, Alec would score his ninth and last competitive goal for Celtic at the same ground. His strike with 12 minutes remaining brought Celtic back into the match at 1-2, with Peter Somers then securing an equaliser before the final whistle. The Celts line-up on this day was follows:

Adams, McLeod & McNair; Young, Loney & Mitchell; Bennett, McMenemy, Quinn, Somers & Semple.

....

Saturday, 30 April 1909
– Alec plays his 100th League game for Celtic

An incredible run of 8 games played in just 12 days takes Alec to his first century of League games as Celtic complete their programme and clinch a fifth consecutive title with a 2-1 victory over Hamilton Academical at Douglas Park. The previous month, a riot after the drawn Scottish Cup final at Hampden with Rangers had denied Willie Maley's side the opportunity to win the Double for the third successive season. The team who lined up with Alec for Celtic in Hamilton as he reached his special milestone that afternoon was as follows:

Adams, McNair & Weir; Young, Dodds & Hay; McLean, McMenemy, Quinn, Somers & Hamilton.

....

Monday, 25 April 1910
– Alec wins his sixth successive League Championship with Celtic

On manager Willie Maley's 42nd birthday, his all-conquering Celtic team stretched their dominance in Scottish football to a record sixth season, with a low-key goalless draw against Hibernian at Celtic Park. This incredible feat would remain unequalled until Jock Stein's great Celtic side won 'nine-in-a-row' more than six decades later. The team who created history in April 1910 was as follows:

Duncan, McNair & Hay; Young, Dodds & Mitchell; Munro, McMenemy, Allan, Johnstone & Hamilton.

....

Saturday, 16 March 1912
– Alec captains Scotland for the first time

In his eighth full international, 29-year-old Alec was given the honour of captaining his country for the first time for the match against Ireland in Belfast. The following Scottish team would win 4-1 in front of 12,000 spectators at Windsor Park:

Brownlie (Third Lanark), McNair (Celtic - captain) & J. Walker (Swindon Town); Gordon (Rangers), Low (Newcastle United) & Bell (Manchester United); Sinclair (Hearts), R. Walker (Hearts), Reid (Rangers), Aitkenhead (Blackburn Rovers) & Templeton (Kilmarnock).

....

Saturday, 11 May 1912
– Alec completes the full set of domestic honours with Celtic

Having missed out on the winning finals twice previously, Alec McNair finally got his hands on his first Glasgow Charity Cup medal on this day, following Celtic's win over Clyde by seven corner-kicks to nil! The match at Hampden had ended goalless, with Willie Maley's side lining up as follows:

Mulrooney, McNair & Dodds; Young, Johnstone & Mitchell; McAtee, Gallacher, Quinn, McMenemy & Brown.

....

Saturday, 9 November 1912
– Alec plays his 200th League game for Celtic

Six weeks before his 30th birthday, Alec celebrates his double-century of League appearances with a 1-0 win over Hearts at Celtic

Park. Jimmy McMenemy scored the only goal, Celts lining up as follows:

Mulrooney, McNair & Dodds; Young, Loney & Mitchell; McAtee, Gallacher, Quinn, McMenemy & Brown.

....

Monday, 18 April 1914
– Alec wins his third and final League and Scottish Cup Double

A 3-0 victory over Hibernian at Celtic Park followed a 4-1 win over the same side in the Scottish Cup final at Hampden two days earlier to clinch Celtic's last Double for Celtic for 40 years, by which time Jock Stein would be the winning captain! The Scottish Cup would now go into cold storage following the outbreak of war that summer. The Celtic line-up for both games was follows:

Shaw, McNair & Dodds; Young, Johnstone & McMaster; McAtee, Gallacher, McColl, McMenemy & Browning.

....

Saturday, 18 December 1915
– Alec plays his 300th League game for Celtic

Six days before his 33rd birthday, and now a widower, Eck reaches 300 League appearances for Celtic as Maley's men extend their recent winning run to five with a comfortable 4-0 win over Partick Thistle at Firhill. That sequence would eventually reach a British record 62 by April 1917! Jimmy McMenemy scored twice with Andy McAtee and Johnny Browning also on target as Celtic lined up as follows:

Shaw, McNair & Dodds; Young, Johnstone & McMaster; McAtee, Gallacher, McColl, McMenemy & Browning.

Saturday, 7 October 1916
– Alec adopts the captaincy of Celtic

An injury to Sunny Jim Young sees Alec installed as interim captain of Celtic. Sadly, Young will never play again for Celtic, the great man eventually announcing his retirement in May 1917, at which point McNair took over on a formal basis.

Saturday, 7 December 1918
– Alec plays his 400th League game for Celtic

Now approaching his 36th birthday, and with the horrific war finally ending after the Armistice of the previous month, the incredible Alec McNair reaches a fourth century of League matches for Celtic. There is disappointment on the day as the Celts go down 3-1 to Motherwell at Fir Park, one of only two League defeats suffered by Maley's men that season. The beaten Celtic team was as follows:

Shaw, McNair & Livingstone; McEvoy, Cringan & Brown; Corcoran, Barber, McColl, McLean & Browning.

Saturday, 10 April 1920
– Alec represents Scotland for the last time

By now over 37 years old, Alec's 15th and final full international match was a crazy encounter against England at Hillsborough, which the hosts edged by the odd goal in nine, despite the Scots having led 4-2 at the interval. The following team had taken the field in front of 35,000 spectators in Sheffield:

Campbell (Partick Thistle), McNair (Celtic) & Blair (Sheffield Wednesday); Bowie (Rangers), Low (Newcastle United) & Gordon (Rangers); Donaldson (Bolton Wanderers), Miller (Liverpool), Wilson (Dunfermline Athletic), Paterson (Leicester City) & Troup (Dundee).

....

Tuesday, 4 January 1921
– Alec is awarded a Benefit match at Celtic Park

A crowd of 30,000 rolled up to Celtic Park to pay tribute to Alec McNair, following almost 17 years of wonderful service to the Parkhead club. The 38-year-old defender had sustained an injury against Clyde the previous day, which would restrict his appearance to the early minutes before he gave way to Willie McStay, who ultimately would replace him in the Celtic team, but not for several years yet! A combined Celtic and Rangers XI were beaten 3-1 by a Scottish League select, which included his old friend and teammate, Jimmy McMenemy, and his current Parkhead colleagues, Tully Craig and Jean McFarlane, the latter pair sharing the goals for the League select on an afternoon where the result was irrelevant, after Patsy Gallacher had opened the scoring. The two line-ups were as follows:

Celtic/Rangers XI: Shaw, McNair (W. McStay) & Manderson; Gordon, Cringan & Murphy; Donaghue, Gallacher, McInally, Cunningham & Morton.

Scottish League: Brownlie (Third Lanark), Neave (Kilmarnock) & Farrell (Clyde); McIntyre (Morton), Townsley (Falkirk) & Marshall (Clyde), McNab (Morton), McMenemy (Partick Thistle), Craig (Celtic), Allan (Clyde) & McFarlane (Celtic).

....

Saturday, 2 October 1921
– Alec wins his 7th and final Glasgow Cup

Almost 15 years to the day of his first cup final win, Alec secures a seventh and final winner's medal in the same competition as Celtic beat Clyde 1-0 to retain the Glasgow Cup. The Celtic side who lined up at Parkhead before 40,000 spectators that afternoon was as follows:

Shaw, McNair & W. McStay; Gilchrist, Cringan & Pratt; McAtee, Gallacher, McInally, Cassidy & McLean.

....

Saturday, 10 December 1921
– Alec plays his 500th League game for Celtic

Another significant landmark in Eck's wonderful career is secured at Somerset Park, as the great man makes his 500th League appearance for Celtic, in a goalless draw with Ayr United. He is just two weeks short of his 39th birthday at this time. The Celtic side who lined up beside him was as follows:

Shaw, McNair & Dodds; Gilchrist, Cringan & McMaster; McAtee, Gallacher, Craig, Cassidy & McLean.

....

Saturday, 29 April 1922
– Alec wins his 12th and final League title

A record crowd at Cappielow, which stands to this day, witnessed a thrilling climax to the Scottish League season, with title rivals Celtic and Rangers neck-and-neck on the final day. One point ahead at kick-off, Willie Maley's men just had to match the result of the Ibrox side to reclaim their crown, and they did so, thanks to a late equaliser from Andy McAtee against Scottish Cup-winners, Morton, whilst Rangers also drew against Clyde at Shawfield. So, some 17 years after that play-off win at Hampden, Alec McNair had secured an amazing 12th League winner's medal. The Celtic line-up was as follows:

Shaw, McNair & Dodds; Gilchrist, Cringan & W. McStay; McAtee, Gallacher, Cassidy, McFarlane & McLean.

....

Sunday, 24 December 1922
– Alec celebrates his 40th birthday…and he's still a Celt!

Just 24 hours before his 40th birthday, on Saturday, 23rd December, Alec plays against Kilmarnock at Celtic Park. An Adam McLean goal looked to have clinched the points before two late strikes from the visitors inflicted a rare home defeat on the defending champions. The full Celtic team was as follows:

Shaw, McNair & W. McStay; Gilchrist, Cringan & J. McStay; McAtee, Gallacher, McLean, McFarlane & Connolly.

....

Saturday, 31 March 1923
– Alec wins his 6th and final Scottish Cup

A solitary Joe Cassidy header saw Willie Maley's men beat a Hibernian side managed by his brother Alec 1-0 at Hampden to clinch Celtic's 10th Scottish Cup, thus equalling the record held by Queen's Park since 1892/93. Incredibly, Eck McNair had played in six of those winning finals. The Celtic line-up that afternoon was follows:

Shaw, McNair & W. McStay; J. McStay, Cringan & McFarlane; McAtee, Gallacher, Cassidy, McLean & Connolly.

....

Saturday, 26 January 1924
– Alec plays his 57th and final Scottish Cup-tie for Celtic

Alec McNair's next match in the Scottish Cup would not be so memorable, Celts beaten 2-0 by Kilmarnock at Rugby Park in the first round to lose their grip on the famous old trophy. This would prove to be Eck's last appearance in the competition. Alec Thomson, born almost two decades after McNair, featured at inside-left in the following Celtic team:

Shaw, McNair & Hilley; J. McStay, W. McStay & McFarlane; McAtee, Gallacher, Cassidy, Thomson & McLean.

....

Saturday, 10 May 1924
– Alec wins his 34th and final honour with Celtic

Now halfway through his 42nd year, Alec wins an incredible ninth Glasgow Charity Cup medal on this day, taking his overall tally to an unbelievable 34, following Celtic's 2-1 win over Rangers at Hampden, thanks to goals from Patsy Gallacher and Willie McStay. A young Jimmy McGrory played on the left wing, as Willie Maley's side lined up as follows:

Shaw, McNair & Hilley; J. McStay, W. McStay & McFarlane; Connolly, Gallacher, Cassidy, Thomson & McGrory.

....

Saturday, 11 April 1925
– Alec plays his 584th and final League game for Celtic

At the grand old age of 42 years, 4 months and 18 days, Eck McNair makes his 584th and final League appearance for Celtic, a 1-1 draw with Queen's Park at Celtic Park in the penultimate match of the campaign. Celtic's goalscorer was Paddy Connolly. Seven days earlier, that incredible somersault goal from Patsy Gallacher and a last-minute winner from Jimmy McGrory had given Willie Maley's side a record 11th Scottish Cup, following a 2-1 win over Dundee at Hampden. Ironically, McNair's next role in football would be as the manager at Dens Park, where he took over for the beginning of the following season. This last-ever Celtic team to feature the wonderful Alec McNair, Celtic's Icicle, was:

Shevlane, McNair & Hilley; J. McStay, W. McStay & McFarlane; Connolly, Wilson McGrory, Thomson & McLean.

Appendix 1: Alec McNair – Season by season summary of appearances

Season	League	Scottish Cup	Glasgow Cup	Charity Cup	Total
1904/05	6	1	1	0	**8**
1905/06	22	2	1	1	**26**
1906/07	28	9	3	2	**42**
1907/08	19	5	4	0	**28**
1908/09	26	7	7	1	**41**
1909/10	28	3	3	0	**34**
1910/11	34	6	3	2	**45**
1911/12	29	6	1	3	**39**
1912/13	30	3	3	3	**39**
1913/14	32	4	2	2	**40**
1914/15	35	*N/A*	0	3	**38**
1915/16	31	*N/A*	1	2	**34**
1916/17	37	*N/A*	2	2	**41**
1917/18	31	*N/A*	2	2	**35**
1918/19	31	*N/A*	1	1	**33**
1919/20	35	3	3	2	**43**
1920/21	29	0	3	0	**32**
1921/22	39	3	4	1	**47**
1922/23	21	4	1	2	**28**
1923/24	29	1	0	1	**31**
1924/25	12	0	0	0	**12**
Total	**584**	**57**	**45**	**30**	**716**

Appendix 2: Celtic FC – Season by season summary of honours during Alec McNair's career

Season	League	Scottish Cup	Glasgow Cup	Charity Cup	Total
1904/05	**Won (1)**	Semi-final	**Won**	**Won**	**3 (1)**
1905/06	**Won (2)**	Quarter-final	**Won**	Semi-final	**2 (1)**
1906/07	**Won (3)**	**Won (1)**	**Won (1)**	Runner's Up	**3 (3)**
1907/08	**Won (4)**	**Won (2)**	**Won (2)**	**Won**	**4 (3)**
1908/09	**Won (5)**	*Cup Withheld*	Runner's Up	Runner's Up	**1 (1)**
1909/10	**Won (6)**	Semi-final	**Won (3)**	Semi-final	**2 (2)**
1910/11	5th	**Won (3)**	Runner's Up	Runner's Up	**1 (1)**
1911/12	Runner's Up	**Won (4)**	First Round	**Won (1)**	**2 (2)**
1912/13	Runner's Up	Quarter-final	Runner's Up	**Won (2)**	**1 (1)**
1913/14	**Won (7)**	**Won (5)**	Semi-final	**Won (3)**	**3 (3)**
1914/15	**Won (8)**	*N/A*	First Round	**Won (4)**	**2 (2)**
1915/16	**Won (9)**	*N/A*	**Won (4)**	**Won (5)**	**3 (3)**
1916/17	**Won (10)**	*N/A*	**Won (5)**	**Won (6)**	**3 (3)**
1917/18	Runner's Up	*N/A*	Semi-final	**Won (7)**	**1 (1)**
1918/19	**Won (11)**	*N/A*	Runner's Up	Semi-final	**1 (1)**
1919/20	Runner's Up	Quarter-final	**Won (6)**	**Won (8)**	**2 (2)**
1920/21	Runner's Up	Quarter-final	**Won (7)**	**Won**	**2 (1)**
1921/22	**Won (12)**	Quarter-final	Runner's Up	Semi-final	**1 (1)**
1922/23	3rd	**Won (6)**	Runner's Up	Semi-final	**1 (1)**
1923/24	3rd	First Round	Semi-final	**Won (9)**	**1 (1)**
1924/25	4th	**Won**	Runner's Up	First Round	**1 (0)**
Total	**12 (12)**	**7 (6)**	**9 (7)**	**12 (9)**	**40 (34)**

*The figures in brackets denote a winner's medal won by Alec McNair.

No 86—ALEXANDER M'NAIR, Celtic F.C.
The Captains of
CELTIC